THE FABLIAUX

Volume 24

Mary Jane Stearns Schenck

The Fabliaux
Tales of Wit and Deception

MARY JANE STEARNS SCHENCK

THE FABLIAUX

Tales of Wit and Deception

JOHN BENJAMINS PUBLISHING COMPANY
Amsterdam/Philadelphia

1987

Library of Congress Cataloging in Publication Data

Schenck, Mary Jane Stearns.
  The fabliaux.

  (Purdue University monographs in Romance languages, ISSN 0165-8743; v. 24)
Bibliography: p.
1. Fabliaux -- History and criticism. I. Title. II. Series.
PQ207.S34   1987   841'.03'09   87-9188
ISBN 90 272 1734 3 (European) / ISBN 0-915027-89-5 (US) (alk. paper)

Purdue University
Monographs in
Romance Languages

Volume 24

MARY JANE STEARNS SCHENCK

THE FABLIAUX
Tales of Wit and Deception

JOHN BENJAMINS PUBLISHING COMPANY

Table of Contents

Acknowledgments

My love for literary studies and modern criticism first developed at FPC/ Eckerd College where three talented professors, Everett Emerson, Howard Carter, and Réjane Genz, taught me more than they imagined. One day during my graduate years, I happened to notice in a bookshop window on the Cours Mirabeau in Aix Propp's *Morphologie du conte,* which had just appeared in French translation. Having been fascinated for some time by French structuralism and linguistics, I imagined from its title that Propp's work might provide a method for analyzing the Old French fabliau. My sense that a subgenre of the narrative could be defined by common structural characteristics (not as much of a commonplace then as now) was borne out by this reading. I owe a great deal to Alan Knight's open-mindedness and advice while I was writing my dissertation and to The Pennsylvania State University for awarding me a Sparks Fellowship to support a year of research in France. After the dissertation came a fortuitous conversation with Larry Crist at a SAMLA meeting. The interest he showed in my early work and the guidance he gave me into the field of semiotics were invaluable. I learned much also during an LSA Summer Institute with Thomas Sebeok, an NEH Summer Seminar with Peter Haidu, and the School of Criticism and Theory with Wayne Booth, Michael Riffaterre, and Hillis Miller who guided my reading of Derrida and my work on irony. I appreciate also the University of Tampa for awarding me two faculty development grants for time during several summers to write this book.

Two portions of this book first appeared in journals as follows: "Functions and Roles in the Fabliau," *CL,* 30 (Winter 1978), 22-34, and "The Morphology of the Fabliau," *Fabula,* 17 (1976), 26-39.

All of these intellectual mentors cannot eclipse, however, personal sources of inspiration and support. To my parents, Amy Anne and Frank Stearns, my husband, David, and my children, Tyson and Katie, I owe much more—without them the task and the results would be quite hollow. Finally I thank my typists, Ruth Cash and Theresa Martinez, for their tireless pursuit of perfection.

M. J. S.
Tampa 1985

List of Abbreviations

AnM   *Annuale Mediaevale*
CL   *Comparative Literature*
CLS   *Comparative Literature Studies*
FEW *Französisches Etymologisches Wörterbuch*
HF   *The Humor of the Fabliaux*
HLF   *Histoire Littéraire de la France*
IJSLP *International Journal of Slavic Linguistics and Poetics*
KRQ *Kentucky Romance Quarterly*
MLN *Modern Language Notes*
MLR *Modern Language Review*
MP   *Modern Philology*
MR   Montaiglon and Raynaud's edition of *Recueil général et complet des fabliaux*
NM   *Neuphilologische Mitteilungen*
PMLA *Publications of the Modern Language Association*
REW *Romanisches Etymologisches Wörterbuch*
RF   *Romanische Forschungen*
RomN *Romance Notes*
RPh   *Romance Philology*
RR   *Romanic Review*
SN   *Studia Neophilologica*
SSF   *Studies in Short Fiction*
ZRP   *Zeitschrift für Romanische Philologie*

Introduction

The artist usually sets out—or used to—to point a moral and adorn a tale. The tale, however, points the other way, as a rule. Two blankly opposing morals, the artist's and the tale's. Never trust the artist. Trust the tale. The proper function of the critic is to save the tale from the artist who created it.
                                                                D. H. Lawrence

For the critic who wants to save the tale from the teller, the Old French fabliau offers a fertile field of study. Unlike the narrators of modern fiction, whether they be the supposedly absent ones of a Robbe-Grillet novel or the self-conscious ones of a Donald Barthelme short story, the artist/narrator of the short verse narrative called a fabliau does not play complicated games with the reader. Although following Lawrence's advice is not a simple or even entirely legitimate critical exercise with any fiction, the simplicity of the fabliau's narrative structure is tempting. The artist is ostensibly the narrator, and he is neither aloof nor tricky. He interrupts the narrative occasionally to offer his point of view, and he almost always introduces himself as well as the tale. Few of these artists are able to resist the temptation to explain their tales, to get in one last point, by tacking on a moral or a proverb as the final word. Thus the critic's task appears to be quite simple. Ignore the framing comments and occasional interruptions in the text; then analyze the narrative that remains.

An analysis of the form and meaning of the narratives as texts with an integrity of their own is central to this study. I trust the tale(s), and I even presume to explain its meaning as has not yet been done. I will not, however, ignore the clearly didactic statements of the narrators for several reasons. Like most folk literature, these tales are unabashedly moral, and any discussion of their meaning must clarify the relationship between the funny, even obscene narratives and the serious framework supplied by the narrators. Also, one of the basic problems in any study of Old French fabliaux is determining which tales should actually be included in the corpus. The narrators' use of the term within the text provides not only a first clue to its meaning but also an initial criterion for establishing the corpus.

From the sixteenth to the nineteenth century, the word *fabliau* has been used loosely to refer to any slightly ribald tale. A review of the prominent critics' definitions and descriptions of the texts reveals as much about the critical bias of the period as it does about these tales which so many intuitively group as a genre. It was only after Montaiglon and Raynaud's late nineteenth-century edition of 152 tales that the corpus was firmly established.[1] The definition of the term itself, however, remained quite vague, especially after the most influential critic of these texts, Joseph Bédier, defined them as "funny short stories."[2] When other critics have attempted to define the term, there have been frequent references to the ribald nature of the narratives, their verse form, and prominent themes such as adultery. Yet the thorny problem of what differentiates the fabliau as a form from anecdotes on similar subjects has not been resolved. Given the healthy status of medieval studies since the Second World War, it is surprising that so few major studies on this genre exist. In fact, during the last ninety years only two major works, *Les Fabliaux* by Bédier (1893) and Per Nykrog's work of the same title (1957),[3] could be considered comprehensive analyses of all the texts. A flurry of dissertations and articles has appeared in the last twenty years, but most of these do not offer satisfactory interpretations of the form and meaning of the genre.

The first of two major goals of this study is to define the term *fabliau* and to determine whether the term can correctly be used to describe a subgenre of the narrative. Previous critics have struggled with the definition, and their opinions are important to consider; so too are the implications drawn from the narrators' use of the term. In spite of the obviously light-hearted themes and frequent ribaldry of the tales, the narrators make it clear that fabliaux are didactic as well as entertaining, but the lessons are not quite the expected *moralités*. They warn the reader about deception, changes of fortune, and the inevitable nature of retribution for wrongdoing. The clear moral thrust naturally calls into question the fabliau's relationship to the exemplum. Some critics have assumed that the exemplum was a model for the fabliau. Others have actually applied the term *fabliau* to a few of the tales from collections such as the *Disciplina Clericalis* and Marie de France's *Fables*. Therefore, an important element in this study will be the description of the formal differences and the direction of influence between these two genres.

To determine whether common, formal structures exist among the tales, I begin with a close textual analysis of those texts identified as fabliaux by their narrators. Sixty-six such tales provide a considerable group for analyzing narrative structure. Their tripartite form—introduction, narrative, and concluding remarks—shows the fabliau's connection to medieval didactic literature, but it is not a particularly distinctive trait. Thus, the case for establishing the fabliau as a specific subgenre of humorous narrative must rest in the analysis of the narrative portion alone. The most appropriate method for analyzing a host of texts with the purpose of revealing their similarities is based on a linguistic model that allows the critic to distinguish deep structure from surface features. Vladimir Propp, in his study of Russian fairy tales, provided a seminal model for all structural studies of narrative that have followed.[4] His method of isolating functions and roles, as those ideas have been modified by contemporary French structuralists and semioticians, proved to be especially useful in analyzing the rather heterogeneous group of texts identified by their authors as fabliaux.

Using Propp's method, I isolated nine functions—arrival, departure, interrogation, communication, deception, misdeed, recognition, retaliation, and resolution—in these tales. Even more significant is the fact that the nine functions work equally as well in describing the narratives in seventy of the remaining eighty-eight texts in the complete corpus. Thus these functions, expecially the central ones—deception and misdeed—constitute an initial definition of the majority of *all* texts previously considered to be fabliaux. The structural definition becomes complete with finding that only two central roles, victim and duper, are played by characters in these tales.

The analysis of the narratives confirms a remarkable similarity in deep structure among texts which have plots about a range of antisocial behaviors, from adultery to horse theft. They are not, in short, just a collection of funny short stories. **A fabliau is an independent, brief, verse narrative with a tripartite macrostructure whose narrative is a humorous, even ribald, story with a cautionary moral. In the narrative, dupers and victims engage in repeated acts of deception and misdeed, such as adultery, theft, or cheating. The cyclical pattern of aggression and retaliation may be brought to an end in a pseudo-judicial scene or it may remain unresolved, but in no case does a heroic figure emerge to establish harmony or a just conclusion to the conflict.**

Since this is a structural rather than a formalist study, it is not an analysis of form devoid of content. Even in the search for functions and roles, the semantic content of these elements is of primary importance. For all of their significance as delimiters of the genre, the identification of functions and roles is no more than a preliminary step in the search for meaning. They may be the most convincing evidence to support a taxonomy, but they do not capture the dynamics of the text nor can they constitute an interpretation of these tales. The second major goal of this study is to hold up to question various theories about the meaning of the tales and to challenge assumptions about their values and social context. My interpretation begins with one complete text, *Le Meunier*, which is not one of the self-proclaimed fabliaux. The analysis demonstrates the subtle relationship between the narrator's comments, the interplay of functions and roles, the value system behind the figures of speech; and, by implication, the validity of the structural definition of the genre.

Discovering meaning in these texts about deception and misdeed demands a fresh approach to one of the central problems recurring in all fabliau scholarship. Many critics have assumed, almost without question, that fabliaux are satiric, and much space has been dedicated to their supposed anticlericalism and antifeminism. The difficulty lies in the fact that for every text that proves such a bias, another one may prove just the opposite. Bédier was the only one of the important critics of the genre to reject the notion that they are satire and to suggest that they are ironic instead. He did not develop his point, but I will by using classical definitions of irony as well as more contemporary ones from Northrop Frye and Paul de Man. The humor in the fabliaux stems naturally from their verbal and dramatic irony, which has not gone entirely unappreciated by previous critics. As a rich source of ironic humor, the fabliau has been best appreciated by Chaucer scholars, but the aim of their studies is quite naturally on Chaucer's narrative art. The dramatic irony of the fabliau, however, is as fine as any, and what has not been appreciated is the extent to which these narratives foreground the use of ironic language as an ultimate weapon used to distort and call into question sensory perceptions of reality. The duper of the fabliau, like the philosopher or artist Paul de Man refers to in his discussion of irony, understands that language can constitute a self and a reality independent of the normative experiences of the other characters. Behind all of the multiple ironies of these texts lies the mode of this genre itself. If we accept that there are only dupers and victims, then we can recognize the ironic mode, as Frye would define it, by the absence of a hero. Understanding the fabliau as an ironic genre clarifies many of the conflicting interpretations of the meaning of these narratives. They do not spring from the reforming spirit of the satirist, but rather are akin to narratives in the great wisdom tradition that casts an ironic glance at a fallen, non-heroic world of common people trying to survive.

From the didactic frame, to the narrative structure that focuses on deception, to the powerful manipulations of language by unprincipled dupers, these texts promote the value of practical wisdom, pleasure, and success. This ethic is undoubtedly rooted in a social context, but it is not a simple matter of one specific class. They have been identified as bourgeois due to their ethic of practicality and hedonism, or as aristocratic due to their supposed inversion of courtly love triangles. Nevertheless, it is quite difficult to prove a clear tie with one class to the exclusion of all others. Although the issue has always been couched in terms of the genre springing from or appealing to a particular social class, the fabliau is better understood as reflecting a locale and a mentality. The small towns and villages, where the upwardly mobile peasantry were a significant social force and where the thriving economy made companions of a heterogeneous cast of characters, constitute the fabliau world. By virtue of their tone and subject matter these tales are, after all, not far removed from folk literature. Their earthiness, pragmatism, and admiration for cunning betray a peasant background, but they are not at all the naïve tales of magical objects we find in other folk literature. Their ironic vision, celebration of intelligence, and raucous pursuit of individual success reflect new values brought into medieval society by the economic expansion and increasing urbanization of the countryside. The fusion of these values with the wisdom of the common man may make the fabliau the first written form of that urbane Gallic wit that scorns stupidity and authority while celebrating the pleasures of both mind and body.

1

The Genre and Its History

A study of the Old French fabliau necessarily begins as a genre study because the word from the time of its first use in the late twelfth century has meant a certain type of story:[1]

> Seignor, se vous volez atendre
> Et .I. seul petitet entendre,
> Jà de mot ne vous mentirai,
> Mès tout en rime vous dirai
> D'une aventure le fablel.
>
> (*Des trois boçus* MR I: 2, vv. 1-5)[2]

These opening lines of the fabliau *Des trois boçus* recall similar lines in the *Lais* where Marie de France contrasts the *aventure* and the *lai*.[3] It is evident that *aventure* in *Des trois boçus* refers to an event or story known to the author who now renders it in verse. *Fablel* is either a certain part of the *aventure* or the author's designation for his own composition. In *Des trois avugles de Compiengne* (MR I: 4), Cortebarbe indicates that it is merely a type of story, a class such as *conte* or *dit*:

> Une matère ci dirai
> D'un fablel que vous conterai.
> On tient le menestrel à sage
> Qui met en trover son usage
> De fère biaus dis et biaus contes
> C'on dit devant dus, devant contes.
> Fablel sont bon à escouter:
> Maint duel, maint mal font mesconter
> Et maint anui et maint meffet.
> CORTEBARBE a cest fablel fet.
>
> (MR I: 4, vv. 1-10)

He is going to recite the *matère*, the plot, of a *fablel*, but his own composition is a *fablel* also. These opening lines are particularly rich in information

1

about this genre and the role of the *menestrel* vis-à-vis his material. His worth lies in "finding" good *contes* or *dits,* in the literal sense of discovering them in written and oral sources, and in the proper sense of composing, remaking, hitting upon just the right combination of words and deeds to make a good story. The purpose of the stories is quite clearly stated: they are a literature of escapism which helps to dissipate grief and unhappiness; but other tales equally emphasize their moral purpose:

> Par cest fablel poez savoir
> Que *cil ne fet mie savoir*
> *Qui mieus croit sa fame que lui:*
> *Sovent l'en vient honte et anui.*
> (*Les .IIII. souhais Saint Martin* MR V: 133, vv. 187-90)

The suggestion that these funny stories may be didactic has prompted much discussion about their purpose, and these arguments will be more thoroughly examined in the following chapter.

It is widely accepted that the genre flourished during the thirteenth century, although as Rychner remarks, "presque tous les fabliaux sont indatables."[4] At the time, the art of making a fabliau was not only very popular but also a very conscious literary or academic exercise. Fabliaux are not just recordings of market place stories, for almost all have been arranged in a tripartite macro-structure, consisting of introduction, narrative proper, and conclusion.[5] The narrators also take pride in putting a pre-existing story into verse:

> Chascuns se veut mès entremètre
> De biaus contes en rime mètre
> Mais je m'en sui si entremis
> Que j'en ai .I. en rime mis.
> (*Le Cuvier* MR I: 9, vv. 1-4)

> Ma paine metrai et m'entente,
> Tant com je sui en ma jovente,
> A conter .I. fabliau par rime
> Sanz colour et sanz leonime;
> Mais s'il i a consonancie,
> Il ne m'en chaut qui mal en die. . . .
> (*De .III. dames qui troverent .I. vit* MR V: 112, vv. 1-6)

Octosyllabic verse, the accepted narrative form of the period, allowed authors to demonstrate a certain artistic virtuosity even in telling a common tale. The conceit of the *jongleurs* and a sense of competition can be seen in the verses quoted above. In one of his fabliaux, Jean Bodel suggests that he is trying to improve his version by taking a tale from Jehan de Boves:

Cil qui trova d'el Morteruel,
. . . .
D'un autre fablel s'entremet,
Qu'il ne cuida jà entreprendre;
Ne por Mestre Jehan reprendre
De Boves, qui dist bien et bel,
N'entreprent-il pas cest fablel,
Quar assez sont si dit resnable;
Mès qui de fablel fet grant fable,
N'a pas de trover sens legier.

(Des .II. chevaus MR I: 13, vv. 1, 14-21)

He obviously intends to surpass the common herd by turning his fabliau into a *grant fable,* one which will have some meaning and value. Whether the octo-syllabic verse form merely reflects the dominant mode for narrative at this time or whether it serves as a memory aid, emphasis is put on the fact that a fabliau reworks another story and that originality consists in having put it into verse:

Il est bien droiz que je retraie,
Puis que nus hons ne m'en deloie,
D'une aventure que je sai
. . . .
L'aventure est et bone et bele,
Et la rime fresche et novele,
Si con je la fis l'autre jour. . . .

(Du prestre teint MR VI: 139, vv. 1-3, 7-9)

The word *fabliau* clearly refers to a rhymed narrative—this much we learn from the texts themselves, but the origins and exact meaning of the term are not completely clear. The etymology of *fabliau,* the Picard form of *fableau* adopted by Bédier and subsequent critics, is not agreed upon by Bédier and Nykrog. Bédier gives a Latin root *fabula + ellus > fableau.*[6] But Nykrog gives *fable + el > fablel* and asserts: "Le mot est ainsi de pure formation française et aucune origine latine directe n'est acceptable. . . ."[7] No doubt the term and the specific form are genuine products of the thirteenth century, but it is also probable that both etymologies figured in the formation of the word. It signifies, in either case, a type of fable, a diminutive or variant of this genre. We also know that many words—*conte, fable, trufle, dit, exemple,* and *lai,* all signifying story—were used quite loosely in the twelfth and thirteenth centuries.

Whether and how the term *fabliau* differs in meaning from other genre terms has been central to much of the criticism devoted to these tales, even if only implicitly. Not all editors or critics attempt a definition of the genre, but it can be inferred from their discussions of the fabliau's sources and meaning or from the texts they choose to include. The history of fabliau scholarship reveals a fluctuation of interest in these tales, varying motivations for studying or publishing them, and most especially definitions and patterns of interpretation based on the critical bias of an era or a critic's taste.

Fabliau literary history begins with Claude Fauchet's *Recueil de l'origine de la langue et poésie françoise ryme et romans*. Given that this late Renaissance work is a catalogue of Old French poets and texts, it represents one of the earliest attempts to classify and distinguish medieval genres. Under the name Raoul de Houdanc or Houdon, for instance, Fauchet says that he never saw Raoul's *roman*, "ains seulement un fabliau, qui est un conte faict à plaisir; comme une nouvelle meslée de fables, où volontiers à la fin il y a quelque interprétation morale."[8] Although he mentions that fabliaux are mixtures of the *nouvelle* and fable, it is clear that *fabliau* and *fable* are distinct genres in his mind, because the fabliau is not entirely serious or moral. For instance, he qualifies *De pleine bourse de sens* as "moral," and he does not call *Du vair palefroi* a fabliau, perhaps because of its serious, courtly tone.

Fauchet lists Jonglet as an author of a fabliau about a nasty trick played on a naïve boy by a *jongleur*.[9] It is not identified as a fabliau in the text, so the reader might wonder whether Fauchet was copying his information from another source. It is more likely, however, that he feels there is something about the text which places it in this group. Its most striking quality is a scabrous plot, placed in a framework that teaches a lesson. He also attributes two fabliaux to Rutebeuf, "qui fut un menestrel, duquel on trouve plusieurs fabliaux (c'est-à-dire contes de plaisir et nouvelles) mis en ryme. . . ."[10] Rutebeuf does, in fact, designate *De la dame qui fit .III. tors entor le moustier* as a fabliau, but the other text, *De la pucelle que vouloit voler*, is neither signed nor identified as a fabliau. This story is as obscene as Jonglet was scatalogical, so for Fauchet, like many later critics, the presence of obscenity or at least a ribald tone is an identifying characteristic of the genre. Fauchet's implied definition is that fabliaux are not genuinely moral, nor courtly, but short verse tales whose humor definitely includes the obscene.

In spite of Fauchet's attempt to remind the French of their literary heritage and keep Old French texts from oblivion, his interest was not shared by men of letters who followed him, especially in the classical period. During the Enlightenment, interest in historical studies led a new generation of scholars to search old manuscripts for details about French society during its earliest periods. Medieval texts were by this time not only unfamiliar but also unreadable for the public and even for many scholars. Thus scholarly activity consisted largely of compiling dictionaries, writing studies of old texts, and publishing modern versions of some of them. A taste for risqué stories also played a role in the publication of certain texts.

The first significant discussion of the fabliau in the eighteenth century is found in the "Mémoire sur les fabliaux" given by the Conte de Caylus before the Académie Royale des Inscriptions between 1744 and 1746.[11] Caylus, known primarily as an *amateur des arts* and antiquarian, situates the fabliau historically by placing it in the tradition of classical myths or fables. His description of the fabliau reflects a classical definition of poetry that seems inappropriate for the nature of the tales he describes. "C'est un poëme qui renferme un récit élégant d'une action inventée, petite, plus ou moins intriguée quoique d'une certaine étendue, mais agréable ou plaisante, dont le but est d'instruire ou d'amuser."[12] In calling it a poem, he alludes to its octosyllabic verse form, but he points out that it contains a well-constructed narrative and is not lyric. He also differentiates the fabliau and the *roman*.[13] In an apparent attempt to separate fabliaux from classical fables that include personifications of animals and from medieval works such as *miracles,* he stresses the fact that fabliaux have neither anachronisms nor absurd events. He further de-emphasizes any symbolic significance by asserting that they were meant to be pleasing and, more importantly, by saying that they are neither a *sentence, proverb, dictum,* or *apothegem,* "le récit même de l'action est l'essentiel au fabliau."[14]

His presentation of the fabliau is classical not only in its echoes of the Horatian formula, *dulce et utile,* but also in his reluctance to discuss in public many of the tales for fear of offending his audience. Although he describes the genre, he banishes from public discussion any text which might violate good taste, since he holds a classical, prescriptive view of literature.

Yet it may be precisely the obscenity which motivated Caylus's "rediscovery" of the fabliau. Known as one of the first French archeologists (*Recueil d'antiquités égyptiennes, étrusques, grecques, romaines et gauloises,* 7 vols., 1752-67), he protested in public about the ribald nature of the fabliau but was himself the author of "quelques œuvres badines qu'on daigne parfois encore remettre sous le manteau."[15] In fact, his works include not only adaptations of several very ribald fabliaux but also some frankly pornographic Latin poems as well as his own erotic tales.[16] As Lionel Gossman says of Caylus, "he had a penchant for amusing erotic tales which were hardly in the grand manner."[17]

The definition Caylus offers of the fabliau tells us less about the tales than about literary tastes at the time; but, he did regard them as a distinct group worthy of some consideration. Even if he personally appreciated them more for their sexual frankness and obscene language than for their literary merit, the attention he focused on them had fortunate results. According to Nykrog, Etienne Barbazan, who was influenced by Caylus's "Mémoire," decided to publish the first edition of fabliaux (1756-60).[18] In his preface, Barbazan differentiates several genres by stating that a *dit* is a didactic work that narrates a good or bad action; a *lai* is also a *récit d'aventure* focusing on an individual to be praised or blamed. The didactic quality of the other genres is not part of his definition of the fabliau, "Les contes ou récits d'aventure gaies, vraies ou fausses, pour divertir et amuser se nommoient Fabel, Fablel ou Fabliau."[19]

The fact that he emphasizes their lighthearted nature and publishes some of the most obscene ones lends credence to the idea that their entertainment value must certainly have been as crucial a factor as their historical value in making the decision to publish them. He is, however, sensitive to the possibility that the tales would offend standards of public, if not private, taste. He goes to some length to apologize for their vulgarity, and he attributes it to the naïveté of the medievals.

The vulgarity and obscenity of the fabliaux, euphemized in most definitions as *gaieté,* was probably the reason for their success, although it was rationalized in order not to reflect poorly on the editor or critic who devoted his time to the subject. In some cases the tales were bowdlerized before publication, as in the collection of modern French adaptations done by Le Grand d'Aussy in 1779.[20] The growing interest in medieval tales resulted in further editions but not necessarily in further refinements in the definition of the genre. A later edition of the Barbazan collection, completed by Méon in 1808, does nothing to further a clarification of the term because it includes a great variety of genres—*miracles, contes, fabliaux, débats, allégories, congés, lais, contes courtois, nouvelles,* as well as essays on Old French and didactic works. The cohesiveness of Barbazan's collection and the definition it implied are lost because Méon's purpose is to edit the contents of several unpublished manuscripts rather than to publish, for whatever reason, one type of story as Barbazan had done.

Medieval scholarship owes the Romantic period a great debt for having expanded upon and genuinely popularized an interest in the Middle Ages that Enlightenment scholars had initiated. Quantities of manuscripts were published because the texts offered glimpses of life during the distant, exotic past so appealing to the disenchanted moderns. Fabliaux were appreciated at this time for qualities important to the Romantics, if we can judge by Auguis's description (1820) of the fabliau, which contains echoes of Rousseau:

> Ce génie original étoit un mélange de franchise, de saillie, des sensibilité et de grâce ingénieuse, où l'on ne sentoit travail, ni recherche, ni affectation d'esprit et de savoir, mais le seul épanchement d'un âme loyale, tendre et gaie. Ce caractère tout particulier fut désigné sous un nom qui n'appartient proprement qu'à la nation françoise; c'est lui de *naïveté.*[21]

Mid-century scholars, influenced by realism and literary theories epitomized in the work of Taine, regarded medieval literature as a treasure trove of historical fact. In 1856, Victor Le Clerc published the essay "Fabliaux" in the *Histoire Littéraire de la France,* in which he states, "Nous regardons les contes comme de fidèles peintures des mœurs du temps. Quelques-uns néanmoins viennent de sources antiques ou orientales; d'autres sont des imitations d'écrits latins presque de même age."[22] His interest in explaining the sources of the

Oriental and Latin ones as well as in explaining the social types seen in these tales outweighs any concern for a definition of the term. In fact, he includes all types of tales (*miracles de la Vierge, aventures d'ermites, contes moraux, lais* and fabliaux) in his discussion because he draws quite heavily on the collections of Méon and Le Grand d'Aussy. His rather vague definition, "Ces contes en vers faciles et populaires . . . ,"[23] also indicates that *fabliau* has lost all specific meaning for him. His study indicates that interest in Old French popular tales was once again increasing, but his remarks do not contribute much to an understanding of the genre.

The lack of precision with which editors and critics referred to the fabliau prompted Anatole de Montaiglon, who was later joined by Gaston Raynaud, to bring more clarity to the editing process. Between 1872 and 1890, they published their six-volume edition, *Recueil général et complet des fabliaux des XIIIe et XIVe siècles,* which has been the primary edition of these tales until the first volumes of a new, complete edition appeared in 1983 and 1984.[24] A collection of 155 tales, the *Recueil* contains, with very few exceptions, those tales which are recognized as fabliaux. Other fabliaux, unknown to Montaiglon and Raynaud, have been published since 1890, but their edition is still largely the corpus accepted today.

Editions and studies since the time of Barbazan enlarged the reading public's awareness of stories in Old French, but they had tended to obscure any precise definition of the term *fabliau.* Motivated by this situation, Montaiglon made very clear his own concept of the genre:

> Maintenant que les publications d'anciens textes français . . . se sont accumulées, il convient forcément d'être plus sévère au point de vue du genre, et, si l'on s'occupe des Fabliaux, de s'en tenir à ce qui est le vrai Fabliau, c'est-à-dire à un récit, plutôt comique, d'une aventure réele ou possible, même avec des exagérations, qui se passe dans les données de la vie humaine moyenne. Tout ce qui est invraisemblable . . . historique . . . pieux . . . d'enseignement . . . fantaisie romanesque . . . lyrique ou même poétique, n'est à aucun titre un Fabliau."[25]

He is precise in defining the genre, stressing that it is a humorous short narrative recounting one situation at a time in a manner that keeps it "au-dessous" of either poetry or drama:

> Il est plus naturel, bourgeois si l'on veut mais il est foncièrement comique, souvent, par malheur, jusqu'à la grossièreté. C'est . . . relativement court, sans former de suite ni de série, un conte en vers, plus long qu'un conte en prose, mais qui n'arrive jamais à être ni un roman ni un poëme.[26]

In addition to separating the fabliaux from tales in collections and serious *contes* or *romans,* Montaiglon suggests their tone is "bourgeois," a notion that would have important consequences in the history of their interpretation.

The Montaiglon and Raynaud collection was so valuable because they viewed their edition as a purely scholarly enterprise and therefore published all the known texts—even, as Montaiglon said, the silliest or stupidest ones. He felt he did not have to apologize for their obscenity because the public could not or would not have any interest in reading them, "ceux qui les liront seront ou des philologues ou des historiens, nous n'avons à nous préoccuper ici ni de jugement, ni de choix, ni d'extraits, ni de suppressions."[27]

If the eighteenth-century men of letters had delighted in the fabliau's obscenity and quaintness, the nineteenth-century philologists were seriously interested in their language and history. The need for edited texts was met by Montaiglon and Raynaud's edition because it presented one reliable version of each tale as well as some of the fragments in notes. Once the corpus of texts was established, important scholars, such as Charles Formentin, Charles Langlois, and Gaston Paris,[28] devoted their attention to other issues—the origins of fabliaux and the picture they present of medieval society.

Joseph Bédier's doctoral dissertation, *Les Fabliaux,* was born of a desire to discredit the Orientalist theory of their origins promoted by his mentor, Gaston Paris. His study marks the beginning of modern scholarship on the genre and is the first serious attempt to discuss their literary value. Devoting a doctoral thesis to fabliaux was audacious at this time because they were considered, at best, a gentleman scholar's pastime, and at worst, a group of filthy stories not worthy of anyone's serious consideration. Brunetière, for one, publicly pronounced them lacking in all literary value.[29] Nevertheless, scholarly studies on the folktale abounded, giving an academic justification for Bédier's dissertation. Wanting to avoid the accusation that even "science" does not justify elaborate studies of the insignificant, as Claude Bernard had pointed out, Bédier justifies his work by stating that, as popular *contes,* fabliaux naturally pose questions about their origins; and, as a distinct literary genre, their development and relationship to other medieval genres should be studied.[30] It is Bédier who not only legitimized fabliau studies but also paved the way for subsequent structural ones.

Drawing on the distinction between fundamental and accessory characteristics, Bédier asserts that what makes popular tales interesting is not their commonplaces but the accessory characteristics, the local coloring of a particular nation or region at a particular historical moment—an insight later used by Vladimir Propp when he developed his morphology of the fairy tale. Bédier turns away from an appreciation of the individual poem, as such, to a study of the attitudes reflected in fabliaux, their authors and their public. He points to the weaknesses of some—careless versification, low style, and grossness of thought and diction—but he also appreciates their good qualities—briefness, truthfulness, and naturalness. As he makes clear in his brief definition, he sees them as funny stories, some reaching for the lowest means to provoke a laugh and none attaining the heights of satire:

L'esprit qui anime cette masse est fait de bon sens frondeur, gai, d'une intelligence réélle de la vie courante du monde, d'un sens très exact du positif. Pas de naïveté, mais un tour ironique de niaiserie maligne; ni de colère ni d'ordinaire, de satire qui porte; mais la dérision amusée, la croyance, commune à tous au moyen âge, que rien ici-bas ne doit ni ne peut changer, et que l'ordre établi, immuable, est le bon; l'optimisme, la joie de vivre, un réalisme sans amertume.[31]

His definition, "Les fabliaux sont des contes à rire en vers,"[32] simplifies earlier ones, its conciseness and breadth no doubt accounting for its having become the textbook definition. Based on this definition, Bédier eliminates sixteen tales from Montaiglon's collection because they either lack a narrative, are not funny, or are too moral or *dévot*. The boundaries between *nouvelle sentimentale, lai, conte moral,* and fabliau are admittedly obscure, and Bédier's choice to include or exclude certain tales is ultimately subjective. On the whole, however, his list is valid if only because he makes his selections with keen intuitive insight into the tales' essential similarities. Although his list of fabliaux contains a few debatable titles, he can be credited with establishing the canon through his very good grasp of what a fabliau is and the range of attitudes it reflects. His work is perhaps best known for his suggestion that fabliaux were created for and by the bourgeoisie, an argument that will be taken up later in connection with Per Nykrog's work and my theory of their social origins.

The search for sources of the genre and its relationship to other medieval genres (by implication the boundaries of the genre) continued with Edmond Faral's "Le Fabliau latin au moyen âge."[33] He attempts to prove that fabliaux spring from medieval Latin comedy. The themes and tone of the comedies are certainly similar to those of the fabliau, and the dramatic qualities of the fabliau have frequently been pointed out, but there are many different types of literature using similar themes without necessarily being formally related. Faral's assertion that "le fabliau du XIIIe siècle, en tant que genre littéraire est issu du conte latin du XIIe siècle, et . . . remonte par cette intermédiaire à l'antique comédie latine,"[34] has not received wide acceptance.

Gustave Cohen in a major work, *La Comédie latine en France au XIIe siècle,*[35] mentions that Faral had referred to the comedies as fabliaux, and Cohen points out that some of the comedies' antifeminism reflects the fabliau spirit. He does not, however, make any case for a connection between the genres, and it is clear from his study that the outcome of the Latin comedies (marriage) and the prominant role of the servant distinguish them from fabliaux even at the most obvious level of plot. Jürgen Beyer points out these and other dissimilarities—the absence of the cunning servant figure, the emphasis on rhetoric, and the lack of moral implications.[36] It is true that a few have fabliau-like elements, but only one, *De mercatore,* has an actual fabliau analogue (*Enfant de neige*). The most obvious and reasonable explanation for common themes is that these themes circulated not only through some written sources but also through popular oral tales, later to be cast in various literary genres.

Although the search for specific literary sources proved unsuccessful, the desire to find their origins in a specific social milieu offered another approach to situating and understanding what a fabliau is. In *Chaucer and the French Tradition*[37] Charles Muscatine draws heavily on Bédier for his ideas about bourgeois literature. His comments on the fabliau's realism, however, demonstrate the much-refined analytical skills of a textual critic in the tradition of American new criticism. He points out that medieval bourgeois literature is not mimetic in the usual sense of the word:

> It is full of exaggeration, of caricature and grotesque imagination. . . . I use the terms "realistic" and "naturalistic" then, loosely—for lack of better ones—to indicate that for the Middle Ages, and particularly in contrast to the courtly tradition, this literature has a remarkable preoccupation with the animal facts of life.[38]

In his Aristotelian analysis of the fabliau, he points to the variety of characters, the dramatic and vital nature of the action, the obscene and jargon-laden diction, and the rhythms of its direct discourse which "supports the representation of *action*—direct, violent, practical—which is one of the chief ends of the whole style."[39] Muscatine recognizes that the bourgeois style, since it is not realistic in the nineteenth-century sense, was a convention like the courtly style. He believes the term *bourgeois* describes the origin and character of the style but not "its free literary currency in the Middle Ages."[40] Muscatine has read Bédier carefully and knows that Bédier points out the circulation of fabliaux in aristocratic circles as well as the contamination (Bédier's word) of the courtly style by the bourgeois. As Muscatine points out, the reverse is also true; some fabliaux have courtly elements.

The importance of Muscatine's discussion of fabliaux is his demonstration that both styles are conventional and, to a certain extent, mixed in works that pre-date the *Roman de la rose*. Although he only reinforces Bédier's identification of fabliaux as bourgeois literature, his analysis is more subtle and points the way toward better stylistic analyses.

The most significant challenge to Bédier's theory was published the same year as Muscatine's study. Per Nykrog in *Les Fabliaux* argues that Bédier consigned these texts to a mediocre status by identifying them as bourgeois:

> Mais les ecrivains "fin de siècle," tirés eux-mêmes à la fois vers l'idéalisme d'une poésie pure et vers une conception naturaliste du monde, ont assigné au genre une place méprisée sur le plan le plus bassement terrestre, en lui infligeant l'injure la plus forte dont ils disposaient: celle de l'appeler "bourgeois."[41]

There is an element of truth here because Bédier himself mentioned the weaknesses of the genre. Yet he surely did not use "bourgeois" society in its pejorative sense. Nykrog goes to great lengths to discredit Bédier's theory, and he does not give Bédier credit for admitting a mixture of audiences. In fact, Bédier does say that two literatures, fabliau and courtly genres, correspond to two different audiences, the bourgeoisie and the aristocracy. Calling his own idea *simple*, he says it is partially true not only because the fabliau flourished in the developing commercial area of Picardy and Flanders but also because some of the authors were bourgeois. He is quite aware, however, that the audiences were often aristocratic:

> D'ailleurs, s'il est vrai de dire que les fabliaux sont l'œuvre de l'esprit bourgeois, les textes ne nous montrent pas qu'ils fussent considérés comme un genre méprisable, bon pour le seul *popellus*. . . . Ils n'étaient point, comme des serfs, proscrits des nobles cours; mais, indistinctement, ils prenaient rang auprès des poèmes les plus aristocratiques.[42]

It is important to note that he distinguishes between the spirit that promoted them and the audience that may have enjoyed them.

Nykrog's central thesis is that fabliau themes are related to courtly themes which only an aristocratic audience could have appreciated. He bases his argument on the fact that 100 or 150 themes found in the fabliaux are erotic (any opposition between the sexes). Although the non-erotic themes represent nearly one-third of the total, he characterizes them as the less important ones and devotes only five pages to them. For Nykrog, the erotic themes and the judicial scenes common to many fabliaux prove that the audience was aristocratic. For him, courtly literature and the fabliau are merely reverse images of each other:

> Le triangle courtois a ainsi deux visages, l'un pénible, l'autre sublime, et du point de vue littéraire il y a entre eux une différence de *style*: le conte romantique place la femme et l'amant au premier plan, en repoussant le mari à l'arrière-plan comme une menace vague; le conte comique insiste sur les relations entre le mari et la femme, l'amant étant souvent réduit à l'état d'ombre ou de "ressort" pur.[43]

Even if the relationship between the two literatures is clear, the real proof of his theory would be to show conscious parody of courtly literature. He does demonstrate several points of comparison: stylistic parody of the *roman courtois* and the *jugement d'amour,* similarity of verse form in the fabliau and the *roman,* an occasional *conte de fée* framework, and parody of the epic as well as didactic works. This last argument is rather weak, however, because, at best, he demonstrates parodic elements scattered throughout the tales. He has not identified a given work as a systematic parody. Also, even the parody that is demonstrable is more likely aimed at the courtly audience and its conventions. Nykrog cleverly asserts, however, that fabliaux are actually burlesques not parodies; the satiric intent is focused not against the aristocracy but against the bourgeois and *vilains* who cannot live up to courtly standards:

> Non seulement les parodies des genres aristocratiques sont de loin les plus fréquentes, mais elles ont presque toutes un même caractère: elles ne raillent nullement les personnages aristocratiques et authentiquement courtois; bien au contraire toute la satire se dirige contre les personnages de rang inférieur, qui singent les manières des nobles. . . .[44]

To prove this point, he maintains that the fate of the characters reveals sympathy or antipathy toward certain social classes. In a schema incorporating sixty-one conflicts, Nykrog shows that aristocratic lovers are victorious and that clerical, bourgeois, or peasant lovers are never victorious over an aristocratic husband. While it may be true that a given lover may not be punished, it is hardly accurate to say that in many of the examples any real triumph is implied for the lover. For instance, asserting that the husband "triumphs" over the cleric in *Le Dit des perdriz* misses the point of the story. Nykrog's results are falsified by the nature of his analysis, emphasizing as it does the conflict between males. In most fabliaux, either the wife triumphs or one character hoodwinks another; lovers are usually mere stage props in the drama, as Nykrog himself pointed out (see above). The questions he poses and the answers he presents reflect more his preoccupation with courtly love triangles than they do what is significant or unique about fabliaux. The falseness of this last argument and the fact that he left out of consideration so many of the tales unfortunately vitiates an intriguing argument.

As Rychner has pointed out, Nykrog is concerned solely with what he thinks the meaning of the fabliaux is, and he expounds on themes and subjects to the detriment of any careful study of formal properties:

> Mais M. N. [Nykrog] donne la preuve la plus apparente de la prédominance qu'il accorde au sujet sur la forme lorsqu'il admet au nombre des fabliaux certains contes de la *Disciplina Clericalis* et certaines fables de Marie de France, qui traitent, il est vrai, d'authentiques thèmes de fabliaux, mais accusent par cela même la différence de *style* considérable qui sépare ces *genres.*[45]

Omer Jodogne also rejects the inclusion of tales from the *Disciplina* or the fables, saying these tales had never had an independent existence outside of the collections. He qualifies Nykrog's inclusion of them as, ". . . impertinentes au sens étymologique du terme."[46] By implication then, one of the prominent defining characteristics, recognized by almost all critics, is the fabliau's independence from any framework or collection. Nykrog's preoccupation with themes blurred a fundamental distinction which was always drawn between fabliaux and fabliau-like short narratives embedded in framing texts. It is worth noting here that the *Nouveau recueil général des fabliaux* does not include any of the tales from Marie de France's works or the *Disciplina Clericalis.*

For all of its valuable insights into mixtures of styles, Nykrog's theory claims too much and is too one-sided. Later critics have pointed out the flaws in his analysis of the characters, the social implications of their status, and the questions of audience.[47] By resurrecting Le Clerc's nineteenth-century view of the fabliau as burlesque and satire, Nykrog explains the tales in terms of ideals and attitudes external to them, rather than in terms of the diverse situations within the tales or their formal properties. There is an inevitable distortion of their broadly comic nature in this approach. Even Nykrog himself seems to have realized that his insistence on an aristocratic audience was counter to common sense and historic reality. In his article "Courtliness and the Towns-people,"[48] he admits that fabliaux had an audience in the towns, but he maintains nonetheless that they stem stylistically from courtly literature. In the final analysis, his work did not refine the definition of the genre or present a credible reinterpretation of its meaning.

At the time Nykrog's thesis appeared, Jean Rychner was also working on the fabliaux, and he re-oriented his own work to be a study of variants and an edition of them. *Contribution à l'étude des fabliaux* presents careful textual analyses to solve the thorny problems of variants and versions of the fabliaux.[49] This work is most useful for his studies of specific fabliaux and his valuable ideas on the issue of audience. He argues, for instance, that by comparing versions such as those of *De Berangier au lonc cul,* one can see *remaniement* as a function of audience. One version reflects antibourgeois sentiments, while the *remaniement* reworks the tale for a bourgeois audience. Whether it was the demands of audience or mere rhetorical choice, as Nico van den Boogaard shows in his article on the *contes* of Haiseau,[50] Rychner's argument is valuable because it shows each version as worthy of comparative stylistic analysis. His statements are not a complete refutation of Nykrog's theory; he asserts that some of the original versions may have been burlesques of courtly literature destined for both aristocratic and bourgeois publics.[51] He does, however, bring balance to the debate by saying, "Ainsi, le genre ne se situait pas pour tous au même niveau et comportait des styles bien inégaux."[52]

Concerned as he was with close textual analysis of individual fabliaux, it is not surprising that Rychner offered no definition of the genre. In a paper given at Strasbourg in 1959, he makes it clear that "after-dinner story" is an adequate definition.[53] In his article on the fabliau for the *Dictionnaire des lettres françaises* (1964), however, his description of them is more focused:

Les sujets sont traditionnels et conventionnels et se retrouvent bien souvent dans le folklore de plusieurs pays. Ils comportent presque toujours une duperie: c'est aux dépens d'une victime, souvent un dupeur dupé, que l'on enseigne ou que l'on fait rire. . . .[54]

Others before him had noted the motif of the *dupeur/dupé,* but Rychner does not make much of his own observation. It is, however, a central mechanism of their structure, as will be seen in Chapter 3.

Several other definitions have been advanced in recent scholarship. Knud Togeby defines the fabliau by comparison with another genre. A fabliau is a "nouvelle de niveau bas du XIIIe siècle,"[55] but this definition offers little of a specific nature. Omer Jodogne defines a fabliau as, "un conte en vers où, sur un ton trivial, sont narrées une ou plusieurs aventures plaisantes ou exemplaires, l'un et l'autre ou l'un ou l'autre."[56] More elaborate than Togeby's, Jodogne's definition still fails to capture much that is essential about these tales.

The impact of Nykrog's and Rychner's work was to reawaken serious scholarly interest in the fabliau. All of the important questions raised in their works begged further inquiry, and new forms of literary criticism inspired another generation of scholars to offer new interpretations. One of the most fascinating and perplexing characteristics of these tales which makes them so popular is their humor. Ten critical essays, gathered in *The Humor of the Fabliaux,* edited by Thomas Cooke and Benjamin Honeycutt,[57] propose some answers about why and how they are funny. The fact that five of the ten authors in this collection had recently written dissertations on the fabliau or closely related literature is a small indication of the growth in fabliau studies since the time of Nykrog's dissertation. In this collection, the complexity of the genre is reflected in analyses that contradict each other; some claim that a fabliau is parody, travesty, or allegory and they elaborate upon the focus of the humor (Togeby, Honeycutt, and Helsinger); others claim it is ironic (Lacy) or merely comic (Theiner) and irreducible to satire of particular social classes. Several of these articles will be taken up in more detail in Chapter 5.

The pace of fabliau scholarship accelerated during the 1970s, but the results have not provided medieval scholarship with the advances seen in research on the epic and courtly literature. Cooke and Honeycutt's volume includes some very interesting articles but nothing to alter radically our understanding of the genre. The most significant contribution in recent years to the debate over the *milieu* of the fabliau is Charles Muscatine's article "The Social Background of the Old French Fabliau."[58] With his characteristic depth of research and keen analytical skill, Muscatine shows that the fabliau reflects the materialism and attitudes of the medieval town, not the values of the court. His ideas will be discussed further in my conclusions about the social origins of the fabliau.

Thomas Cooke's *The Old French and Chaucerian Fabliaux: A Study of Their Comic Climax*[59] is a comparative study similar to Muscatine's earlier work. Eschewing all theoretical arguments about genre, the nature of comedy, or the *milieu* of the fabliau, Cooke does a traditional analysis of characters, setting, action, and dialogue. He focuses on their most important feature, a carefully prepared but surprise comic climax. By focusing on the arrangement of events to achieve their comic effect, Cooke clearly places the fabliau as most American critics have, in the tradition of the broadly comic popular tale. Nevertheless, he denies that the tales could be examples of comedy or irony in Northrop Frye's sense of the terms.

The two most recent book-length studies, Marie-Thérèse Lorcin's *Façons de sentir et de penser: Les Fabliaux français*[60] and Philippe Ménard's *Les Fabliaux: Contes à rire du moyen âge*,[61] offer little to advance the definition of the genre or explain its meaning. Lorcin's work may be useful for social historians who want to study cultural elements reflected in the fabliaux. She has not based her selection of texts on any definitions of the term and seems to ignore most of the past critical work on the genre. Her study is in the vein of Le Clerc's and Langlois's analyses of medieval society "après les fabliaux," redone in a twentieth-century social scientist's vocabulary. As his title indicates, Ménard takes the fabliau to be a "conte à rire" as Bédier did. Ménard rejects the idea that common structures can be found in this large corpus of texts, perhaps because he misunderstands the theoretical basis for structural studies. Being a catalog of themes and elements, his work is a general introduction to the genre in the tradition of French university criticism.

Although the complexity of the issues in fabliau scholarship has been demonstrated repeatedly by the conflicting and intriguing theories advanced, few scholars have applied innovative critical approaches to these texts. A few exceptions are the essays by Roy Pearcy, Willem Noomen, Michel Olsen, Larry Crist, and Nora Scott. Olsen's and Crist's articles will be discussed in conjunction with the analysis of narrative structure in Chapter 3. In "Investigations into the Principles of Fabliaux Structure,"[62] Pearcy presents his own form of semiotic and structural analysis. This article and an earlier one, "Modes of Signification,"[63] attempt to prove that the mechanisms of humor and style are related to medieval epistemological theories. He presents four patterns of comic action based on the communication between senders and receivers of verbal or sensory messages. To a certain extent, this is a discussion of irony in Jakobsonian terms. Pearcy defines a fabliau episode as a sequence of reciprocal messages. He proposes elaborate formulas to describe the action in the fifteen tales that fall into each of his four patterns, but these formulas are unnecessarily complicated for his conclusion that individual texts belong to the group called fabliaux. His primary purpose is to show that "the essential, definitive characteristic of the fabliaux is a comic structure founded on logical relationships."[64] Yet he admits that his sample is rather small to support generalizations about the genre. In both articles, Pearcy presents the fabliau as a reflection of the intellectual debates of the Middle Ages. For the theory to hold, of course, Pearcy would have to demonstrate that logical fallacies are not found in folktales that use the common device of the fool or the trickster. He is careful to avoid drawing an absolute connection between the universities and the fabliau, but it is clear that these articles have the common aim of showing the influence of Aristotelianism on the fabliaux.

Willem Noomen, in his "Structures narratives et force comique: Les Fabliaux,"[65] makes a similar point that the narratives are constructed around a disruption of communication or of a protagonists's project. Citing the theory of Koestler that comedy is "bisociative," Noomen points out that discrepancies in interpretation of words, in the identification of persons or objects, or in patterns of perceived behavior create a contrast that provokes a laugh. The clash is caused by the discrepancy between two or more "matrices" to which the behavior or words belong. Narrative technique consists of choosing characters and situations that will provoke for a specific audience the sense of distance and aggression necessary for the contrasting elements to seem funny. Noomen's primary goal in this brief article is to suggest a method for analyzing these elements, and he cautions that any generalizations must be based on a large number of individual analyses.

Noomen's sense that a classification of comic elements is possible suggests, as have many critics and editors, that common narrative elements exist and could constitute a precise definition of the genre. In *Contes pour rire*,[66] Nora Scott admits genre terms may not have been used with much precision during the Middle Ages, but she maintains that certain "tendances" can be identified initially by an intuitive grasp of resemblances among texts commonly identified as fabliaux. As she notes, the formal description, a narrative told in octosyllabic rhymed couplets without strophic breaks, also describes most thirteenth-century narratives. The particular tendencies of the genre, however, are its briefness, condensation, close connections between cause and effect, and the presence of a moral or lesson. In emphasizing their didactic qualities, Scott is echoing Paul Zumthor's definition of the short narrative.[67] Although many critics tend to discount the explicit *moralités* and judgement framework, these elements cannot be ignored, as will be seen in the discussion of the fabliau's relationship to the exemplum in Chapter 2.

In one respect, the most recent criticism is the most ambitious but also the least satisfying if the reader looks for more than allusions to the possibility of describing the structure and meaning of the fabliau. Some of the recent studies rework tired clichés about the genre; some obfuscate in jargon and formulas what needs to be made clear. Others, daunted perhaps by the size of the corpus and the diversity of the tales, stop short and claim, as does Scott, that this is "une tache réservée à l'avenir. . . ."[68]

It is precisely this task that I take up, beginning with an inductive analysis of the texts in order to offer a structural definition which forms the basis for a reinterpretation of the meaning and values informing these texts. Starting with a large corpus including every text that either Bédier or Nykrog referred to as a fabliau, the analysis then narrows to the self-proclaimed ones for the initial phase only of establishing a formal description. Once that is accomplished, I then demonstrate its validity and application to the majority of *all* texts in the corpus. The subsequent interpretations of the genre are based on the group I would identify as typical fabliaux. There is an inevitable circularity in taking Bédier's and Nykrog's lists as the corpus, then defining the genre by reason of characteristics found there. I am heartened, however, by the fact that in preparing the *Nouveau recueil complet des fabliaux* van den Boogaard and Noomen also took the traditional corpus as their starting point. After much research into additional manuscripts, they were able to add only one text to the group. Taking this corpus as a given is a conservative approach to the research task, but nothing precludes taking the results presented here and applying them to new or debated texts at some later point. In the discussion which follows, three fragmentary texts are excluded from the combined list of Bédier and Nykrog, leaving 165 tales with which to begin a search for the meaning and definition of the word *fablel*.

2

The Didacticism of the Fabliau

Among the many generic terms for short story, such as *conte, dit,* or *trufle,* found in the 165 tales in the fabliau corpus, the word *fablel* occurs in sixty-nine texts.[1] As was mentioned in Chapter 1, most of these tales have a tripartite structure consisting of the narrator's introduction, the narrative proper, and the narrator's conclusion. By narrator, I mean storyteller in the broadest sense, be he *trouvère, jongleur, menestrel,* or *remanieur,* for that distinction is not at issue here. These narrators most often use the term *fablel* in their introductions and conclusions, and certain implications can be drawn from these contexts about the sources and meaning of the narratives. It quickly becomes obvious that for them, the fabliau has not only entertainment but also practical value. Part of the definition of fabliau depends upon clarifying the question of their didacticism, their relationship to the exemplum, and the implications of their concluding morals.

Fablel is rarely found within the narrative itself, unless the author interrupts to reflect on his art. For example:

> Or sai-je bien qu'il me covient
> Dire par quel réson Jehans,
> Qui molt ot cele nuit d'ahans,
> Remist les .II. prestres ensamble:
> Se ne le vous di, ce me samble,
> Li fabliaus seroit corrompus.
>
> (*D'Estormi* MR I: 19, vv. 250-55)

The use of *fablel* in the introductions provides only sketchy clues as to its meaning. Often *fablel* and the verb form *fabloier* are mere synonyms for *conte* and *conter*: "Seignor, oiez .I. noviau conte / Que mon fablel dit et raconte . . ." (*De la damoisele qui ne pooit oïr parler de foutre* MR III: 65, vv. 1-2). At times the word *fablel* is modified, as in these lines from *Du prestre ki abevete* (MR III: 61, vv. 2-3): "Se vous me volés escouter, / .I. flablel courtois et petit [vous raconterai] . . . ," but the word *courtois* must be understood in terms of

19

the story which follows. Here the word is ironic because the story depicts one of the crudest seduction scenes in the collection. The stories introduced by the term *fablel* are fabricated from components referred to as *conte, aventure,* or *matère,* which the author had heard, perhaps at the market place:

> Dès or, que que j'aie targié,
> Puisqu'il m'a esté enchargié,
> Voudré je un fabliau ja fere
> Dom la matiere oï retrere
> A Vercelai devant les changes.
>
> *(De la grue* MR V: 126, vv. 1-5)

The sources may also have been written, for the narrators in several fabliaux give credit to their sources. Even if the specific attribution is false, some written source may have existed:

> Sans plus longuement deslaier,
> M'estuet conter d'un chevalier
> Et d'une dame l'avanture,
> Qui avint, ce dit l'escriture,
> . . . .
> Pierres d'Anfol, qui ce fablel
> Fist et trova premieremant. . . .
>
> *(Du chevalier qui recovra l'amor de sa dame* MR VI: 151, vv. 1-4, 248-49)

Although the introductions contain more than twenty-five references to *fablel* where the word means a type of story, there are few indications as to the nature of the tale. Two ideas, however, are frequently expressed: fabliaux are good for people because they teach by example and because they are amusing:

> Qui biau set dire et rimoier,
> Bien doit sa science avoier
> A fere chose où l'en aprenge,
> Et dire que l'en n'i mesprenge.
> Et cil ne fet mie folie
> Qui d'autrui mesfet se chastie.
>
> *(Du vilain au buffet* MR III: 80, vv. 1-6)

> Flabel sont or mout entorsé;
> Maint denier en ont enborsé
> Cil qui les content et les portent,
> Quar grant confortement raportent
> As enovrez et as oiseus,
> Quant il n'i a genz trop noiseus,
> Et nès à ceus qui sont plain d'ire,

> Se il oent bon flabeau dire,
> Si lor fait il grant alegance . . .
> *(Du chevalier qui fist les cons parler* MR VI: 147, vv. 1-9)

There are implications that the humorous ones risk offending a sense of propriety and are an inferior form of entertainment. In a *débat* between two *jongleurs* (this is not a fabliau although it was published in the Montaiglon collection), one accuses the other of being an unsuccessful, low-class storyteller. He then brags about his own repertoire, which consists of aristocratic genres, epics, and romances. In response, the accused *jongleur* brags about all of his famous acquaintances and his repertoire, listing *contes* and fabliaux by title. The implication is that the *jongleur*, who brags most about his *dits*, *contes*, and fabliaux, irritates the company with his inferior works and provokes the wrath of the *menestrel*:

> Diva! quar lai ester ta jangle:
> Si te va séoir en cel angle,
> Nos n'avons de ta jangle cure,
> Quar il est raison et droiture
> Par tot le mont, que cil se taise
> Qui ne sait dire riens qui plaise.
> *(Des deux bordéors ribauz* MR I: 1, vv. 1-6)

Comments in many fabliaux show that contemporary audiences realized that the fabliau was a genre associated with material destined to violate certain social conventions. The opening lines of *Du fotéor,* a tale about a man for hire, surprisingly state:

> Qui fabloier velt si fabloie,
> Mais que son dit n'en affebloie
> Por dire chose desresnable;
> L'en puet si bel dire une fable
> Qu'ele puet ainsi com voir plaire.
> (MR I: 28, vv. 1-5)

This tale relates a ribald adventure, but the author has followed his own warning, because it does not become *desresnable*. There is also a playful recognition of the risqué nature of these tales, as can be seen in the final verses of *Du sot chevalier,* "Et li sos ot apris à foutre. / A cest mot est mon fablel outre" (MR I: 20, vv. 317-18).

Jean Bodel seems very apologetic about their limitations, although he wrote nine fabliaux:

> Seignor, après le fabloier,
> Me vueil à voir dire apoier,

Qar qui ne sait dire que fables,
N'est mie conterres regnables
Por à haute cort à servir. . . .
                    (*Del couvoiteus et de l'envieus* MR V: 135, vv. 1-5)

His attitude is significant in that, as an author of diverse genres, he has
seemingly enjoyed writing fabliaux but makes no pretense about their status
compared to the genres enjoyed by a "high court." It is only in making something out of a fabliau, he says, that it can assume a higher meaning. "Mès qui
de fablel fet grant fable, / N'a pas de trover sens legier" (*Des .II. chevaus*
MR I: 13, vv. 20-21). Here Bodel implies that a *fablel* has value if it assumes
the didactic power of a fable.

Many critics have agreed with Bédier that because fabliaux are funny, they
are not moral tales. Bédier admits that there are fabliaux which come close to
being *dits moraux* and that ultimately we must categorize tales by questioning
whether the author is attracted to his subject because the story amused him
or whether he imagined the story to prove a point. For him, fabliaux are
essentially "contes à rire," not moral tales.[2] If we accept, however, what the
authors say about their stories, then we must recognize that fabliaux were
seen as lighthearted by some, but also as capable of demonstrating a moral
by others. In fact, the references to their didactic qualities are more numerous.[3] One author perceives the double function of the genre:

Vos qui fableaus volez oïr,
Peine metez à retenir;
Volentiers les devez aprendre,
Les plusors por essample prendre,
Et les plusours por les risées
Qui de meintes gens sont amées.
                    (*De la dame qui se venja* MR VI: 140, vv. 1-6)

A hesitation to accept fabliaux as didactic stems from familiarity with
the saints' lives, religious allegories, and other medieval didactic works. If
didacticism means seriousness of tone and loftiness of subject, then the fabliau
does not fit. Yet, the power of fabliaux to be examples is clearly stated in
the texts, so many critics have made the case that these are counterexamples—
products, for example, of the antifeminism of the Middle Ages. Another
approach to their didacticism is set forth by Zumthor in the *Essai de poétique
médiévale.*[4] As a short narrative form, fabliaux are closely associated with the
lais and exempla, all of which Zumthor calls "nouvelle" forms to distinguish
them from the *grand chant courtois* and the *roman.* The *roman* plays out
its significance from *aventure* to *aventure* and is an open form. The *nouvelle*
forms, on the other hand, are a "durée close," compressing the narrative to
its barest essentials and eliminating ambiguity, for the narrative only serves

to reveal a point. "Cette structure se manifeste généralement en ceci que l'aboutissement de l'action constitue un 'pointe': une cause finale par laquelle est produit et en vertu de laquelle s'organise ce qui la précède et l'amène."[5] Zumthor emphasizes that the compactness of the *nouvelle* form means that the conclusion plays out the premises of the opening, so that rarely are there any causes that impinge on the action from outside the narrative system. Thus, as opposed to the *roman,* a moral or "senefiance" is implied by the narrative itself and is usually explicitly stated by the narrator:

> La "senefiance" d'un roman s'établit à partir de chaque détail ou épisode, et comporte ainsi, normalement, une multiplicité qui peut aller jusqu'à la contradiction; par la même, elle n'est définissable qu'à un haut degré d'abstraction. La "senefiance" d'une "nouvelle" a pour signifiant le texte entier comme tel et, sauf exception, elle a quelque chose d'obvie et comme concret.[6]

Zumthor's analysis clarifies for us that didacticism in the fabliau must not be taken to mean preaching Christian morality. It is no doubt because readers have expected tales with morals to be serious that they have rejected the morals attached to fabliaux as sarcasm or mere after-thoughts designed to appease the Church. Jürgen Beyer says that fabliaux use the form of a moral but destroy its value. "The moral actually documents the unfitness of the fabliau for moralization."[7] But for Zumthor, the fact that morals may be ironic does not change the fact that the narratives are structured to teach a lesson. "Qu'elle [la morale] soit parfois ironique ou mensongère ne modifie pas le système: La narration est, fondamentalement le lieu d'un enseignement."[8] His theory that *lai,* fabliau, *fable,* and exemplum are less separate genres than forms of the *nouvelle* would explain in part the ubiquitous and apparently undiscriminating use of these very terms in the texts themselves. It is apparent that fabliau writers got the stories or anecdotes from a range of written and oral material and that they referred to both their sources and their own compositions by a variety of generic terms. As Zumthor and others have remarked, "Certains 'fabliaux' sont en relation matérielle directe avec des *exempla* latins."[9] Although he makes no reference to how many fabliaux might actually be versions of exempla, Zumthor's discussion leaves the impression that many may be, and that lines of demarcation between these genres are not clear. Nevertheless, the effort to distinguish these *nouvelle* genres, as Zumthor would call them, is not hopeless. The fabliaux can definitely be distinguished from exempla on the basis of formal criteria, and lessons in the conclusions to fabliaux offer some insight into the unique qualities of these tales.

Exempla are essentially anecdotes on a great variety of subjects and were used during sermons to exemplify Christian doctrine. The critics who study primarily exempla usually distinguish them from fabliaux by virtue of their lack of humor, because exempla were required to have a seriousness of tone befitting the pulpit. The anecdotes are explanatory and descriptive by nature. As J.-Th. Welter explains in *L'Exemplum dans la littérature religieuse et didactique du moyen âge,*

> Cette matière [the narrative] se répartit en deux classes: l'une comprenant la description de la nature, des phénomènes célestes et terrestres, des propriétés des pierres, des plantes, et des animaux, l'autre comprenant celle de l'activité des êtres animés.[10]

There is a difference, however, between any sort of illustration of a point and an exemplum, which is, strictly speaking, a narrative or tale. As Joseph Mosher explains in *The Exemplum in Early Religious and Didactic Literature of England,*

> It is quite likely that some writers considered any illustration whatever an *exemplum*. Others, perhaps recognizing a distinction between an example and an *exemplum,* may have carelessly confused the two at times.[11]

Nevertheless, according to Mosher, the true tradition in the Church was that an exemplum was a brief narrative involving human characters, a trait that separated exempla from related forms such as fables, bestiary and lapidary passages, apothegms, and figures of speech.[12]

Welter makes a formal distinction between an exemplum and an ordinary tale or anecdote on the basis of length. The exemplum consists normally of only eight to twenty lines, and if it becomes longer the moralist has become a *conteur* interested in pleasing rather than making a point.[13] Briefness is relative, of course. The average of 300 lines for a fabliau would distinguish it from an exemplum for Welter but would make the two similar for Zumthor when he compares them to the *roman.* Yet, the comparison shows that fabliaux, by virtue of their length, are not just skeletal anecdotes and do go beyond making a point. The majority of those fabliaux which do have exempla analogues, however, are under 150 lines.

In addition to the formal difference in length, the exempla differ from fabliaux in that the former are prose tales whereas fabliaux are in octosyllabic verse. The fact that the authors say they are reworking a well-known story into rhyme reinforces the notion that these tales were conscious literary creations rather than mere illustrations of doctrine. The verse form also indicates that they were no doubt recited in circumstances where the rhyme added to their entertainment value. The exempla, on the other hand, were not supposed to entertain or evoke gratuitous pleasure. According to M.-M. Davy, Etienne de Bourbon, the author of a treatise on sermon making and compiler of exempla, described their purpose with appropriate seriousness:

Selon lui, l'exemplum, qui est à la fois un récit, un enseignement moral et religieux, une application immédiate à l'homme, peut faire mieux comprendre les vérités de la religion chrétienne et les graver à jamais dans les cœurs.[14]

The distinction between a story that is good *for* something and a good story cannot always be made, but it is easy to recognize the extremes. There is no doubt that obscene or lascivious tales were not considered didactic and were therefore unfit for sermons. Th.-M. Charland in his work *Artes Praedicandi* discusses one of the ornaments of style: the *opportuna jocatio*.[15] The medieval sermon-makers advocated the inclusion of a few funny stories or jokes in order to recapture a sleepy audience's attention, but there were to be no more than three and they could not be obscene.[16] The theoreticians were clear in their rejection of theatrics and obscenity. Alain de Lille, one of the most important theorists, said that in sermons there should be " 'ni bouffoneries, ni puerilités, ni mélodies cadencées ou vers bien tournés, qui servent plus à charmer les oreilles qu'à former l'esprit.' "[17]

According to Davy, Jacques de Vitry also spoke against buffoonery, "il défend rigoureusement les histoires vaines, les paroles bouffonnes, voire obscènes."[18] The Latin from which Davy has translated is more precise, and we can see a direct attack against the verse tales, presumably the fabliaux, " 'infructuosas enim fabulas et curiosa poetarum carmina a sermonibius nostris debemus relegare . . . scurrilia tamen aut obscena verba vel turpis sermo ex ore praedicatoris non procedant.' "[19] This statement, as well as that of Alain de Lille against "melodies cadencées ou vers bien tournés," shows that officially, at least, exempla were not to be ornamented, and the preachers were not to borrow literary tales if the entertainment value surpassed their instructive qualities.

Exempla, like parables, had always been used by the Church, but they were most popular during the thirteenth century due to the creation of the preaching and minor orders. One might assume that fabliaux were outgrowths of the proliferation of moral anecdotes, but as Welter points out, the relationship was more likely the reverse. Fabliaux were sources for the growing collections of exempla. He shows that secular tales designated as *fabula* in Latin were always popular and always decried by the Church from the fourth century to Saint Bernard.[20] For Welter, *fabula,* "idle tales" or "vulgar stories" against which the Church Fathers railed, are synonymous with fabliaux. So from his perspective, the thirteenth century witnesses the culmination of a long tradition of *fabula* that encroach on genuine moral anecdotes. Welter feels that as they became popular, they influenced the sermon makers because of their satiric qualities:

Au XIIIe siècle, le genre des fabliaux se sera définitivement constitué et l'anonymat des auteurs aura disparu. Aussi les fabléaux, comme on les appelait alors,

constitueront-ils la satire sociale la plus réaliste et la plus vraie à la fois. Grâce
à ce caractère satirique, ils finiront par envahir la chaire principalement avec les
prédicateurs des ordres mendiants.[21]

From whichever perspective one sees the influence, fabliau authors drawing on exempla collections, or sermon makers dipping into popular tales for
their material, the fact remains that very few actual analogues between the two
genres exist. In a recent study, I searched among fabliaux in the Montaiglon
collection and five major exempla collections but found only fifteen tales with
analogues in both genres.[22]

Furthermore, the most important formal distinction to be made between
one form of didactic literature—the exemplum—and another—the fabliau—is
that fabliaux are independent tales and exempla are always part of a larger
work. Bédier used this criterion as a major one in accepting tales into the
corpus of fabliaux; but, as was mentioned in Chapter 1, Nykrog challenged
this tradition by calling tales from the *Disciplina Clericalis* and Marie de
France's *Isopet* fabliaux. Most critics, including the editors of the *Nouveau
recueil complet des fabliaux,* have not agreed with Nykrog, and non-indepen-
dent tales seem to be definitively excluded from the corpus of fabliaux. Still,
there is a tendency to take exempla, separate them from their context, and
treat them as independent tales when analyzing them. Collections of exempla,
especially those without moral lessons attached, such as Jacques de Vitry's
Sermones Vulgares, appear to be anthologies of short stories. But this is a
misconception of the word *exemplum.* When an anecdote is placed in a compi-
lation that is used as a preacher's encyclopedia of illustrations or when it is
actually part of a sermon, the anecdote undergoes a formal change, losing its
individual status by becoming part of a new whole. It is then interpretable in
terms of the framework that surrounds it, especially the biblical intertext to
which that framework refers.

A comparison of the exemplum and fabliau analogues "The Woman Who
Made Her Husband a Monk" from Jacques de Vitry's collection and the fabliau
Des .III. dames qui trouvèrent l'anel will demonstrate how two similar anecdotes have different meanings.[23] Jacques de Vitry's tale relates the story of a
woman who gets her despised husband drunk and then runs to tell certain
monks that he has expressed a desire to join them. Because he is a rich man,
they happily accept the proposed contract, accompany the wife to her house,
tonsure him, and carry him back to the monastery. There is no moral conclusion after the narrative, but the man's reactions carry the interpretation. He
feels shame because his drunkenness and naïveté have led him to this condition. The moral order external to the tale regulates the outcome of the narrative because there is no questioning of the appropriateness of his condition
or effort made to change it.

Two versions of similar fabliaux incorporate this anecdote in a longer tale entitled *Des .III. dames que trouvèrent l'anel* (MR I: 15 and MR VI: 138). The frame story in each version tells of three ladies who find a precious ring and decide to give it to the woman who best deceives her husband. The MR I: 15 version contains some interesting additions to the exemplum version. Following the narrative statements which present the frame and motivation for the women's individual stories, the first woman enlists the help of her lover, who brings wine and a monk's robe to the house. Once the husband has fallen into a stupor, they dress and tonsure him, carry him to the monastery, and leave him against the door. There is an amplification of the action and characters by virtue of the lover's presence, but there is also a difference in arrangement of the narrative in comparison with the exemplum. The wife and lover carry out one narrative sequence together without the help of the monks. The fabliau also continues with an entirely new narrative sequence. In the morning, the husband sees his new condition and, instead of lamenting it, sees God's hand at work and gladly accepts his new calling. The husband initiates a second narrative sequence when he petitions to enter the monastery, confronts his wife with his sudden conversion, begs permission to leave her, and finally attains his goal. The end fulfills the desires of both parties.

The narrative possibilities exploited in this fabliau, which are very typical of the genre, involve an amplification of the number of actors and to a small extent their characterization. The most important innovation is in new action which branches from the initial sequence. The narrative moves beyond a simple opposition between the original antagonists to reverse the situation, giving an apparent victory to both sides. The second sequence of events, based on a false understanding of the earlier events, demonstrates an idiosyncratic response on the husband's part; the man misses the point and merrily dupes himself into a monk's life. Beyond the marvelous comic input such a twist provides, the man's response demonstrates that the meaning of events is challenged within the narrative itself. As opposed to the accepting, passive husband in the exemplum who understands why he is in the predicament, i.e., vice led to his downfall, the husband in the fabliau questions his situation and decides that God must have performed a miracle. The anecdote of the exemplum, arranged to illustrate a moral value system implied by the framework text, offers an exemplary character, one who conforms to the values and accepts the ordered world of the "Christian intertext" as the audience is also supposed to do. In the fabliau, on the other hand, the expanded narrative holds those values up for scrutiny in two ways. One is by having characters react according to their own interpretation of the situation, and the other is by placing the action in a context where the audience is asked to evaluate the action.

Other comparisons between fabliau and exemplum analogues reinforce the point that the fabliaux increase the action of the anecdote in linear fashion;

events move literally beyond the final point of the exemplum. The events act out reactions to the kernel situation through either a new sequence of events for a protagonist or the judicial scene which is an enacted interpretation of the preceding action. The exemplum, its plot reduced to a brief sketch of events, depends upon the values of its framework text, whereas the fabliau shows a tendency to play out the implications and even challenge the moral order the exemplum illustrated. The narrative of a fabliau may be similar to that of an exemplum and even conclude with a moral; but the fabliau, as an independent tale, creates its own world of meaning. Its didacticism, as Zumthor suggests, is a result of its narrative arrangement. What Zumthor does not go on to explore, but what is crucial to our discussion, is how the morals reveal the nature of the tales and their own very particular frame of reference.

If, then, the distinction between exemplum and fabliau has been established, three texts from the *Disciplina Clericalis* must be eliminated from the initial group of self-proclaimed fabliaux with which I began my study. Of the sixty-six remaining ones, thirty-five conclude with a moral, seven with a proverb, and three by asking the audience to judge which of the characters has won the conflict depicted in the story. The proverbs concluding some of these fabliaux serve the same function as the moral because they reiterate or interpolate the point of the story. The *jugement* framework also can be seen as a variation on the explicit moral because the capacity to exercise judgement is literal rather than implied. The total number of morals, proverbs, or judgements— forty-five—means that almost seventy percent of these self-proclaimed fabliaux conclude with some manner of moral reflection.

The morals are usually preceded by formulas such as, "Par cest fablel vueil enseignier," or "Par cest flabel poez savoir." The moral itself may consist of only a few lines followed by an *explicit*:

> Par cest fablel prover vous vueil
> Que cil fet folie et orgueil
> Qui fame engingnier s'entremet;
> Quar qui fet à fame .I. mal tret,
> Ele en fet .X. ou .XV. ou .XX.
> Ainsi ceste aventure avint.
> *(Des .II. changéors* MR I: 23, vv. 283-88)

The fabliau may combine a proverb and an expanded moral:

> Cest fabliaus nos dit et raconte
> Q'an son respit, dit li vilains,
> *Que à celui doit l'an del pain*
> *Q'on ne cuide jamais veoir;*
> Car l'an ne cuide pas savoir
> Tel chose qui vient mout sovant.
> *(Le Povre Clerc* MR V: 132, vv. 242-47)

In a few cases the proverb is stated by one of the characters and the narrator's presence is therefore not quite so obtrusive. The majority of these conclusions, however, constitute a clear break from the story, a final comment by the narrator. When the *jugement* framework is used, the call for audience participation in evaluating the story definitely breaks away from the *récit* to substitute a new set of characters, the audience, as arbitrator and moralizer.

The fact that the moral conclusions are structurally independent of the narrative and have little impact on the narrative if removed may have created the impression that they are not related to the narratives or are not genuine. When the narratives and morals are compared, however, it is evident that they are fitting. For example, in *Du provost à l'aumuche* (MR I: 7), a provost steals a side of bacon during a feast in honor of his master. He hides the bacon under his hat and is caught because the fat, heated by a nearby fire, starts to drip down his face. According to the moral drawn by the author, the discovery of the theft and the subsequent beating that the provost receives are examples of ill-gotten gain being lost.

A few of the morals could be characterized as oblique, or drawn from a secondary point in the narrative. For example in *Des trois boçus* (MR I: 2), the jealously guarded wife of a hunchback accidentally suffocates three musicians who have been secretly entertaining her. Her ruse to get rid of the bodies also results in her husband's death. Yet the moral drawn is not against women and their craftiness but against the husband. We know from the opening lines that the *boçu* was an ugly creature who was able to marry the beautiful girl only because he was rich. The moral is directed against him for having thought that money could buy the affection of a beautiful girl:

> DURANS, qui son conte define,
> Dist c'onques Diex ne fist meschine
> C'on ne puist por denier avoir;
> . . . .
> Por ses deniers ot li boçus
> La dame qui tant bele estoit.
> Honiz soit li hons, quels qu'il soit,
> Qui trop prise mauvès deniers,
> Et qui les fist fère premiers.
> (*Des trois boçus* MR I: 2, vv. 285-87, 292-96)

Another indication of the didactic purpose of these tales can be seen in the wording of this particular passage in *Des trois boçus*. The word *definer* is normally a synonym of *finer*, "to end" or "to finish," especially when it is the final verse. *Des tresces* (MR IV: 94) ends with this verse: "Ici vueil definer mon conte" (v. 434). It can, however, mean "define" from *definire* and when the word *fabliau* is its direct object, it would seem the more likely translation, as in the phrase "DURANS, qui son conte define." *Definer* precedes the moral here and seems to reinforce Durans's wish to summarize the story and reiterate his point. According to von Wartburg, *definer* in Scholastic philosophy signifies "Faire connaître par une formule précise ce qu'est une chose, ce qu'on entend par un terme; fixer le sens d'un point de dogme; déterminer avec precision" (FEW, III 30a). Thus a phrase such as "Tout ainsi cis fabliaus define" (*Le Cuvier* MR I: 9, v. 150) could be read, "in this way this fabliau makes its definition [of a problem] or explains a point," rather than the simple "thus this fabliau ends." This reading of the word *definer* reinforces the didactic intention of the narrators.

Furthermore, there is only one example of a blatantly sarcastic moral. *Du chevalier à la robe vermeille* (MR III: 57) tells of a man who comes home unexpectedly, surprising his wife, who has time to hide her lover but not to pick up his clothes or other belongings. According to the wife's quickly fabricated story, the various items are gifts sent by her brother. When the husband awakens from a nap and asks for them, she tells him he must have been dreaming. The moral is as follows:

> Cis fabliaus aus maris promet
> Que de folie s'entremet
> Qui croit ce que de ses iex voie;
> Mès cil qui vait la droite voie,
> Doit bien croire sans contredit
> Tout ce que sa fame li dit.
>
> (vv. 307-12)

What then is the thrust of the moral reflections? Among the forty-five fabliaux with moral conclusions, several present a double message, so there are fifty-one in all. They refer to: deceptive women (21), poetic justice (11), fools (6), the need for others (3), lechers (2), and misuse of money or goods (2). They advise people not to make fun of others (2), to beware of bad company (1), and to persevere in love (1). Finally there is a statement that *clercs* are more clever than *chevaliers*. Almost all of these reflections or opinions, although they may seem at first to be rather disparate ideas, can be grouped under several related headings. For example, the audience is admonished to be wary of those who would deceive us: women, lechers (especially clerics), and bad company:

> Par example cis fabliaus dist
> Fame est fète por decevoir;
> Mençonge fet devenir voir,
> Et voir fet devenir mençonge.
>
> (*Le Dit des perdriz* MR I: 17, vv. 150-53)

> Cis fabliaus moustre par example
> Que nus hom qui bele fame ait,

Por nule proière ne lait
Clerc gesir dedenz son ostel. . . .
(De Gombert et des .II. clers MR I: 22, vv. 184-87)

In Jean Bodel's fabliau *De Barat et de Haimet,* a poor fellow who had briefly
associated with two robbers never succeeds in recovering the ham stolen by
his crafty friends. Bodel concludes with a proverb: "Por ce vous di, seignor
baron: / *Male est compaignie à larron*" (MR IV: 97, vv. 531-32).

The reader or listener is also warned not to deceive himself as the fools do,
or deceive others by tricking them or by being an imposter. Often in the
tales of adultery, the conclusion is similar to the one in *Du prestre ki abevete*
(MR III: 61), where the husband is ridiculed for being a fool:

Ensi fu li vilains gabés
Et decheüs et encantés
Et par le prestre et par son sans
Qu'il n'i ot paine ne ahans,
Et, pour ce que li uis fu tuis,
Dist on encor: *Maint fol paist duis.*

(vv. 79-84)

A man can also be a fool about money, overestimating its power to buy love,
as in *Des trois boçus* discussed above. Greed also makes men foolish, as in
De Brunain where the *vilain* naïvely believes the priest when he says that God
returns twofold to the cheerful giver. The *vilain* almost loses his only cow by
giving it to the priest, but the greed of the priest who accepts the gift is punished
in this case because the *vilain*'s cow not only returns home but drags the
priest's cow with her. Those who act under false pretenses are also criticized.
In *De Berengier au lonc cul* (MR IV: 93) the wife of a boastful husband discovers the secret of his "valor" when she sees him denting his armor against
a tree and inflicting superficial wounds on himself. She in turn deceives and
humiliates him. The author advises men not to brag of anything they cannot
live up to:

Por ce deffent à toute gent,
Qui se vantent de maint afere
Dont il ne sevent à chief trere,
Qu'il lessent ester lor vantance.

(vv. 274-77)

Related to the idea of being aware of deceivers is the advice given in several
of the fabliaux to esteem properly one's need for other people. These stories
advocate the creation of alliances in order to eliminate the possibility of that
person's trickery or in order to create allies as a defense against a third party's
deceit. In *Le Cuvier* (MR I: 9), for instance, a wife tricks her husband by hiding

her lover under an overturned wash tub. Just as the husband enters, the neighbor from whom the wife had borrowed the tub sends her servant to request its
return. Fortunately, the neighbor can guess by the friend's refusal that it is
needed for the specific purpose. Therefore, she is able to help her friend by
paying a fool to cry "au feu," which causes a commotion in the street and
allows the lover to escape. The author concludes:

> Or puet cele son cuvier rendre,
> Qui moult a esté effraée.
> Ainsi s'est cele délivrée,
> Qui moult savoit de la chevance,
> Quar apris l'avoit de s'enfance;
> S'ele n'éust besoing éu,
> Ele n'éust jamès séu
> Le grant besoin de sa voisine.

(vv. 142-49)

Even more pointed is the conclusion to *Le Povre Clerc* (MR V: 132) where a
woman is betrayed by a young cleric to whom she had refused food. Brought
back into the home by the husband, the cleric begins to reveal the presence
of the wife's lover. The author cites the proverb *"Que à celui doit l'an del
pain / Q'on ne cuide jamais veoir"* (vv. 244-45). We are not being admonished
to give food to strangers out of a sense of charity, but because we never know
when that person will be in a position to either help or hurt us.

Within the moral framework of the tale, poetic justice or an immediate
retributory justice is the ultimate threat to the deceiver, and at the same time
the consolation for the deceived. It is a familiar theme in the conclusions
to see the idea expressed that someone received their just desserts. For example
in *Du fotéor* (MR I: 28), the conclusion tells a little of the young man's later
life during which he was very successful until he was eventually defeated by his
overconfidence. The final verses are:

> Mais Fortune, à qui il servi,
> L'en dona ce qu'il deservi.
> L'en dit pieça: qui va, il lesche,
> Et qui toz jors se siet, il sèche.

(vv. 379-82)

The fabliau often reiterates in its conclusion the idea that there is a direct
correspondence between a character's type and his actions, or specific situations and the set of stereotyped reactions generated by them. Thus fabliaux
reflect the desire for an orderly world where events do not occur randomly;
characters want to restore order or balance, but they may not be able to do so.
It is not surprising to find in the conclusions that the capacity to render a
judgement or justice is overtly stated, justice being the capacity to "right"

imbalances. Nevertheless, in the majority of cases when justice is sought, it is perverted by a corrupt judge. Justice is also an open system; it can be "suspended," as in the cases when the author asks for the audience's opinion:

> Or dite voir, n'i ait menti,
> Et si jugiez réson et voir
> Laquele doit l'anel avoir.
>
> (*Des .III. dames* MR I: 15, vv. 276-78)

The theme of justice returns later in the discussion in Chapter 5, but even in these conclusions we can see that justice is a secular, not sacred, notion. Audience participation in rendering a decision reinforces the idea that justice is of this world. Unlike the morals of exempla, fabliaux do not allude to damnation or heavenly rewards, although God may be credited with having established the system of earthly justice. The results of one's behavior are immediate and tangible, as in the case of the priest who is humiliated and loses all of his money because he tried to seduce the daughter of an honest bourgeoise (*Du prestre et d'Alison* MR II: 31). The final verses of *Du prestre qu'on porte* (MR IV: 89), another tale of a priest who is killed because of lechery, express this quite clearly:

> Por le siecle fali et vuit
> Qui mal se preuve et est provés
> Chaitis en cest siecle est trovés.
>
> (vv. 1162-64)

All but two of the conclusions to these tales can be encompassed by two related themes: the need to avoid deception and the promise or threat of retributory justice.[24] Their lessons are practical and relate especially to some very common experiences. Looking at the relative importance accorded to various types of deception, it is immediately apparent that women are perceived to be the arch deceivers, although they are by no means the only ones capable of deceit. In the introductions and conclusions there are strong indications that these tales have not only to do with trickery, but most especially the treachery of women.

A further proof that by the thirteenth century, the word *fablel* had come to signify tales about deception and especially the wiles of women, is apparent through a study of the manuscripts of the *Disciplina Clericalis*. Nykrog included some of these tales not only because they resembled fabliaux plots but also because some are actually called fabliaux in one of the Old French manuscripts. Setting aside the Arabic or earlier Oriental versions, I looked at Pierre Alfonse's twelfth-century Latin translation. He begins by saying that he has translated the work in order for men, clerics in particular, to better themselves. His teachings come from a variety of writings, "Partim ex prouer-

biis philosophorum et suis castigacionibus, partim ex prouerbiis et castigacionibus arabicis et fabulis et uersibus, partim ex animalium et uolucrum
similitudinibus."[25] These separate examples are incorporated in the story of
a philosopher teaching his son by telling anecdotes interspersed with the
father and son's comments. The Latin designations for the genres indicate
nothing more than classical proverbs, fables, and teachings. In the conversation that precedes the first tale about a bad wife, the son asks his father to
speak to him of *fabulis* or *proverbiis* on the subject of women's treachery.
Throughout the text the terminology used to refer to the tales is limited
to those terms, or *narracio* and *legentes*.

There are two versions of the *Disciplina* in Old French, both of which
date from the thirteenth century, and a Middle English version from the
fifteenth century. In comparing these three translations of the Latin, it is
apparent that two are rather faithful translations of the Latin, at least in
regard to the literary terms of interest here. These two are Version B of the
Old French, which is in the Anglo-Norman dialect, and the Middle English
one. For example, the father has told his son to beware of bad company,
which provokes a long diatribe against women. The son then asks for some
illustrations:

> Dixit quidam discipulus magistro suo: Legi in libris philosophorum quibus pre-
> cipiunt ut ab ingenio femine peruerse custodiat se homo. Et Salomon in *prouerbiis*
> hoc idem admonet. Sed tu si super ingenio illius siue de *fabulis* siue de *prouerbiis*
> aliquid memoriter tenes, uellem renarrando me instrueres.[26]

In Old French (Version B) this becomes:

> Et dist le fiz. "Mult me plerreit
> Oïr de femmes, ke ke seit,
> Kar cum plus les conuistreie,
> De tant meuz guarder n'en purreie."[27]

And in Middle English:

> Suche a disciple saide to his Maister. "I have rad in wordis of Philosophres whiche
> comaunden a man to kepe hym from the forward wit and engyne of wymmen.
> And [Salomon] only in the same *proverbes* amonestith and warneth. If thow
> therfor any thing above the wiles of hem memoratief holdist I wold with tellyny
> thow woldist teche and lierne me, outher of *fables* outher of *porverbis*."[28]

In Version A, the Old French text in Continental French (as the editors Hilke
and Soderhjelm call it),[29] the son uses the term *fablel* in this passage:

> "Chiers pere, mout ai grant talent
> D'oïr de lor contenement;

De lor uevres et de lor tors,
De lor engienz et de lor mors
Orreir volentiers parler
Por saveir mei d'eles garder;
Aucun *fablel,* aucune *rien*
M'en dites, si fereiz mout bien!"[30]

This is not the first instance in which *fablel* is used in Version A. In the introduction, the Old French translator describes Pierre Alfonse's work. He mentions its classical origins and then says that Pierre Alfonse wanted to make the learning process more enjoyable:

Por ce que plus s'i delitast,
Qu'i li sist ou qu'i li coitast,
I mist deduiz et beaus *fableaus*
De genz, de bestes et d'oiseaus.[31]

In the corresponding passage of Version B the term *fablel* is not found; in fact it is never used in the Anglo-Norman text. In the Continental version *fablel* occurs five times, the first and second occurrences in the passages quoted above, and the third immediately following the first tale, *De la male fame,* when the son comments on the story saying:

Ce dist le fiz: "Iceste espose
Esteit veirement engignose:
Par grant engien fu delivree
De ce dont el ert encombree.
A grant profit li tornereit
Qui teus *fableaus* auques orreit."[32]

The father then tells another story *D'une autre male fame,* and because his son seems to appreciate them thoroughly, he promises him a third. " 'Beaus fiz, le tierz *fablel* orras, / Et à itant m'en sofferras.' "[33] The son is so overwhelmed by the treachery of women that he exclaims:

"Deus!" dist li fiz, "et il coment?
Qui cuidast que si sodement
Peüst hom ne feme trover
Si grant engien ne porpenser?
Qui trestot l'or m'aportereit
Qui est en Arabe et dorreit,
Nes voudreie je oblïer,
Se nes cuidoue recovrer
Cez treis *fableaus* que dit m'avez."[34]

The three stories are very similar: the wife in each tale is entertaining her lover when the husband returns unexpectedly, and she manages to fool him so that he remains unaware of the situation. It is interesting that these tales are characterized as fabliaux by the scribe of Version A, whereas he uses *fable, conte,* and other literary terms for all the other tales in the work. In the Latin version there is no distinctive label attached to these stories; they are either called fables, proverbs, or narratives.

The importance of this use of *fablel* in Version A is clear. In France during the thirteenth century when the version was written, *fablel* designated a specific type of story and these stories influenced the translator to add this generic term to the Latin text. At least for him, the connotation of *fablel* is that these are stories about the wiles of women. Although similar stories existed in Oriental tale collections before the Old French tales, they were not designated by any particular term. Thus, Version A shows us that by the thirteenth century on the Continent, an Old French genre, the fabliau, had an identity and life of its own.

By studying the implications of the use of *fablel* in the introductions and conclusions of tales, we can see a precise definition of a fabliau emerging. A fabliau is a brief narrative poem with a tripartite macrostructure whose narrative is a humorous, even ribald, story arranged to teach a lesson. The narratives appear to be specifically about the trickery and changes in fortune; the moral reflections in the conclusions contain warnings about deception and a secular system of punishments. The next step is an analysis of the narratives themselves.

Deception and Misdeed: The Morphology of the Fabliau

Studies of narrative structure inspired by the French structuralists have so complicated our vocabulary for analyzing plot and character that the reader might anticipate intricate diagrams or esoteric jargon when an analysis of narrative structure is proposed. The insightful modern methods of narrative analysis can be used, however, to clarify the subject rather than to obfuscate it, if judicious choices are made. One such choice is to return to the source of modern theories because the groundbreakers, for all of their shortcomings, wrote clear and penetrating analyses. From a post-structuralist perspective, the method used here to analyze the fabliau would seem hopelessly bourgeois because it aims at clarity, but the method may be justified by its appropriateness for a genre that is given to frankness and even graphic clarity.

Behind much of what Lévi-Strauss, Bremond, and Greimas have advanced as theories of narrative structure lies the work of Vladimir Propp. He, in turn, was influenced by the outstanding critic of the fabliau, Joseph Bédier. In his attempt to prove fabliaux did not come from Indian tales, Bédier repeated the distinction Gaston Paris made between essential and accessory traits of the tale. Bédier identified this essential core as W and the accessory characteristics as a, b, and c, which are, "par nature transitoire et mobile. Ils sont les accidents du conte, dont W est la substance. Ils sont, par définition, arbitraires et peuvent varier d'un conteur à l'autre."[1] Bédier used this formulation not to analyze the narrative structure but to demonstrate that the presence of similar accessory traits would prove a filiation between tales. Propp saw in Bédier's attempt to separate the essence of a tale from its accidental properties a fundamental truth about narrative that Bédier himself simply did not pursue. Propp, however, developed a method for separating and identifying the fundamental elements of diverse tales which he published in *Morphology of the Folktale*. This classic Russian Formalist study of narrative structure first appeared in 1928 but was not translated into English until 1958 and into French until 1970.[2]

The essence of Propp's method was to isolate from the confusion of surface details in the plots of all Russian fairy tales, the essential predicates or "functions" of the action. As he said, "Function is understood as an act of a character, defined from the point of view of its significance for the course of the action."[3] Propp stresses that functions are the basic components of the tale, and that they are not dependent on specific characters. "Functions of characters serve as stable, constant elements in a tale, independent of how and by whom they are fulfilled. They constitute the fundamental components of a tale."[4] The specific characters who perform the functions may vary, and the manner in which they accomplish them may also vary. Propp does establish similar abstractions from the specific characters, designating them as roles, which are similar to functions in being stable elements in all of the tales.

Working originally with the English version, Lévi-Strauss, Greimas, Bremond, and others wrote critiques of *Morphology of the Folktale,* at once embracing its fundamental method and pointing out its limitations.[5] Much of what later commentators have amended in his system of functions and roles is based on the binarism inherent in Saussure's linguistics that influenced, if not engendered, all French structuralism.[6] Bremond points out that functions do not occur in one set sequence, as Propp had maintained, but in logical pairs. Each function, according to Bremond, also has three phases: (1) *virtualité,* (2) *actualisation ou absence d'actualisation,* and (3) *but atteint ou but manqué.*[7] In the analysis of the fabliau, I have in mind these refinements of Propp's system as well as Lévi-Strauss's admonition that a structuralist study must not separate content and form.

The seminal nature of Propp's work is clear from the hundreds of studies inspired by it, and his greatest achievement was to show the feasibility of isolating common elements from a large group of distinct texts. Taking into account later corrections to his system, Propp's method of analysis by functions and roles is still useful for analyzing fabliaux because they too include short narratives with relatively uncomplicated plots. The total corpus of tales is also approximately the same size as Propp's group of Russian fairy tales. Inspired by this method, I analyzed the sixty-six self-proclaimed fabliaux, attempting to isolate functions from the many actions in the narratives. I was not attempting to find those functions Propp had isolated in the fairy tale, because the fabliau differs greatly from the fairy tale by virtue of its humor, its sex-related themes, and its almost total lack of magical elements. It was therefore surprising to find a few crucial functions that do coincide in the two genres, but that comparison will figure in a later discussion.

As is commonly recognized, fabliaux plots often relate a battle of the sexes, and tales of adultery or seduction abound. As has already been discussed at length in Chapter 1, Nykrog based his thesis on what he referred to as the "erotic triangles" that occur in approximately two-thirds of the tales. In *Les Transformations du triangle érotique,* Michel Olsen bases his Greimasienne analysis of the erotic triangle in fabliaux and *nouvelles* on the same corpus.[8] Unfortunately, Olsen does not add significantly to an understanding of the fabliaux because he depends too heavily on the weakest parts of Nykrog's analysis for his own conclusions. For instance, he reproduces Nykrog's table that correlates the success and failure of lovers to their social status (see above p. 12). Nykrog's and Olsen's studies overemphasize the erotic triangles and imply thereby that the focus of the fabliaux is on love or permutations of love triangles. The advantage of a functional analysis is its capacity to identify the crucial elements in the action of most tales in this diverse corpus, rather than the action in just those that include an "erotic triangle." In the small corpus of self-proclaimed fabliaux that form the basis of the initial search for functions and roles, adultery and seduction plots are definitely prominent. Nevertheless, the fabliau will be shown to focus primarily on tricks and anti-social acts of varying kinds; many do not even have a male/female conflict.

Before reading the following discussion, it may be helpful to the reader to refer to Figure 1 to gain an overview of the functions of the fabliau. The list of functions represents a revision of an earlier analysis published else-where.[9] The method of analysis is the same, but changes have been made taking into consideration a rereading of the tales and especially the suggestions of Larry Crist and James Lee in their article "L'Analyse fonctionnelle des fabliaux," which is, in part, an analysis of my earlier work.[10] The analysis by functions pertains only to action within the narrative proper, following the author's introduction.

The initial part of the fabliau narrative includes elements called, following Greimasienne terminology, qualifying statements, which are descriptions of actors and the scene. Qualifying statements occur occasionally throughout the narrative, but I am concerned here primarily with those occurring prior to the narrative sequence that initiates the action. The opening qualifying statements of a fabliau are generally of two types: those that introduce the main characters and explain their relationships to each other (QS-1) and those that introduce only one character and do not explain his relationship to other characters who are eventually introduced into the narrative (QS-2).

In QS-1, the characters are presented very briefly:

> Il avint, si com j'oï dire,
> C'uns clers amoit une borjoise
> Qui mout estoit sage et cortoise.
> (*Des braies au cordelier* MR III: 88, vv. 6-8)

> Jel di por une damoisele
> Qui ert fame à un escuier,
> Ne sai Chartain ou Berruier.
> La damoisele, c'est la voire,

F-1	*Arrival*	
	a	arriving
	b	returning
F-2	*Departure*	
	a	departing
	b	going on errand
F-3	*Interrogation*	
	a	questioning/challenging
	b	propositioning/offering
	c	requesting/summoning
F-4	*Communication*	
	a	informing/answering
	b	proclaiming
	c	giving/receiving object
F-5	*Deception*	
	a	lying/fabricating a story
	b	hiding
	c	disguising/substituting
	d	cheating
	e	playing on words/riddling
	f	using magic
F-6	*Misdeed*	
	a	disobeying
	b	attempting/committing adultery
	c	seducing
	d	insulting/embarrassing
	e	stealing
	f	cheating
	g	tricking
	h	assaulting
F-7	*Recognition*	
F-8	*Retaliation*	
F-9	*Resolution*	

Fig. 1. The Functions of the Fabliau

Estoit amie à un provoire.
(*De la dame qui fit .III. tors entor le moustier* MR III: 79, vv. 16-20)

By introducing the characters and conveying crucial information about their relationships to one another, QS-1 immediately creates expectations in the minds of the audience. The two preceding passages as well as many others like them announce, in effect, that an adultery plot will follow. At times the qualifying statements are quite lengthy, but usually the relationships are briefly sketched and stock situations conveyed. Jean Bodel begins *Du vilair de Bailluel* (MR IV: 109) by describing the *vilain* who is on his way home:

Il estoit granz et merveilleus
Et maufez et de laide hure.
Sa fame n'avoit de lui cure,
Quar fols ert et de lait pelain,
Et cele amoit le chapelain.

(vv. 8-12)

Even without the last verse, the audience anticipates the wife will deceive her husband.

These qualifying statements are characteristic of those plots that relate conventional male/female conflicts such as adultery, seduction, or lovers' quarrels. They are not unknown, however, in the plots that present a conflict between males. This indicates that the specific relationship between the males, usually a conventional dominance pattern, is also important for the outcome of the story. In *Du vilain au buffet* (MR III: 80) there is a long passage describing the mean, petty seneschal who begrudges the generosity of his master toward all of the little people of his realm. Due to his position and the description of his personality, the reader can anticipate his aggressive behavior against an innocent *vilain* who arrives at the banquet. In *De Barat et de Haimet* (MR IV: 97), the split between Traver and his two disreputable companions, who later steal from him, is signaled from the beginning:

Cis fabliaus dist, seigneur baron,
Que jadis furent troi larron
. . . .
Li uns avoit à non Travers;
As autres .II. n'apartenoit,
Mès lor compaignie tenoit.

(vv. 1-2, 6-8)

The other qualifying statement (QS-2) presents one character whose relationship or kinship to other characters is not explained. Usually the other characters are not even introduced at the outset. In *De Boivin de Provins* (MR V: 116) Boivin is introduced, and his departure for the fair is described. The action has begun before Mabile, the prostitute who will try to rob him, enters. In *Le Povre Clerc* (MR V: 132) the author presents the poor cleric, and the action begins immediately when he stops at the house to ask for food. It is only at this point that the woman and her maid are introduced. *Le Povre Clerc* makes a good comparison with the adultery plots introduced by QS-1. The same characters often used in either adultery or seduction plots are present: a cleric, a married woman, and her maid. The fact that they are not introduced together at the beginning means the audience does not anticipate this type of plot; and, in fact, the cleric and the woman do not have a sexual relationship. If the tale opened with QS-1, the audience might have anticipated a conventional plot. Thus, the use of QS-2 signals an unusual plot will follow.

In *Du fotéor* (MR I: 28), for example, there is an adultery plot but with an important twist—namely that the lover is just a young man for hire who tricks both the wife and husband. The story begins with a QS-2 introducing the young man and his background, without mentioning the woman. The same is true in *Les .IIII. souhais Saint Martin* (MR V: 133), the story of a husband and wife who trick each other. Only the husband is introduced at the beginning, and it is impossible to judge from the opening lines what type of plot will follow. It is an unusual one because the only sex-related aspect of the conflict is that husband and wife try to out do each other by making obscene wishes. The fact that the wrongdoing is accomplished by magic is also a marked departure from the norm.

The qualifying statements, by virtue of their brevity, are an appropriate introduction to the quick-paced action that follows. Among all of the diverse events presented in these narratives, it is possible to isolate nine basic functions which encapsulate all of the significant action. They are: arrival F-1, departure F-2, interrogation F-3, communication F-4, deception F-5, misdeed F-6, recognition F-7, retaliation F-8, and resolution F-9. The entire plot of a fabliau can be separated into these functions, as may be seen in the three examples presented in Appendices A, B, and C. A given fabliau may not utilize each one of the functions, and the functions do not necessarily appear in numerical sequence. This is not to imply, however, that they can occur randomly. For example, F-1 and F-2 are transitional functions (arrivals and departures) that can occur in inverted order and at various points throughout the tale. Certain functions are logically related; misdeed precedes retaliation, for instance, but the entire sequence of functions from F-3 to F-9 is at best an ideal form rarely seen in actuality. All fabliaux include functions F-5 and F-6, and some stop after the misdeed is committed. The majority, however, elaborate upon the sequence, repeating functions and recycling through an abbreviated series such as going from F-7 back to F-3, F-4, and F-5. The question of sequence is rather complex and will be discussed more fully in Chapter 4. The reader should bear in mind that there is a causal relationship between certain functions, but the numerical sequence does not imply a direct correlation with the chronology of events in the tale.

What then is the relationship of functions to events in these tales? Every action or move of a character is not necessarily a function; a function is significant action which is defined in terms of the consequences it provokes. For example, if a man steals a ham or violates a maiden, he has committed an action that has significant results for the narrative, i.e., his antisocial act (misdeed) harms another character and may provoke a desire for revenge. Also, several specific actions may be necessary to constitute a function, or conversely, one action may be several functions. For example, if a man makes a statement that is misunderstood by others, he may have committed a misdeed (F-6) by insulting them as well as by deceiving himself (F-5) if the statement is inadvertent. A specific action may be designated as one function in one tale and a different function in another context. But the relationship between specific elements in the tales and functions was made clear by Propp.

> Without concerning ourselves with the question of the priority of this or that particular meaning, we must nevertheless find the criterion which in all such cases would permit us to differentiate among elements without respect to similarity of actions. In these instances it is always possible to be governed by the principle of defining a function *according to its consequences.*[11]

Before elaborating on the functions of the fabliau, the reader should note that the primary setting for a fabliau is a house, and arrivals and departures refer to the house in which the characters are placed by the initial situation. The courtyard of a house, an inn, or any dwelling place may be used to suggest the same type of setting. One fabliau takes place in a church and six other fabliaux take place entirely outside,[12] but they are somewhat atypical in this respect. The conventional house or inn reinforces the idea that the fabliau is truly domestic comedy.

The first of the two transitional functions, the arrival F-1, refers to two different circumstances: an outsider arriving (F-1a) or a non-outsider returning (F-1b). Normally the tale is initiated by the function F-1; and, naturally, the transitional functions mark a change of scene during the tale.

When a stranger arrives (F-1a), it is often a seducer (*De Gombert et des .II. clers* MR I: 22 and *De Frere Denise* MR III: 87) or someone who offers something to the main character. In *Du fotéor* (MR I: 28), a young man asks who the most beautiful woman in town is, and then arrives at her house to offer his sexual services. Sometimes the stranger meets up with other characters outside (*Les .IIII. souhais Saint Martin* MR V: 133 and *Del couvoiteus et de l'envieus* MR V: 135), but the action may move inside at a later point. F-1a does not always pertain to a complete stranger. It may be the arrival of a character, known to other characters in the tale, who nonetheless does not belong in the house. In *Du prestre ki abevete* (MR III: 61), for example, the priest and the wife have a relationship prior to the day he arrives to trick the husband. The outsider may also be someone who has been summoned—a lover or potential victim called to the house by a wife. In *Du chevalier à la robe vermeille* (MR III: 57), the wife sends a message to her lover indicating that her husband has left for Senlis, and he hastens to her side:

> Et, quant cil oï la novele,
> Robe d'escarlate novele
> A vestu, forrée d'ermine.
> Comme bacheler s'achemine,
> Qui amors metent en esfroi;
> Montez est sor son palefroi,
>
> . . . .
> Et est venuz droit cele part
> Où il cuida trover la dame.
>
> (vv. 29-34, 44-45)

F-1a is also the arrival of a friend who has been sent for and who will be sent on an errand (*De la male Honte* MR IV: 90 and *De deux angloys* MR II: 46). Even a stranger may be summoned in order to help the main character carry out a task (*Des trois boçus* MR I: 2).

F-1b, returning, refers to a character who left the house on his own or was sent away. This character, in contrast with the character who is arriving (F-1a), belongs in the house by virtue of ownership or association. Most often it is a husband, who catches the wife and lover off-guard when he returns unexpectedly. In *Des braies au cordelier* (MR III: 88), the wife hastens her husband's departure for the market by waking him long before dawn. When he goes to meet his friend, however, he is told to go back to bed:

> Atant s'en est d'iluec tornez;
> A son ostel s'en est alez,
> Dont vient à l'uis, et si apele.
> "Dieus, com ci a pesme nouvele,
> Biaus douz amis," ce dit la dame!
> "Mes sires est à l'uis par m'ame,
> Nos somes mout mal asené. . . ."
>
> (vv. 109-15)

F-1b can also be a planned return that involves a character who left the house specifically to set up a trick. In *Des .III. dames qui trouvèrent l'anel* (MR I: 15), for example, the wife presumably leaves for the market, but actually is gone for a week with her lover. She re-creates the same scene on entering as the day she left, and then convinces her husband and the neighbors that he is crazy to have accused her of having been gone.

The other transitional function, the departure, F-2, also has two variations. In F-2a, a character is departing from the house, indicating that his role in the action has been completed or that new action can begin due to his absence. In F-2b, a character is going on or is sent on an errand, and in this case a change of locale will be presented.

F-2a is the counterpart of F-1a because the action initiated by the arrival has been completed and the character leaves the scene. A lover enjoys his lady's company and decides to leave before everyone is awake, as in *Des braies au cordelier* (MR III: 88):

> Et li clerc vint isnel le pas
> A la dame, si li a dit:
> "Bele amie, se Dieus m'aït,
> Orendroit m'en covient aler:
> Qui aime, il doit s'amor celer,
> Por ce m'en vueil aler matin,
> Que ne me voient li voisin
> Hors issir de vostre maison."
> . . . .
> Atant li clers d'iluec s'en part.
>
> (vv. 202-37)

When a non-outsider leaves the house, the move allows action to develop in his absence. This form of the departure function is common in tales of adultery where the husband must be absent or must leave at the very beginning of the tale in order for the wife to be free. If the departure is not presented, having taken place before the narrative begins, then the husband is usually said to be going to work or the market. This allows his wife to set up a tryst with her lover:

> Chascuns se veut mès entremètre
> De biaus contes en rime mètre
> Mais je m'en sui si entremis
> Que j'en ai .I. en rime mis
> D'un marchéant qui par la terre
> Aloit marchéandise querre.
> En sa meson lessoit sa fame. . . .
>
> (*Le Cuvier* MR I: 9, vv. 1-7)

It is sometimes the wife rather than the narrator who announces the departure in a message to her lover:

> Mais conter vos vueil tot à tire
> Comment une cointe borgoise,
> Qui estoit mignote et cortoise,
> Li [the priest] ot mandé, n'est mie guile,
> Que ses sires à une vile
> Devoit cel jor au marchié estre.
>
> (*Du prestre et de la dame* MR II: 51, vv. 8-13)

The departure of a non-outsider means the absence of a character who has authority over the one left at home. The departure allows the other character to act freely, inevitably against the will of the authority figure. For example, in *De la grue* (MR V: 126), a *chatelain* has his daughter closely guarded by an old woman. As she is preparing food one day, the old woman runs out to get a dish she needs:

> .I. jor par une matinée,
> Vost la norice aparellier
> A la damoisele à mengier.
> Si li failli une escuelle
> Tost maintenant s'en corut cele
> A lor ostel qui n'est pas loing
> Querre ce dont avoit besoing;
> L'uis de la tour overt laissa.
>
> (vv. 26-33)

A clever young man arrives and takes advantage of the open door. When an F-2a departure occurs, the narrative does not elaborate upon what the character does who has left. Since the F-2a is a gratuitous, unplanned, and often coincidental action, the action of the departed character is not important after he leaves. F-2a differs in this respect from F-2b, which is planned with the subsequent action of the fabliau in mind.

F-2b is an act that moves the narrative away from the original locale. A character may leave when sent on an errand (*De la male Honte* MR IV: 90) or may leave to set up a trick. The wife often leaves home in order to set up a situation designed to fool the husband (*Des .III. dames qui trouvèrent l'anel* MR I: 15); or, as in *D'Auberée* (MR V: 110), the go-between leaves her house to go to another woman's where the action takes place. The difference between the feigned separation (F-2a) and the departure to set up a trick (F-2b) is that in F-2b the scene shifts at least momentarily, focusing on the deceiver while away from home and describing the deception he or she sets up for the victim. This action is a necessary element in the plot, whereas in F-2a the mere absence of the specific authority figure is all that is necessary. A character may also be tricked into leaving on an errand, so his departure combines both separation and departure on an errand. In this case the narrative relates both what happens to the character while away and what goes on in the house (*Del fol vilain* G 2 and *Des braies au cordelier* MR III: 88). This action would be designated F-2a + b, illustrating the fact that one action in a tale may represent several different aspects of a function, or even several functions.

The third function, interrogation, F-3, has three primary forms, each of which has several different nuances. F-3a is questioning or challenging, F-3b propositioning or offering, and F-3c requesting or summoning. The purpose of the interrogation is to gather information in the broadest sense. It is a type of reconnaissance in that a character seeks information in order to know whether he can proceed to a new action, or he may simply be curious about a new situation. It is a straightforward and usually guileless investigation into a specific environment where the character needs to be provided with an answer or an object signifying that he is to proceed.

Questioning, F-3a, is most often done by a character who leaves himself open to deception by demonstrating his naïveté. In *De la grue* (MR V: 126), the young girl calls out a window to a boy, asking him what kind of bird he is carrying and what she could give him for it. He guesses correctly by her manner that she will be easy to fool. The question can generate a sincere offer of information as in *Du fotéor* (MR I: 28), where the young man asks who the most beautiful woman in town is, and he is given her name. The question can also become a challenge in reaction to a new situation where a character thinks he has discerned that something is amiss. In other words, challenging may follow a recognition or a partial recognition of a misdeed. When a wayward wife comes home, the husband may ask, as in *Des .III. dames qui trouvèrent l'anel* (MR I: 15), "Pute, où avez-vous tant esté?" (v. 160).

F-3b, propositioning, is often a straightforward sexual advance that is not an attempt to deceive the propositioned person, although this person's legitimate partner might be deceived were the proposition to be accepted. A lecher may arrive and make advances to the wife or daughter (*Du fotéor* MR I: 28 and *Du prestre et d'Alison* MR II: 31), or a woman may approach a man (*De la viellete* MR V: 129). A character may also propose a non-sexual venture such as in *De Brunain* (MR I: 10) where the *vilain* proposes to his wife that they take their cow to the priest:

> "Os," fet li vilains, "bele suer,
> Que noz prestres a en convent:
> Qui por Dieu done à escient,
> Que Diex li fet mouteploier;
> Miex ne poons-nous emploier
> No vache, se bel te doit estre,
> Que pour Dieu le donons le prestre."
>
> (vv. 10-16)

F-3b may also be in the form of offering. In *Les .IIII. souhais Saint Martin* (MR V: 133), Saint Martin appears to the peasant and offers him four magic wishes as a reward for his faithful devotion. Likewise in *De Brunain* (MR I: 10) after the husband and wife have discussed the matter, the husband goes and in all sincerity offers his cow to the priest:

> Li vilains s'en entre en l'estable,
> Sa vache prent par le lien,
> Présenter le vait au doien.

> Li prestres ert sages et cointes.
> "Biaus Sire," fet-il à mains jointes,
> "Por l'amor Dieu Blerain vous doing."
>
> (vv. 22-27)

Requesting, F-3c, is a specific demand for help in the form of food, money, or lodging. In both *De la dame escolliée* (MR VI: 149) and *Le Povre Clerc* (MR V: 132), a stranger arrives at a house and asks for lodging or food. In *D'Auberée* (MR V: 110) and *De la male Honte* (MR IV: 90), a person's help is requested in carrying out a task. In the last-mentioned fabliau, the gentleman, Honte, calls on a friend to deliver his belongings after his death to the king:

> Honte ert le preudom apelez,
> Quant vit que tant fu adolez.
> Et que il vit qu'il ne vivra,
> .I. sien compere en apela:
> "Compere," dit Honte, "prenez
> Mon avoir que vos là veez
> En cele male qui là pent;
> Por Dieu vos pri omnipotent,
> Se ge muir, portez la lou roi."
>
> (vv. 11-19)

Another form of requesting is summoning which precedes an actual request for help or a lover's tryst (*Du chevalier à la robe vermeille* MR III: 57). As an F-3 function, summoning is a straightforward action like the proposition, but it may nevertheless yield deceptive results. In *De la grue* (MR V: 126), for example, the girl summons the young man, thinking that he can undo the harm he has done her; but, of course, she is later deceived by being *défoutue*. In each case the interrogation is intended as a candid request for information, for a reaction from the other person, or for cooperation. The reaction to it can be either a straightforward communication, F-4, or a deception, F-5.

F-4 is called communication in order to imply not only the transfer of information but also the exchange or communication of objects, and it has three forms: informing or answering F-4a, proclaiming F-4b, and giving or receiving an object F-4c.

The most common form of communication, F-4a, answers a question or offers unsolicited information. In response to the question "Que faites vous là, bone gent?" asked by the priest in *Du prestre ki abevete* (MR III: 61, v. 33), the *vilain* answers, "Par ma foi, sire, nous mengons" (v. 35). In *Du fotéor* (MR I: 28), the maid is sent to ask who the young man is who has waited outside the door of the house, and he answers, " 'Ge sui fouterres, bele suer. . . . / Et bone joie vous doint Diex!' " (vv. 131, 133). The information may also be obtained through hearsay, as in *De la damoisele qui ne pooit oïr parler de foutre* (MR III: 65) in which the girl's reputation for fainting at the mere mention of *foutre* is widely known. The information is sometimes offered gratuitously, thus leaving the question F-3a implied. Although this information is gained by hearsay or offered spontaneously by another character, it is nevertheless vital to the development of the plot.

F-4b, proclaiming, is the affirmative form of propositioning (F-3b). Instead of asking for an opinion or offering something to see if it might be accepted, the proclamation is a statement that may even be irrelevant to the immediate circumstances, but it becomes incorporated into the action, confusing rather than clarifying a given situation. It is not, however, a purposefully deceptive statement. It differs from F-4a in that it is not the answer to a question and seems unmotivated by the context. In *Du sot chevalier* (MR I: 20), for example, the chevalier is trying to remember a lesson on sex that his mother-in-law has given him when a party arrives and asks for lodging. He tells them they are welcome and then proceeds to mumble to himself a key phrase from his lesson, " 'Li plus lons ert foutuz, / Et li plus court sera batuz' " (vv. 131-32). The messenger overhears this statement and misunderstands it, thinking the *chevalier* is planning to attack them. In *De la male Honte* (MR IV: 90) the *vilain* arrives at court and makes the unsolicited and apparently insulting remark, " 'Sire,' fait il en son langaige, / 'La male Honte vos aport . . .' " (vv. 34-35).

In F-4c, the communication involves the physical giving or receiving of an object which serves the same function as information because it motivates the ensuing action. In *Des trois boçus* (MR I: 2), for example, after the wife discovers that she has accidentally smothered the musicians, she hires a porter to carry them to the river. She requests the service (F-3c), and then the porter receives the bodies (F-4c). Frequently the object is found by chance. In *Des .III. dames* (MR IV: 99) and its variant (MR V: 112), three women making a pilgrimage find some male genitalia over which they argue fiercely. Finding a dead body is the motivation for each new sequence of action in the long tales such as *Le Dit dou soucretain* (MR VI: 150), *Du segretain* (MR V: 123), *Du prestre qu'on porte* (MR IV: 89), and *De Constant du Hamel* (MR IV: 106). Although F-4 is usually preceded by F-3, it can stand alone, as is the case with F-4b and in tales where objects are found accidentally (F-4c). The communication involved, however, is equally important to the development of the plot whether the interrogation is explicit or implicit.

The fifth function, deception, has six different forms, arranged here in order of descending frequency. These different methods of deception are: lying or fabricating a story F-5a, hiding F-5b, disguising or substituting F-5c, cheating F-5d, playing on words F-5e, and using magic F-5f. The deceptive act is not an end in itself but rather a function that serves as a means to accomplish or cover up a misdeed (F-6).

According to these tales, lying or fabricating a story, F-5a, is the easiest and most obvious way to deceive another character. This particular form of deception represents a negative form of the functions of interrogation (F-3) and communication (F-4). When the wife in *Des braies au cordelier* (MR III: 88) hears her husband return, she uses a deceptive question in order to convince him that she is very suspicious of everyone who comes to the door. She keeps asking him who he is and pretends not to recognize his voice. In *De la dame qui se venja* (MR VI: 140), the wife has arranged for her lover to be with her, knowing her husband will return home. In order to avenge herself and frighten her lover, she receives the husband in the bedroom, asks him for wine, and pretends to offer it to her lover who is hiding under the covers. When her husband asks to whom she is speaking, she says, " 'A mon ami / Qui en mon lit gist delés mi' " (vv. 157-58). The husband thinks she is kidding, but she pursues her ruse by asking him, " 'Sire, se je le vos moutroie, / Qu'en feriez vos?' " (vv. 161-62). This deceptive question provokes a threat from the husband which frightens the lover, but it also allows the wife to make a joke that keeps the husband from realizing she has told the truth.

Devious propositions can also be made, as in *Des .II. changéors* (MR I: 23) where the wife wants to scare her lover; she proposes to her husband that he enter the bath where the lover is hiding. The husband does not know, of course, who is in the tub, so she tells him that it is a shy, ugly woman. Her proposal to the husband is understood by the lover as an actual threat to reveal his presence, but she has already told the husband that he is only to scare "the ugly woman" by pretending to enter the tub. One of the more common devious offers is illustrated by *De Gombert et des .II. clers* (MR I: 22), in which the cleric seduces a girl under cover of night by offering her an iron ring that he says is gold. Summoning is also frequently counterfeited when a woman summons a priest or other potential lover in order to rob him. In *Du segretain ou du moine* (MR V: 123), for example, the wife has told her husband of the priest's proposition, and he suggests the extortion plot. She then goes to the church and lies to the priest, pretending to accept his advance:

> "Sire, par la foi que vous doi,
> Vostre volenté ferai toute.
> Venés ent, et si n'aiiés doute,
> En maison n'est mie mesire;
> Mais une rien vous veul jou dire,
> Et si vous fac bien asavoir,
> Ne venés mie sans l'avoir. . . ."

(vv. 122-28)

Fabricating a story is not only the most common form of false communication, it is also one of the most imaginative and humorous functions in a fabliau. When a husband has challenged (F-3a) his wife's absence, for example, she will often respond with an incredible story about what she has been doing. In *De la dame qui fit .III. tors* (MR III: 79), the unfaithful wife is caught by her husband as she returns very late one night, and he immediately accuses her of infidelity. She manages to convince him that she is pregnant and has been at church doing various things to devine whether the child will be a boy or girl. The adulterous wife often wants to set up a situation to get rid of the husband, and so she uses a false proclamation. In *Du vilain de Bailluel* (MR IV: 109), the wife greets her husband with a false alarm about how sick he looks and then declares that he is dead. Even an object can be received deceitfully, as in *De Brunain* (MR I: 10) where the priest takes the cow offered by the *vilain,* although he realizes that the *vilain* has misunderstood the biblical quotation about the cheerful giver receiving twofold from God. He thinks he has fooled the *vilain* and enriched himself, but the situation is later reversed. Thus, lying and fabricating stories are used either to extricate a character from a difficult situation or to set up a situation in which he can proceed with his wrongdoing.

Hiding, F-5b, is another common form of deception used to cover up a misdeed. For example, a man trying to steal something can hide it in order to have his theft go unobserved (*Du provost à l'aumuche* MR I: 7). In many of the adultery tales the wife hides her lover when the husband comes home unexpectedly (*Le Cuvier* MR I: 9, *Des braies au cordelier* MR III: 88, *Du chevalier à la robe vermeille* MR III: 57, and *Du prestre et de la dame* MR II: 51). Hiding a dead body is also a frequently used technique (*Du prestre qu'on porte* MR IV: 89, *Du segretain* MR V: 123, and *Le Dit dou soucretain* MR VI: 150). In these tales the dead body is hidden in one place and then another; each time the person who discovers it either thinks he has somehow killed the man, or at least will be implicated, so he hides it elsewhere. Hiding can even be used to prevent misdeeds, as when goods are hidden in order to thwart a thief (*De Boivin de Provins* MR V: 116 and *De Barat et de Haimet* MR IV: 97), or to set up a situation in preparation for a misdeed. In *D'Auberée* (MR V: 110) the go-between hides a man's jacket under the bed of a married woman, knowing that her husband will find it and throw her out of the house. The go-between will then be able to take advantage of her misfortune to promote an affair with a young boy.

Lying about an actual event, making up a story to create a false situation, or hiding the truth are all closely related deceptions. In each case the duped person is fed unreliable information which he accepts for one reason or another. Part of the hiding technique is the interference with sensory perception; either the object cannot be seen or the eyesight of the victim is blocked.[13] Disguises or substitutions, F-5c, are also often used to dupe people into reacting incorrectly to a situation. One of the best instances of a disguise being used to an unfaithful wife's advantage is in the fairly elaborate tale *Des tresces* (MR IV: 94). A wife's lover is caught by the husband as the lover tries to get into the bed. Thinking he is a robber, the husband leaves his prisoner in the wife's care while he goes for a lantern. The wife lets the lover escape, but the husband realizes it was not an accident and throws her out of the house. She sends a disguised friend back to the house to take her place and then goes off with her lover. The husband thinks it is his wife who has returned and so he beats her, cuts her hair, and throws her out again. The next morning the wife goes back and can easily convince her husband that the entire night was a bad dream.

Cheating, F-5d, as a form of deception only occurs in two fabliaux. It is perhaps more frequently seen as a form of the function misdeed, to be discussed next. In other words, the hostile action toward another character (misdeed) is a matter of cheating him out of money or goods. Cheating can be a means to attain another end, however, and in this case it is a form of deception, F-5d. In *Do pré tondu* (MR IV: 104), for example, the wife argues with her husband; her wrongdoing or misdeed is disobedience. She wins the argument, however, through deception because she cheats and uses sign language in an argument over terminology. In *Des .II. chevaus* (MR I: 13) the priest has proposed a tug-of-war between the *vilain*'s horse and his own in order to determine which one is better; and the winner will get to keep both horses. The horses are tied together by their tails and the tug-of-war begins. When the priest sees that he is losing, he fools the *vilain* by cheating at the game, i.e., he cuts the horses' tails.

Another form of deception is playing on words, F-5e. The use of figures of speech, riddles, euphemisms, or words unknown to the naïve character is a common method used to outsmart a victim. Euphemisms and *double entendre* are especially favored by seducers to entrap naïve girls in sexual play. The sexual conquest of the girl who could not bear to hear the word *foutre* proceeds by the use of euphemisms for various parts of the body (*De la damoisele qui ne pooit oïr parler de foutre* MR III: 65 and MR V: 111). In *De la grue* (MR V: 126) the boy seduces the girl by playing on her ignorance of the word *foutre*. Using it as a noun, he convinces her it is an object she has on her person and he will look for it. There is also the deception that occurs in *De deux angloys* (MR II: 46) when the Englishman misuses words by speaking broken French. He thinks he is asking for *agnel* but actually says *asnel*, so the butcher profits from the obvious mistake and gives him donkey meat.

The other form of deception, magic F-5f, is not frequently used, but it does occur in several fabliaux. In contrast with much medieval literature, there is almost no mention of Christian supernaturalism, although magic is incorporated into several tales as a means of deception. The use of magic may be a carryover from the Oriental sources of these specific tales or a reflection of their connections to folk literature. In either case, it is never used more than incidentally in the fabliaux. In *Les .IIII. souhais* (MR V: 133), the *vilain* has been given four wishes by Saint Martin. The wife begs to be able to use one and then deceives her husband by using this magic wish to accomplish a hostile action against him. The husband retaliates by using the second wish to cause her harm, and then they have to use the other two wishes in order to undo their foolishness. In *Del couvoiteus et de l'envieus* (MR V: 135), magic wishes are also used as a means of tricking and eventually harming another character. Inevitably the duped person is insensitive to his environment or too dull-witted to perceive the obvious and is in a constant state of self-deception because he cannot see events as they really are.

The sixth function, the misdeed F-6, marks the climax of the fabliau. All of the preceding functions prepare for this act; and, once it is accomplished, the narrative may end. The misdeed may be defined as a hostile action by one character against another that violates societal norms or personal ethics. Only eight categories of misdeeds have been isolated from the group of self-proclaimed fabliaux, indicating that the fabliaux reflect only certain aspects of man's capacity for antisocial, hostile, or cruel actions. The eight categories are: disobeying F-6a, attempting or committing adultery F-6b, seducing F-6c, insulting or embarrassing F-6d, stealing F-6e, cheating F-6f, tricking F-6g, and verbally or physically assaulting F-6h.

Disobeying, F-6a, is common in male/female conflicts and refers specifically to women who do not respect the role they are expected to play. A wife will disobey her husband by arguing with him (*De Sire Hain et de Dame Anieuse* MR I: 6), by constantly contradicting him (*Do pré tondu* MR IV: 104), by eating some things she is supposed to prepare for him (*Le Dit des perdriz* MR I: 17), or by demanding too much sexual attention (*De porcelet* MR IV: 101). She may even let a "robber" escape who happens to be her lover, as in *Des tresces* (MR IV: 94):

> Lors l'a la dame aus cheveus pris,
> Et fait semblant que bien le tiegne;
> Mais li sires comment qu'el preigne,
> Por du feu se met à la voie.
> Et maintenant la dame envoie
> Son ami à grant aleüre. . . .
>
> (vv. 126-31)

Attempting or committing adultery, F-7b, is a more serious form of disobedience. It may be mentioned very briefly, and the attempt may be interrupted by a returning husband. In *Du prestre et de la dame* (MR II: 51), for example, the wife and her lover have not even tasted the meal that she prepared for him, when the husband arrives:

> Li Prestres si esploita tant,
> Et tant de la Dame s'aprime
> Qu'il fu à l'ostel devant prime,
> Où fu receü sanz dangier.
> La baiesse atorne à mengier

> Char cuite en pot, pastez au poivre,
> Et bon vin cler et sain à boivre,
> Et li bains estoit ja chauffez,
> Quant uns deables, uns mauffez,
> Le seignor la Dame amena. . . .
>
> (vv. 16-25)

Usually, however, the couple have enjoyed their time together, and their affair may be described at length. Descriptions of this misdeed and seductions are often ribald but almost always so outrageous that humor prevails over obscenity.

Seducing, F-6c, occurs as frequently as does adultery. A married woman may be taken advantage of or blackmailed (*D'Auberée* MR V: 110 and *De Gombert et des .II. clers* MR I: 22), but most seductions involve young girls, who are taken advantage of because of their naïveté (*De Frere Denise* MR III: 87) or who are seduced by gifts, as in *De Gombert et des .II. clers* (MR I: 22):

> Mès, se vos mes bons consentez,
> Granz biens vous en vendra encor,
> Et si aurez mon anel d'or,
> Qui miex vaut de .IIII. besanz;
> Or sentez comme il est pesanz;
> Trop m'est larges au doit m'anel.
>
> (vv. 64-69)

Insulting or embarrassing, F-6d, is one of the misdeeds that may be construed as a breech of personal ethics. The insult often occurs between lovers, as in *De la dame qui se venja* (MR VI: 140) in which the lover asks an indelicate question at a very intimate moment, deeply offending his mistress. The wife in *De Berangier au lonc cul* (MR III: 86) insults her low-born husband by reminding him of her aristocratic family and their valor in battle. Her insult motivates him to fabricate stories about his own prowess. Making fun of stupid or handicapped people was a great medieval joke, and the fabliaux certainly reflect much disdain of stupidity. Telling an outrageous story when the duper knows it will be believed is actually a form of making fun of the other character's credulity. Making fun as a misdeed may be more specific, however, as when husbands and wives make fun of each others' bodies or personal habits (*De la coille noire* MR VI: 148).

Stealing, F-6e, is another form of hostile action that violates one character's rights of domain. Committing adultery and seducing could even be seen as a specialized form of stealing, although it is useful to isolate the stealing of sexual rights as a specific form of F-6 in order to demonstrate its relative importance in these tales. F-6e refers specifically to the theft of goods (*De Barat et de Haimet* MR IV: 97 and *Du provost à l'aumuche* MR I: 7) and money (*De Boivin de Provins* MR V: 116). In these tales, the thieves think that their victims are too stupid or naïve to realize what has happened, but as often happens, the thief is tricked in return in each one.

Cheating, F-6f, is a distinct form of misdeed as well as a deception. It is a misdeed in *Des .II. chevaus* (MR I: 13), as was mentioned, and also in several other tales where one character cheats his victim out of money or promised goods. In *Du fotéor* (MR I: 28), the glib young man manages to convince the husband that he should be paid because the wife had contracted with him for the afternoon, but he did not receive either sex or money. One of the cleverest ways to cheat someone out of money is for the duper to set up a situation whereby several people are led to believe that the duper's debts will be paid by another person (*Des trois avugles* MR I: 4). In certain cases, characters are owed or can expect money or food from another character who essentially cheats them out of what should be offered (*Le Povre Clerc* MR V: 132 and *Du prestre qui ot mere à force* MR V: 125).

Tricking, F-6g, is what the fabliau is all about in the broadest sense, because each misdeed is either accomplished or covered up by deception. In this sense tricking or deceiving a character could be considered as part of the aggression against the other character. Nevertheless, since there are specific antisocial acts that constitute the actual misdeed (F-6), it is clear that deception is a separate function used to prepare or cover up the antisocial act itself. In some tales, however, the best description for the misdeed itself is a trick. In *Des .II. changéors* (MR I: 23), for example, a lover calls the husband into the bedroom to see his "friend," who is actually the wife. He shows all but her face, and thus the husband does not discover who is in bed. The lover commits adultery before the husband arrives, but his later behavior can only be called a trick. What he does is not an overtly hostile act, it is merely a hoax. Likewise, in *Des trois avugles* (MR I: 4) the cleric only pretends to give money to the blind men, and therefore causes their humiliation later when they cannot pay a bill at the inn. In *Des .III. dames qui trouvèrent l'anel* (MR I: 15) one of the subplots involves tricking a husband into joining a monastery, and in *De la crote* (MR III: 58) the wife tricks her husband into tasting some excrement.

A small number of hostile actions may be loosely grouped under the heading of verbally or physically assaulting another (F-6h). In many cases, physical abuse of a slapstick variety accompanies other misdeeds, such as in *De Gombert et des .II. clers* (MR I: 22) when the clerics add injury to insult by beating Gombert after seducing his wife and daughter. The mean seneschal accompanies with a slap his insulting greeting to the peasant in *Du vilain au buffet* (MR III: 80). In two tales of magic wishes (*Les .IIII. souhais Saint Martin* MR V: 133 and *Del couvoiteus et de l'envieus* MR V: 135), the first wish is a trick that causes physical harm to the recipient. There are also many verbal arguments (*Des .III. dames* MR IV: 99 and V: 112 and *Le Jugement des cons* MR V: 122) which may or may not be accompanied by physical violence. Verbal threats are also used as misdeeds (*Du sot chevalier* MR I: 20).

The basic pattern described thus far is that one character uses devious methods to carry out a hostile or antisocial action against another. In a few fabliaux, the deception and misdeed are not just actions like transitive verbs; they are reflexive. For example, the husband in *Du chevalier à la robe vermeille* (MR III: 57), who believes his wife's crazy story, deludes himself and actually acts upon that self-deception by going on a pilgrimage. The success of many plots is predicated on the self-deception of the victim, and our enjoyment of the story is enhanced by these victims' credulity. The husband in *Des tresces* (MR IV: 94), for instance, accepts a disguised neighbor as his unfaithful wife, cuts her hair, beats her, but the next day is convinced it was all a bad dream when he sees his unblemished wife. The funniest self-deceiving fools are those who become so befuddled by a wife's story that they actually apologize for their suspicions and accusations. When the wife in *De la dame qui fit .III. tors* tells her husband the lie about performing a special ritual to determine the sex of her unborn child, the husband is undone by the false news of her pregnancy:

> "Dame," dist il, "je, que savoie
> Du voiage ne de la voie?
> Se je seüsse ceste chose,
> Dont je à tort vous blasme et chose,
> Je sui cil qui mot n'en deïsse
> Se je anuit de cest soir isse."
>
> (MR III: 79, vv. 161-66)

A radical form of self-deception and self-inflicted misdeed appears in the very short tale *Du provoire qui menga les meures* (MR IV: 92). A priest is on his way to the market one day when he stops to pick mulberries. While he is standing in the saddle in order to reach the high branches, he looks down and wonders what would happen if someone said giddy-yap to the horse. Unfortunately he says this aloud and the horse bolts, throwing him into the brambles. His statement and his fall are both self-inflicted. The reader might hesitate to classify it as a fabliau because it has only the one character, and thus there is no conflict. On the other hand, it can be accepted as the most reduced form conceivable, a tale at the very lower limits of the genre. It bears more resemblance to a joke, of course, as do a few other very brief tales, but I consider them to be fabliaux if they are narratives about deception and misdeeds.

Some fabliaux (*Del fol vilain* G 2 and *Du prestre et de la dame* MR II: 51) utilize the first six functions and then the narrative stops. Most, however, do not merely end with the accomplishment of a misdeed. There is quite often another function, the recognition F-7, even if no action ensues from it. In

Du prestre ki abevete (MR III: 61), the *vilain* sees the priest making love to his wife, as does the *vilain* in *Du vilain de Bailluel* (see Appendix B), but neither victim manages to counterattack. Recognitions of misdeeds are most often made because of physical evidence that can be seen, e.g., the lover's clothes may be left or the lover himself may be found. The discovery of a dead body and the recognition that accusations may follow prompt characters to dispose of the corpse (*Du segretain* MR V: 123 and *Le Dit dou soucretain* MR VI: 150). In several instances a husband recognizes his wife's infidelity because of her unusual behavior.

As is to be expected, it is the victim who most frequently recognizes the misdeed and then can react accordingly. There are tales, however, where the victim learns about the situation from another character. In *De Gombert* (MR I: 22), the cleric thinks he is talking to his friend but is actually revealing his conquest of the daughter to his victim's father. In *De Frere Denise* (MR III: 87) and *De la male Honte* (MR IV: 90), an outsider recognizes the misdeed and clarifies the situation.

There are also humorous variations on the common pattern of a victim recognizing the misdeed and deception or another person revealing it to him. In *De la grue* (MR V: 126), for example, the victim tells her guardian what the young man has done to her, but the girl never understands she has been seduced. In *Le Cuvier* (MR I: 9), the discovery is made by a friend of the duper (the wife), so she helps the wife rather than reveal the situation to the victim. Another clever twist on the recognition function occurs in *De Berangier* (MR III: 86 and IV: 93) when the duper reveals her misdeed to the victim. This seems illogical, but the wife in this case knows she has totally dominated her cowardly husband, so she further humiliates him by revealing that she was his adversary in the mock battle.

When the recognition occurs, the victim may react in a variety of ways. He may accept the situation and resign himself to his fate, as the husband does in *De Berangier*. Or he may recognize the misdeed but not consider himself any the worse for it. In *De deux angloys* (MR II: 46), the Englishman discovers that he has inadvertently bought donkey meat because his friend complains about its toughness. They have a good laugh and the friend's health is restored, so they consider themselves well paid for the mistake. Even if there is no action taken after the recognition, the function is important because it reinforces the cautionary morality of the fabliau. The character's awareness of his deception and the bad consequences that ensued parallels and reinforces the audience's recognition of the dangers of being duped.

On the other hand, the victim in approximately half of the tales may choose to retaliate (F-8) against the duper. This antisocial act comes as a direct response to the injury or offense and is carried out by the victim of the misdeed. Some of its forms are similar to misdeeds, the retaliation being a *quid pro quo* for the first offense. The victims-turned-aggressors also are capable of

using deception as part of their retaliation. The retaliation is identified in
the fabliau as a different function rather than a second misdeed because the
misdeeds are most often not provoked by the victim. The qualifying statements may provide background information on an ugly husband, but if he
is not portrayed as committing a misdeed against his wife, then her action
(adultery) is a misdeed. If, however, he performs a function that can be construed as a misdeed against her, as the husband does in *Des trois boçus* (MR I:
2) when he denies his wife the pleasure of hearing the musicians (at Christmas-
time no less), then her reaction is considered a retaliation (disobedience in
calling the musicians back to play for her). Retaliations take place only because
a definitely hostile action has preceded, and they rely heavily on physical
violence such as beatings and even murder for their success. All of the plots
that involve extortion and the subsequent death of the victims (*Du segretain*
MR V: 123, *Le Dit du soucretain* MR VI: 150, *Du prestre qu'on porte* MR IV:
89, and *D'Estormi* MR I: 19) are initiated by a seduction or proposed seduction misdeed which a married couple decide to exploit for their own monetary
gain. In a similar situation, *Du prestre et d'Alison* MR II: 31, a priest who has
asked for the favors of the daughter of an honest bourgeoise is hoodwinked
into paying her, not for the daughter, but for an evening with a prostitute. He
is also chased out of the house, publicly humiliated, and beaten. It is interesting to note that although retaliations often parallel the tricks used in F-5
and F-6, the greatest number utilize threats, beatings, or more severe violence.
Only in *De Guillaume au faucon* (MR II: 35) is adultery used as a retaliation,
further indicating how atypical this fabliau is.

If physical force guarantees success in most cases, verbal attacks as a form
of retaliation are almost always doomed to failure. The husband who chal-
lenges his wayward wife in *De la dame qui fit .III. tors* (MR III: 79) starts
off very bravely:

> "Dame, orde vilz pute provée,
> Vous soiez or la mal trovée,"
> Dist li escuiers. "Dont venez?
> Bien pert que pour fol me tenez."
>
> (vv. 121-24)

But he is no match for her quick wit.

As we have seen, the fabliau presents a conflict and creates a tension that
can be counterbalanced by a retaliation. If the action progresses from F-1
through F-9, one misdeed has essentially been counteracted by another one,
and there is no reason to believe that the action could not continue with
several more cycles of aggression and counteraggression. The tales of the
hidden body are good examples of the manner in which some fabliaux literally
do repeat the same functions over and over to the point of boredom. The
simplest narratives end with a misdeed, lengthier ones with a retaliation, and

some more complex ones triple or multiply many times the basic sequences. There is only one other type of ending to these narratives, a resolution F-9. It is a function that potentially resolves the uneasy balance, not by countervailing power but by eliminating the source of the conflict. When resolution occurs, the object of contention is removed or neutralized in some way such that the conflict ends. In almost all cases, the function is called for and accomplished by a third party to the conflict.

In the tales where a body is hidden and discovered only to be hidden again because the person is afraid of being implicated in the crime, the story could continue to recycle through the functions as long as the pattern of discovery, assumed guilt (self-deception), and retaliation (hiding the body to cover a crime) was not broken. In each of these tales there is a resolution because someone eventually decides to bury the body. At the end of *Du prestre qu'on porte* (MR IV: 89), the crowd runs to bury the body so that the honor of the abbey where it has been found will be preserved. In the analogues (*Du segretain* MR V: 123 and *Le Dit dou soucretain* MR VI: 150), the abbot or the crowd, neither of whom has been involved in the narrative up to this point, buries the body. In *De Barat et de Haimet* (MR IV: 97), Traver's ham has been stolen and recovered numerous times. In the final confrontation between Traver and the thieves, Traver proposes an end to the conflict by splitting and eating the ham on the spot. Also in *De la male Honte* (see Appendix C), the verbal misunderstanding is clarified when the wise man suggests that they ask the *vilain* what he means by "la male honte." Here the recognition is also a resolution because the mistake and the source of conflict are clarified. In all of these cases, the conflict is defused but the ending is not necessarily a happy one.

There is a form of attempted resolution that occurs when the conflicting parties seek out a third party and ask him to resolve the conflict. This involves a change of scene (F-1 and F-2) and then a request (F-3c) for justice. Often the characters seek out ecclesiastical justice as in *Du prestre qui ot mere* (MR V: 125), *Des .II. chevaus* (MR I: 13), and *De la coille noire* (MR VI: 148). Ideally the ecclesiastical judges should not only resolve the conflict, but also render justice. The latter goal is virtually never attained. In *De la coille noire* (MR VI: 148), the argument resolves itself in the process of telling the story to the bishop, and he does not need to make a judgement. But in *Du prestre qui ot mere* justice miscarries because the old woman lies about the identity of her son, and in *Des .II. chevaus* the bishop never renders his decision. In several tales a solution is advanced that shows the judicial process itself to be corrupt (*De la viellete* MR V: 129 and *Des .III. dames* MR IV: 99 and V: 112). At times, the appeal for justice is left unanswered and, as was mentioned in Chapter 2, the narrators themselves step in to ask the audience to judge.

Resolution (F-9) does not occur in many fabliaux. When it does, it provides an end to the conflict, but not necessarily a just solution. There are a few cases where resolution not only ends the conflict but also punishes the duper and compensates the duped person. In one tale, *De Frere Denise* (MR III: 87), a *chevalière* discovers that Frère Denise is not a boy and then uncovers the story of her abduction. There is a long diatribe against priests, and the lady makes the young monk pay a dowry so that the girl can be properly married. This plot, although it does involve both deception and misdeed, is a bit atypical because of its ending. In *De la male Honte,* the *vilain* who was beaten is at least compensated for his troubles by being allowed to keep the trunk and its contents, but of course the king is not punished for having had the poor man beaten. Since so few tales end with a just settlement and since retaliations, especially brutal ones, are more common than resolutions, the world of the fabliau is not one where problems are actually worked out and resolved. On the contrary, these tales reflect a world of immediate retributory justice administered by the injured party, who, if he is the most clever person, will prevail.

As can be seen by looking at the three fabliaux analyzed in Appendices A, B, and C, the nine functions that have been discussed can fully describe the significant action in these tales. Each of these examples also has a complete macrostructure typical of these tales: an introduction, the narrative, and a conclusion. The extent to which functions F-1 and F-2 are used varies according to the changes of scene and the number of characters arriving and departing. F-3 and F-4 are functions that supply information to help stimulate the action and also are part of the character's expression of his interaction with the others as well as his reactions to events or the situation around him. Thus these functions are usually expressed in dialogue form.

The two most crucial functions that occur in every tale identified as a fabliau are the deception and misdeed. The first two functions are merely transitional moves that mark changes of scene; and the next two functions are used primarily as preparation for the following functions or to add to the complexity of the action. But the misdeed and deception are central to the entire situation developed in the plot. The last three functions are responses to F-5 and F-6, and, if the tale has an extremely simple structure, they may not occur.

There remains much to be said about characters and combinations of functions in sequences. A reading of the three fabliaux in Appendices A, B, and C, however, is an indication of the range of surface plots typical fabliaux may exhibit and the manner in which functions occur. The nine functions we have discussed adequately describe the essential actions of sixty of the sixty-six self-proclaimed fabliaux (see Table 1, at the end of this chapter). Within the group of typical fabliaux, however, there are some which stretch the definition. At the lower limits are simple anecdotes that are more jokes than full-fledged humorous narratives: *Du prestre qui dist la passion* MR V: 118, *Du provoire qui menga les meures* MR IV: 92, *De porcelet* MR IV: 101, *De la crote* MR III: 58, and *De la coille noire* MR VI: 148. *De Frere Denise* MR III: 87 seems a little serious to be keeping company with tales such as *Du fotéor*; and *De Guillaume au faucon* (MR II: 35) is clearly a *conte courtois* until the final sequences. But only six of these self-proclaimed fabliaux should definitely be re-evaluated (see Table 2, at the end of this chapter). Considering the relative newness of the term *fablel* in the thirteenth century, and the mixture of generic labels found in these texts, it is not surprising that a few do not fit a general pattern. It is perhaps more surprising that sixty of sixty-six actually do have so many elements in common. Before dismissing the six odd ones, let us look at the reasons for excluding them from the list of typical fabliaux.

Du vallet qui d'aise à malaise se met (MR II: 44) is the story of a prospering young man who marries a poor girl and then sinks ever deeper into debt as he tries to cope with the financial responsibilities of a household. The tale begins with several familiar functions—a young man who is described as a bit cocky arrives at a town, where he courts and proposes to a young girl. When her parents learn of his intentions, the mother realizes he will marry the girl without a large dowry, so the parents promote the engagement. The mother succeeds in tricking the young man into thinking there is another suitor, which encourages him to agree to a small dowry. If *Du vallet* concluded briefly after the deception, or if the young man discovered the trick and tried to retaliate, the story would be a typical fabliau; but the narrative continues with an atypical event, the marriage. The rest of the narrative relates how naïve he is about finances and the debts he incurs trying to set up the household for his wife. The tale is not a humorous illustration of deception but a serious example of how marriage can financially ruin a man. Bédier also debated about the classification of this tale and ultimately decided to consider it among the fabliaux as an example of a mixture of genres: "*Le Vallet qui d'aise à malaise se met,* par exemple, est-il un conte très faible ou un excellent tableau de mœurs? L'un et l'autre. Il sera bon de respecter l'indécision même des trouvères, et de marquer, en accueillant ce poème dans notre collection, comment les fabliaux peuvent confinir à des genres divers."[14] I will say, on the contrary, that its action is not adequately explained by the nine functions, and therefore, it should not be grouped with the typical fabliaux.

Li Sohaiz desvez (MR V: 131) by Jean Bodel is the account of a woman, neglected by her husband, who falls asleep and dreams of going to a market where there are male genitals for sale. Bodel does not actually refer to his tale as a fabliau, but it has generally been considered as such because of its subject matter. It was included in the group of self-proclaimed fabliaux because the word *fabliau* does appear in the text when Bodel refers to himself as ".I. rimoieres de fabliaus" (v. 210). The action does not correspond to the functions of the fabliau because the principal vehicle of the humor is a dream instead of an actual conflict, and the couple happily make love when she recounts the dream. There is no purposeful deception and the only misdeed is the husband's neglect, which he fully compensates his wife for after they awaken.

Des putains et des lecheors (MR III: 76) parodies an explanatory legend about the origins of the three estates. It begins in a way completely different from the typical fabliau by explaining how God gave land to the *chevaliers*, alms to the *clers*, and work to the *laboranz*. The mock seriousness of the tale becomes apparent as God is besieged by the riff-raff wanting to know where their place in the Creation is to be. Having first asked St. Peter who this noisy group is, God then assigns the lechers to the *chevaliers* and the prostitutes to the *clers*. Thus, according to the author, the prosperous state of the prostitutes indicates that the clerics have taken care of them, and the clerics will be saved because of their good works. There is no conflict and therefore no possibility of analyzing the plot in terms of the nine functions. It is also one of the two tales in the group which does not have a moral conclusion relating to justice or deception. *Des putains* is clearly closer to an explanatory legend than a fabliau.

Trubert is an extended narrative composed largely of fabliau sequences, but its 3000-verse length should set it outside the limits of a genre defined as a short narrative. Trubert's background is briefly mentioned at the outset, and the tale resembles the opening of several *romans* which detail the naïveté of the hero. Trubert's adventures extend over several days, he periodically returns home, and the narrative ends rather abruptly without any sense of closure. *Trubert* may be the first picaresque *conte*, and I feel, as Nykrog did, that it does not belong in the group of typical fabliaux.

In the typical fabliau, a cautionary moral is placed in the conclusion following the narrative proper, which is a self-contained humorous story of deception. The *conte moral* differs in that the narrative itself develops a moral point of view. *De pleine bourse de sens* (MR III: 67) is an example of this difference. In this tale, a philandering husband is asked by his wife to buy her a "plaine borse de sen," (v. 69), and the tale relates his quest and his ultimate realization of her meaning. The story is a literal quest to resolve the moral problem he has created by taking a mistress. The significant action could not be described by the functions of the fabliau, but it is a tale which could easily be analyzed by the same method and its particular functions would give insight into the structure of the *conte moral*.

Du chevalier qui recovra l'amor de sa dame (MR VI: 151) is the story of a *chevalier* who performs all the tasks and obligations of a true courtly lover in order to win his lady's esteem. He requests permission to joust in a tournament with her husband, and she is so impressed with his courage that she decides to bestow her favors upon him that night. She summons him to her chambers late in the evening, but keeps him waiting while her husband falls asleep. Unfortunately, the lover, who is weary from the day's exploits, also falls asleep, and the lady is so offended that she tells her maid to send him away. In order to regain her love, he attempts a test of his courage: he enters and appears by the couple's bed. When the husband awakes and asks him who he is, he replies that he is the ghost of a knight killed that day in the tournament who must seek the lady's pardon before his soul can rest. In true courtly fashion the husband beseeches his wife to forgive the knight, but she refuses. The husband then asks the "ghost" what he had done to offend his wife, but the knight declares he could never reveal the story of the insult. The wife is at last so touched by his bravery that she forgives him.

In this tale there is no misdeed, and the relationships between characters reflect the courtly tradition rather than the antagonisms of the fabliau. The husband and the lover are not in conflict; on the contrary, the husband is eager to have his wife comply with the rules of courtly love by being charitable. The essence of the narrative is not deception and aggression, but tests and good deeds characteristic of the *service d'amour*. Therefore, it does not fit in with our concept of the typical fabliau. *Du chevalier qui recovra l'amor de sa dame,* like each of the six tales, has certain elements in common with the typical fabliau, but the basic structure of these tales differs in significant ways, thereby altering their meaning. As *tableau de mœurs, contes picaresques,* dream visions, *contes morals* or *contes courtois,* they lack the negative dramatic conflict necessary in the fabliau's shifting patterns of deceit and aggression.

The morphology of the fabliau has been established by taking the group of self-proclaimed fabliaux as initial sources; their common structures provide a means of defining the term and setting some boundaries for this subgenre of the short narrative. But what of the other eighty-eight tales in the traditional corpus which may have different or no generic labels attached to them? The structural definition would be almost pointless if it described only those texts already identified as fabliaux by their authors. The nine functions and their patterns of occurence do, however, describe the majority of the remaining tales in the corpus. I have analyzed each one and found that all but eighteen should be considered fabliaux. Therefore, the master list of typical fabliaux in Table 1 now includes a total of 130 texts.

The number of atypical tales is not large, especially considering that the traditional corpus was established on the basis of very broad definitions of the genre. In Table 2, I list the atypical texts, their distinctive traits or points of difference, and what seems to me to be a more appropriate genre label. It should be noted that the lists are entitled "typical" and "nontypical" fabliaux to emphasize that this is a descriptive rather than a prescriptive study. It is not my purpose to banish eternally certain texts. It is my purpose, however, to define the typical fabliau and to analyze the meaning of the genre. For the sake of this project, then, those tales in Table 2 are considered peripheral to the definition and analysis.

My study has shown that even in regard to the action, there is a high degree of conformity to nine basic functions. The specific functions also confirm the implications about the word *fablel* found in the introductions and conclusions. The conflict in a fabliau focuses on deception to prepare or cover up misdeeds, such as adultery, stealing, cheating, and physical aggression. The narratives include cycles of deception and misdeeds counteracted in many cases by physical retaliation and resolved by counterfeit judicial processes. There is little or no harmony achieved and no real conclusion to the problems that generated the conflict. The narratives, in other words, illustrate the warnings in the author's conclusions about deception and a secular system of punishment. The roles the characters assume and the dynamic interplay between functions and roles remain to be considered.

TABLE 1

Typical Fabliaux

C'est de la dame qui aveine demandoit pour Morel sa provende avoir	MR I: 29
*Cuvier, Le	MR I: 9
*D'Auberée, la vielle maquerelle	MR V: 110
*De Barat et de Haimet	MR IV: 97
*De Berangier au lonc cul	MR III: 86
*De Berengier au lonc cul	MR IV: 93
*De Boivin de Provins	MR V: 116
De Brifaut	MR IV: 103
*De Brunain, la vache au prestre	MR I: 10
De celle qui se fist foutre sur la fosse de son mari	MR III: 70
De celui qui bota la pierre	MR IV: 102
De celui qui bota la pierre	MR VI: 152
De Charlot le juif	MR III: 83
De Connebert	MR V: 128
*De Constant du Hamel	MR IV: 106
*De deux angloys et de l'anel	MR II: 46
*De deux vilains	G 3 [RR 15 (1924)]
*De Frere Denise	MR III: 87
De Gauteron et de Marion	MR III: 59
*De Gombert et des .II. clers	MR I: 22
*De Guillaume au faucon	MR II: 35
De Jouglet	MR IV: 98
De la borgoise d'Orliens	MR I: 8
*De la coille noire	MR VI: 148
*De la crote	MR III: 58
*De la dame escolliée	MR VI: 149
De la dame qui fist batre son mari	MR IV: 100
De la dame qui fist entendant son mari qu'il sonjoit	MR V: 124
*De la dame qui fit .III. tors entor le moustier	MR III: 79
*De la dame qui se venja du chevalier	MR VI: 140
*De la damoisele qui ne pooit oïr parler de foutre	MR III: 65
*De la damoisele qui n'ot parler de fotre	MR V: 111
De la damoiselle qui sonjoit	MR V: 134
De la femme qui cunqie sen baron	Bédier, p. 303
*De la grue	MR V: 126
*De la male Honte	MR IV: 90
De l'anel qui faisoit les . . . grans et roides	MR III: 60
De la pucele qui abevra le polain	MR IV: 107
De la pucele qui vouloit voler	MR IV: 108
De la sorisete des estopes	MR IV: 105
De la vielle qui oint la palme au chevalier	MR V: 127
*De la viellete	MR V: 129
*Del couvoiteus et de l'envieus	MR V: 135
De l'enfant qui fu remis au soleil	MR I: 14
*De l'escuiruel	MR V: 121

Continued on next page

Table 1 (Continued)

De l'espervier	MR V: 115
De l'evesque qui beneï lo con	MR III: 77
*Dèl fol vilain	G 2 [*RR* 15 (1924)]
De l'oue au chapelein	MR VI: 143
*De porcelet	MR IV: 101
De Saint Piere et du jougleur	MR V: 117
*Des braies au cordelier	MR III: 88
Des braies le priestre	MR VI: A-I
*Des .II. changéors	MR I: 23
*Des .II. chevaus	MR I: 13
*De Sire Hain et de Dame Anieuse	MR I: 6
Des .IIII. prestres	MR VI: 142
*D'Estormi	MR I: 19
*Des tresces	MR IV: 94
*Des trois avugles de Compiengne	MR I: 4
*Des trois boçus	MR I: 2
*Des .III. dames	MR IV: 99
Des .III. dames de Paris	MR III: 73
*Des .III. dames qui trouvèrent l'anel	MR I: 15
Des .III. dames qui trovèrent l'anel au conte	MR VI: 138
Des .III. meschines	MR III: 64
*De .III. dames qui troverent .I. vit	MR V: 112
Dis de le vescie à prestre, Li	MR III: 69
Dit de la gageure, Le	MR II: 48
Dit de le nonnete, Le	MR VI: A-III
*Dit des perdriz, Le	MR I: 17
Dit dou pliçon, Le	MR VI: A-II
*Dit dou soucretain, Le	MR VI: 150
Do maignien qui foti la dame	MR V: 130
Do preste qui manja mores	MR V: 113
*Do pré tondu	MR IV: 104
Dou povre mercier	MR II: 36
Du bouchier d'Abevile	MR III: 84
Du chevalier à la corbeille	MR II: 47
*Du chevalier à la robe vermeille	MR III: 57
*Du chevalier qui fist les cons parler	MR VI: 147
*Du chevalier qui fist les cons parler	MR VI: 147bis [a]
Du chevalier qui fist sa fame confesse	MR I: 16
Du clerc qui fu repus deriere l'escrin	MR IV: 91
Du fevre de Creeil	MR I: 21
*Du fotéor	MR I: 28
Du heron ou la fille mal gardée	*Romania* 26 (1897)
Du moine	*Romania* 44 (1915-17)
Du pescheor de pont seur Saine	MR III: 63
Du prestre crucefié	MR I: 18
*Du prestre et d'Alison	MR II: 31
*Du prestre et de la dame	MR II: 51
Du prestre et des .II. ribaus	MR III: 62
Du prestre et du chevalier	MR II: 34

Continued on next page

Table 1 (Continued)

Du prestre et du leu	MR VI: 145
Du prestre et du mouton	MR VI: 144
Du prestre ki abevete	MR III: 61
Du prestre qui dist la passion	MR V: 118
Du prestre qui ot mere à force	MR V: 125
Du prestre qu'on porte	MR IV: 89
Du prestre teint	MR VI: 139
Du preudome qui rescolt son compère de noier	MR I: 27
Du provoire qui menga les meures	MR IV: 92
Du provost à l'aumuche	MR I: 7
Du segretain moine	MR V: 136
Du segretain	MR V: 123
Du sot chevalier	MR I: 20
Du vilain asnier	MR V: 114
Du vilain au buffet	MR III: 80
Du vilain de Bailluel	MR IV: 109
Du vilain mire	MR III: 74
Du vilain qui conquist paradis par plait	MR III: 81
Estula	MR IV: 96
Flabel d'Aloul, Le	MR I: 24
Jugement des cons, Le	MR V: 122
Male Honte, La	MR V: 120
Meunier d'Arleux, Le	MR II: 33
Meunier et les .II. clers, Le	MR V: 119
Nonnette, La	*Romania* 34 (1905)
Pet au vilain, Le	MR III: 68
Plantez, La	MR III: 75
Povre Clerc, Le	MR V: 132
Prestre pelé	*Romania* 55 (1929)
.IIII. souhais Saint Martin, Les	MR V: 133
Romanz de un chivaler et de sa dame et de un clerk	MR II: 50
Saineresse, La	MR I: 25
Sentier batu, Le	MR III: 85
Souhaits, Les	G 1 [*RR* 15 (1924)]
Testament de l'asne, Le	MR III: 82
Vilain de Farbu, Le	MR IV: 95

*Denotes those tales in the original group of sixty-six self-proclaimed fabliaux.
[a](2nd version in notes)

TABLE 2

Nontypical Fabliaux

Tales to Be Reclassified

Points of Difference from or
Affinity to Other Genres

A. *Tales from Self-Proclaimed Group*   See discussion on pages 60 ff.

1. *De pleine bourse de sens* MR III:
   67   *conte moral*
2. *Des putains et des lecheors* MR
   III: 76   explanatory legend
3. *Du chevalier qui recovra l'amor
   de sa dame* MR VI: 151   *conte courtois*
4. *Du vallet qui d'aise à malaise se
   met* MR II: 44   *tableau de mœurs*
5. *Sohaiz desvez, Li,* MR V: 131   dream vision
6. *Trubert,* Méon, *Nouveau recueil,*
   I, 192   *roman* or *conte picaresque*

B. *Other Tales in Fabliau Corpus*

7. *C'hest de la houce* MR II: 30   quest marriage, good deed / *conte moral*
8. *De fole larguece* MR VI: 146   serious action / *conte moral*
9. *Des chevaliers, des clers, et des
   vilains,* Barbazan, I, 45   no conflict / mock explanatory legend
10. *Des .III. chanoinesses de
    Couloingne* MR III: 72   storytelling, no conflict / a *jongleur gab?*
11. *Des .III. chevaliers et del chainse*
    MR III: 71   test, challenge met, *judgment d'amour* /
                                              conte courtois
12. *Dit de Dame Jouenne, Romania,*
    45, 99-105   dramatic version of *Do pré tondu* / farce
13. *Du c qui fu fuit a la besche,* Bar-
    bazan/Méon, *Fabliaux,* IV, 194   no conflict / obscene explanatory legend
14. *Du mantel mautaillié* MR III: 55   magical object, good deed, happy ending /
                                              lai or *conte courtois*
15. *D'une seule fame* MR I: 26   battle, test, murder, trial / *dit* (?)
16. *Du prestre qui fu mis au lardier*
    MR II: 32   only verse form makes it differ
17. *Du vair palefroi* MR I: 3   quest, separation of lovers, undesired wed-
                                              ding, lovers reunited, marriage / *conte
                                              courtois*

(Continued on next page)

Table 2 (Continued)

Points of Difference from or
Affinity to Other Genres (Continued)

18. *Du vallet aux .XII. fames* MR
    III: 78   marriage / *conte moral, tableau de mœurs*
19. *Houce partie, La,* MR I: 5   quest, marriage, good deed / *conte moral*
20. *Lai d'Aristote, Le,* MR V: 137   discourse on love, lengthy moral / *conte courtois*
21. *Richeut,RR,* 4, iii, 261-305   extended narrative, birth and life history of protagonist / *roman*
22. *Roi d'Angleterre, Le,* MR II: 52   series of word plays, no conflict / joke
23. *Veuve, La,* MR II: 49   no conflict, long description of widow / *tableau de mœurs*
24. *Vilain qui n'ert pas de son oste sire,Romania,* 62, 1-16   diatribe against *vilain,* description, no conflict / *dit*

4

Victims and Dupers: The Fabliau Dynamic

The characters in the fabliau can be analyzed in a variety of ways—by their social status, their relationships to one another, or their roles within the plot. Historically, it has been their social status that has interested the critics and prompted several lengthy analyses of the society they presumably reflect. The presence of *chevaliers, bourgeois, vilains,* and the ubiquitous *prestre* has provoked animated arguments about the meaning of these tales, but it should be noted that in the group of self-proclaimed, typical fabliaux there are as many characters of indeterminate social standing (*une feme, son ami, les voisins, un bacheler*) as there are characters who clearly belong to the aristocracy, the bourgeoisie, or the clergy.[1] Trying to calculate the number of characters within this group of fabliaux gives at best a sense of the diversity of social classes represented, and it is risky to give much weight to absolute totals. If, for instance, there are more *vilain* or lower class characters, does this mean fabliaux are necessarily proletariat literature? The large number is just as likely due to the numerous secondary characters, who are normally servants (the ethos of the *vilain* is another question, however; see discussion below, Chapter 6). Doubling and tripling of characters, as in *Des .III. dames* (MR IV: 99), *Des trois avugles* (MR I: 4), or *Des trois boçus* (MR I: 2) also alter the numbers even though the presence of three priests or three poor men has virtually no impact on the social implications of the story.

Several factors make it impossible to be categorical about the social bias of the genre. First is the fact that all four major social groups of medieval society—the aristocracy, the bourgeoisie, the clergy, and the lower class—are present, and the first three are almost equally represented. Also, since very few characters are named, the terms *bourgeois* and *vilain* are more a descriptive label than significant social information. *Vilain,* for instance, is frequently used as a derogatory epithet rather than as an identification of social origins; and, likewise, *courtoise* may be applied to a woman to indicate beauty or refinement regardless of her social class. Furthermore, as Rychner and others have pointed out, a given tale may be reworked for different audiences by

71

changing the designations of the characters or by modifying their attributes. In these cases, social standing has less to do with the demands of plot or theme than the demands of an audience.

The diversity of social classes represented should force a re-evaluation of the whole notion that this genre is necessarily identified with a given social class. At least two other types of social information are more pertinent to an understanding of the meaning of these tales. For instance, information about the occupations of the characters and their geographical settings—either explicit or implicit—is crucial to their value system. These aspects of their social background figure in an analysis to follow of *Le Meunier d'Arleux* MR II: 33 (in Appendix D) and in the final chapter. Other pertinent social information includes the relationship between the characters within each text, for if the characters' social class is not always identified, their relationship to one another is always made clear. Relationships may be based on traditional bonds, such as kinship, economics, or friendship. There is even a "negative" bond—those characters who are unacquainted, strangers who are thrown together and therefore play the same roles as characters who are acquainted. Usually these relationships are explained by the qualifying statement or as the characters are introduced. As was mentioned in the discussion of QS-1, the explanation of these relationships between the characters is important because it creates a certain set of expectations in the audience as to the type of plot that will follow.

In the majority of fabliaux, the major characters are related through kinship, the most common form being marriage. Of all the potential kinship patterns that could be expressed, it seems significant that in the group of self-proclaimed fabliaux there are so few describing a relationship other than marriage. In a few cases, a mother/daughter or father/daughter relationship (*Du prestre et d'Alison* MR II: 31, *De la damoisele* MR III: 65 and V: 111, and *De l'escuiruel* MR V: 121) is crucial. One fabliau presents a mother/son relationship (*Du prestre qui ot mere* MR V: 125). Only a few fabliaux include cousins, nieces, or nephews, and they normally are secondary characters, the exception being *D'Estormi* (MR I: 19). Only one among the self-proclaimed group, *Le Jugement des cons* MR V: 122, includes characters who are siblings, and there are no father/son relationships.

The predominate kinship bonds in the fabliau have one salient characteristic in common: they are all relationships where one character has real or potential sexual prerogatives over another one. Certainly the only aspect of marriage which is important is the establishment of sexual rights. In the parent/daughter relationship the same factors obtain because the parent controls the sexual behavior of the daughter until a husband is given these sexual rights. In one tale a surrogate parent plays the role of guardian, although in this case not very successfully (*De la grue* MR V: 126). Even in the case of the mother/son conflict, it is a question of jealousy over the son's sexual behavior which creates a rivalry between the women.

Thus the only aspect of kinship which matters in these tales is sexual "access" to another person, and therefore another relationship can be included in this group. The lover usurps the role of the husband, and the couple form a bond which is similar to marriage, although it exists outside legal sanctions. Counting illicit sexual relationships as a variation of the legal and blood kinship patterns, we see a very high proportion—forty-four of sixty fabliaux—include major characters related by one or another form of kinship.

Economic and social bonds reflect not only the feudal order but also a money economy. There are examples of a *chevalier* and his *escuier* (*Du chevalier qui fist les cons parler* MR VI: 147 and 147 bis), a *chatelain* and *vallet* (*De Guillaume au faucon* MR II: 35), a king and his subjects (*De la male Honte* MR IV: 90), a *chevalier* and his provost (*Du provost à l'aumuche* MR I: 7), and a *conte* and his seneschal (*Du vilain au buffet* MR III: 80). The nascent capitalistic economy is reflected by the many characters who are servants of the bourgeoisie. In most cases they are maids who help their mistresses (*Le Cuvier* MR I: 9 and *Du prestre et de la dame* MR II: 51) or men hired to carry out a specific task (*Des trois boçus* MR I: 2 and *Des .III. dames qui trouvèrent l'anel* MR I: 15). Another aspect of the capitalistic system is seen in the partnerships or cooperative relationships established for economic gain: the merchants in *Le Cuvier* MR I: 9; the robbers in *De Barat et de Haimet* MR IV: 97, *Du prestre qu'on porte* MR IV: 89, *Du segretain* MR V: 123; and the prostitutes in *De Boivin* MR V: 116.

The bond of friendship is not neglected in the fabliau either. This relationship implies a feeling of familiarity and a relative equality not characteristic of the sexual, legal, or economic ties. Some "friendships of the road" may or may not, however, withstand the temptation of individual gain (*Des .III. dames* MR IV: 99 and V: 112, *Del couvoiteus et de l'envieus* MR V: 135, and *Des trois avugles* MR I: 4). At times, good friends trick each other inadvertently (*De deux angloys* MR II: 46) or work together to hoodwink some unsuspecting victim (*De Gombert et des .II. clers* MR I: 22).

Only two fabliaux in this group contain characters who are all complete strangers to each other (*De la viellete* MR V: 129 and *Des .II. chevaus* MR I: 13), and in both cases there are very few characters in the entire tale; the first has only three and the second has two. Usually if a stranger has a significant role in the tale, it is in a context in which the other characters do know each other. In *Des trois avugles* (MR I: 4), for example, the three blind men are friends, but the cleric who tricks them, as well as the innkeeper and priest, are all strangers to each other. The long tales where a body is hidden and discovered several times all begin with a conflict between characters who have a bond of kinship. As the tale progresses, however, the people who hide the corpse are not acquainted with the person who finds it. Strangers are quite common as minor characters; a man in the street may perform a service (*Le Cuvier* MR I: 9) or may be a hapless victim who stumbles into trouble. Strangers can even be primary characters, as is the *fouterres* of *Du fotéor* (MR I: 28). The cleric who helps unravel the plot in *Le Povre Clerc* (MR V: 132) was also a stranger when he first arrived and asked for food at the *vilain*'s house.

The various relationships between characters are important because they indicate the nature of the conflict that will develop. When the characters are related by friendship or are strangers, there is less chance of predicting what type of plot will follow because these relationships can generate various degrees of friendly or hostile behavior. But when they are related by kinship, which is more precisely a sexual bond, the type of tensions inherent in these sexual relationships create predictable behavior. This is also true to a certain extent of those based on economics, because the established hierarchy of lord/vassal or master/servant produces a limited set of behavior patterns. The real meaning of the characters' relationships to one another, however, is significant when they are seen in conjunction with the roles that they play.

In the fabliau, the characters are revealed primarily through their actions; in other words, the functions they execute identify them more clearly than their social status or their bonds with other characters. The characters are not individuals contributing a unique part to the action; they assume an importance in the plot by virtue of the roles they play. The roles are limited to four possibilities: the duper, the victim, the auxiliary, and the counselor. Nevertheless there can be as many as a dozen characters in a single tale, i.e., there is not a one-to-one correspondence between characters and roles as there is not between actions and functions. As Propp indicated, roles are stable elements that are not dependent on the specific individual who fulfills them; several characters may play the same role, or one character may play several roles.[2] Of the four roles, at least the first two, duper and victim, are found in every fabliau and constitute part of its definition.

The duper, arch-villain of the fabliau, carries out the deception (F-5) and the misdeed (F-6). Like the wife in *Des braies au cordelier* MR III: 88, this character is extremely clever and well-versed in the art of deception, "La dame sot mout de renart; / Engigneuse fu de toz tors" (vv. 238-39). The skills of the duper are varied, but his most salient talent is the verbal *tour de force,* at times convincing the victim that he has only imagined what were actual events. The wife in *Du chevalier à la robe vermeille* (MR III: 57) is able to convince her husband that he merely imagined seeing a *palefroi* and *robe vermeille* which she had previously told him were gifts from her brother:

> —Sire," dist ele, "par saint Pere,
> Il a bien .II. mois et demi,

Ou plus, que mon frere ne vi;
Et, s'il estoit ci orendroit,
Ne voudroit il en nul endroit
Qu'en vostre dos fust embatue
Robe que il eüst vestue;
Ce deüst dire uns fols, uns yvres.
Ja vaut plus de .IIII^{XX}. livres
La grant rente que vous avez,
Et la terre que vous tenez:
Querez robe à vostre talant,
Et palefroi bel et amblant,
Qui souef vous port l'ambleüre:
De vous ne sai dire mesure,
Quar vous estes tels atornez
Que toz les iex avez troublez. "

(vv. 244-60)

The sheer bravura of a duper sometimes accounts for his success. In *Du fotéor* (MR I: 28), when the husband returns unexpectedly, interrupting the wife and lover, the *fotéor* greets him boldly and even chastizes him for not returning his greeting:

−Mais vos, qui ci ne me daigniez
Respondre quant ge vos salu,
Quar ge sui cil qui a valu
Plus as gentix dames du mont
Que tuit cil qui el siecle sont;
Quar ge sui un fouterres maistre."

(vv. 340-45)

The *fotéor* then explains with false frankness that he had been hired for the afternoon and is anxious to render his services in order to be paid:

".XX. sols doi ci gaaignier hui,
Bien les i aurai sax encui
La dame qui m'a aloé,
Quar bien la cuit servir à gré;
Mais n'ai encor à lui géu,
N'encore mon loier éu.
Mais or est tens de commencier;
Molt tost la me faites coschier;
Si irai faire mon revel."

(vv. 347-55)

If the duper is characterized by his gift for using language to his best advantage, he also knows that saying nothing is sometimes the best deception. In *De Gombert et des .II. clers* (MR I: 22), for example, the cleric who seduces Gombert's wife goes to her bed and, without saying a word, assumes the role of her husband. When she comments on his unusual sexual prowess, he fore-stalls the disclosure of his identity by letting her chatter while he continues silently with his fun:

> Li clers, qui ne fu pas noiseus,
> En fist toutes voies ses buens,
> Et li lesse dire les suens.

(vv. 128-30)

The duper has not only a great deal of imagination and control of verbal irony (to be further discussed in Chapter 5), but he also has a capacity to respond immediately to adverse circumstances. His reaction to threatened discovery is to obscure the situation either verbally or physically by hiding a person or object. His extraordinary power to manipulate circumstances is perhaps objectified or externalized when the duper commands the forces of magic in his wrongdoing. This power allows a duper to dominate his victim even when the victim is aware of his intentions and tries to prevent the con-sequences. Nevertheless, magic is an unusual tool, and it is more normally his or her own native abilities, especially in the case of women, which permit the duper to hoodwink and then aggress against his victim. The duper is also usually distinguished by his self-possession and spirit of playfulness, calmly executing a caper and then watching the developments with detachment. In *Des trois avugles* (MR I: 4), for instance, after the cleric has pretended to give the blind men some money, he watches with glee as they try to figure out which of them has the money to pay the innkeeper:

> Li clers, qui fu à biaus harnas,
> Qui le conte forment amoit,
> De ris en aise se pasmoit.

(vv. 176-78)

When the deception is used as a reflexive function, i.e., the character dupes himself, he is usually the antithesis of the skillful deceiver. Two good examples of the stupid character who fools himself are found in Gautier le Leu's tales *Del fol vilain* (G 2) and *De deux vilains* (G 3). The self-deceived duper mistakes one person for another or an object for another one which causes an embarrass-ing moment. Instead of perceiving situations accurately, these characters become confused or think they have done something they have not. Under-standably these characters also lack the sense of humor and self-assurance of their counterparts. The personality traits that these self-dupers demonstrate are therefore often similar to those of the other main character in the fabliau, the victim.

If the duper is known for his quick-wittedness, the victim is identified by his slow and stupid ways, his dull mind being confirmed by his rough physical appearance. The husband who believes his wife when she tells him he has died is introduced as an ugly sluggish dolt:

> Il estoit granz et merveilleus
> Et maufez et de laide hure.
> Sa fame n'avoit de lui cure,
> Quar fols ert et de lait pelain,
> . . . .
> Ez vous le vilain qui baaille
> Et de famine et de mesaise.
>
> (*Du vilain de Bailluel* MR IV: 109, vv. 8-11, 20-21)

The victim is most often taken in by the duper because of naïveté or the inability to respond quickly to situations. Naïve girls inevitably trust the wrong men and are seduced (*De Frere Denise* MR III: 87 and *De la grue* MR V: 126), a husband comes home and fails to recognize that something is amiss (*Du prestre et de la dame* MR II: 51), or the victim fails to grasp that there is obviously a misunderstanding between him and his opponent (*De la male Honte* MR IV: 90). The least alert of the victims are those who never recognize (F-7) the misdeed, or must have it revealed to them by another person.

There are some victims, however, who are clever enough to discover a misdeed when the evidence is too blatant to be overlooked (*Des braies au cordelier* MR III: 88 and *De la dame qui fit .III. tors* MR III: 79), but who allow themselves to be deceived a second time by the more clever duper. There are also instances in which a victim cannot keep pace with the verbal barrage from the duper and finally recognizes that his protest is of no avail, so he falls silent and accepts his fate. In *Des trois avugles* (MR I: 4), for example, the innkeeper is cheated by a cleric who uses a priest to accomplish the misdeed. The cleric pays the priest a small sum to say a mass for the innkeeper who the cleric says has gone mad; meanwhile he tells the innkeeper that the priest will reimburse him for the cleric's debts. After a scene of demands for money countered by pastoral solicitude, the innkeeper realizes he has been caught in a game he cannot win:

> Et li borgois s'est toz cois teus;
> Corouciéz est et moult honteus
> De ce qu'il fu si atrapez;
> Liéz fu quant il fu eschapez;
> A son ostel en vint tout droit.
>
> (vv. 327-31)

The duper has a strong and distinctive personality, but his victim is usually just an innocent, or an average "nice guy" like Sire Hain who is dominated by his wife. He responds to her insolence and disobedience with Casper Milquetoast phrases instead of strong protest:

"Diex!" fet Hains, "com tu me tiens cort!
A paines os-je dire mot;
Grant honte ai quant mon voisin m'ot,
Que tu me maines si viument."
(*De Sire Hain et de Dame Anieuse* MR I: 6, vv. 76-79)

Contrary to the duper, who always emerges as a real presence in the fabliau, the victim may be a faceless stranger who just happened along at an inopportune moment. Some victims are mistaken for someone else and suffer the consequences without even knowing what has happened. In *D'Estormi* (MR I: 19), for example, the uncle does not want to tell Estormi that there are three corpses to be buried, so he waits until Estormi has returned from burying one, then tells him that the corpse has returned. After the third corpse has finally been buried, a priest happens by as Estormi is leaving the graveyard, and Estormi thinks it is the corpse trying to escape again:

N'ot gueres alé quant il ot
.I. prestre devant lui aler,
Qui de ses matines chanter
Venoit, par sa male aventure.

(vv. 514-17)

We know nothing more about this victim than is presented in these few lines because Estormi attacks and kills him before he can protest.

The auxiliary is any character used by the duper as an assistant or someone caught up in the misdeed by virture of his association with the victim. Almost every fabliau has one or more characters who serve as auxiliaries to the main characters or who are encountered accidentally.[3] They may assume an active part, as maids often do when they are sent on errands or when they relay information. Hercelot in *Du prestre et d'Alison* (MR II: 31) knows that her mistress is going to substitute a prostitute for the daughter, so she gleefully sets off to notify the priest that all is ready for his arrival:

"Sire, bon jor puissiez avoir
De par celui qui vos salue,
Qui est vostre amie et vo drue,
De par Marion au cors gent."

(vv. 216-19)

The auxiliary may also help to administer the misdeed or retaliation, expecially when physical force is used. In *De la male Honte* (MR IV: 90), for example, the king asks his men to get rid of the *vilain* and to discourage him from coming back.

Many auxiliaries, however, are characters who are only marginally involved in the action and who are almost nothing more than props added to the scene.

The lover is always an auxiliary to the wife's deception of her husband, but he may have only a small part in the action. In *Le Cuvier* (MR I: 9), we learn that the wife is with her lover, "Et ele se fesoit baingnier / Avoec .I. clerc de grant franchise . . ." (vv. 12-13). We know nothing more about him until the wife frees him and he runs away during the confusion caused by the man yelling "Fire!" Even the man in the street who was hired by the neighbor has a larger role and some dialogue with her. Nevertheless, none of the auxiliaries, whether they play an active or passive part in the action, are described at length.

A special type of auxiliary provides something to a main character and then withdraws from the action. These donor-auxiliaries are unusual because normally an auxiliary is asked by a main character to help with a task or is involved with the main character by association. The donor-auxiliaries, on the contrary, appear at the beginning of the story, and although they have no special connection with the main character, they offer him a gift. In each of the four cases where this occurs (*Del couvoiteus et de l'envieus* MR V: 135, *Les .IIII. souhais Saint Martin* MR V: 133, and *Du chevalier qui fist les cons parler* MR VI: 147 and 147 bis) the gift is magic power. It is not surprising to find this form of donor-auxiliary here because these particular tales are clearly related to fairy tales where there are donors, according to Propp.[4] Nevertheless, as has been pointed out before, magical elements are unusual in the fabliau corpus and so too are the donor-auxiliaries.

In approximately one-third of the fabliaux a fourth role, the counselor, appears to perform the resolution (F-9). As the name *counselor* indicates, this character is capable of understanding the situation which exists between the duper and victim and able to render advice that would resolve the conflict. In *De la male Honte* (MR IV: 90), for example, the character who fills this role exemplifies its ideal qualities. The king has just ordered his men to seize the *vilain* when a wise man comes forward:

> Quant .I. hauz hom s'est avant mis,
> Qui saiges ert et entendanz
> Et de parole molt saichanz.

(vv. 122-24)

He is therefore able to make a suggestion that prevents another misdeed from occurring and resolves the conflict.

> "Sire," fait il, "vos avez tort
> Se le vilain aviez mort;
> Mais,ençois que li façoiz honte,
> Sachiez que est la male Honte."

(vv. 125-28)

A counselor offers his advice gratuitously as in the preceding example, or he may be asked for his opinion. In *De Sire Hain et de Dame Anieuse* (MR I: 6), the unrepentant wife, Dame Anieuse, shocks a neighbor, who asks his own wife, Aupais, what she thinks. Aupais then gives Dame Anieuse a lecture on behaving as a good wife, which motivates the final resolution of the conflict between Sire Hain and Dame Aneiuse. In *Du sot chevalier* (MR I: 20) the wife is unhappy with her stupid husband and consequently turns to her mother for advice. The mother plays the role of counselor because she instructs her son-in-law about sex and thus resolves his marital problems.

The counselor is not often described in detail, but he reveals his wisdom by correctly analyzing the situation. In *De deux angloys* (MR II: 46), the brother who has been fed donkey meat analyzes the bones and can tell they are not from a lamb. When he sees the hide, he is certain that Alein has been cheated:

> "Alein," fait-il, "tou diz merveilles.
> Si fait pié, si faite mousel
> Ne si fait pel n'a mie ainel.
> Ainelet a petite l'os,
> Corte l'eschine et cort le dos;
> Cestui n'est mie fils *bèhè.* "

> (vv. 98-103)

Another counselor, the *conte* of *Du vilain au buffet* who is "preus et sages" (MR III: 80, v. 55), wants to hear the *vilain*'s side of the story before punishing him for having slapped his seneschal.

The counselor not only can analyze situations clearly, but is also supposed to make judgements in the sense of settling disputes between the duper and his victim. Many of the characters asked to play the role of counselor are judges, but they reveal themselves to be inadequate, corrupt, and profiteering. In the tales *Du prestre qui ot mere* MR V: 125 and *De la viellete* MR V: 129, the counselor is given incorrect information and therefore makes an incorrect judgement. In the two tales *Des .III. dames* (MR IV: 99 and V: 112), the women who are arguing seek out a counselor to judge their case. The judge is an abbess who decides to trick them and keep the object over which they are arguing:

> Assez a ore bien jugié
> Ici ma dame l'abaesse;
> Mout fist que fausse tricherresse
> Qui leur toli par covoitise.
> (*De .III. dames* MR V: 112, vv. 104-07)

She has resolved the conflict between the women by removing the object of contention; thus she is a counselor. But she also plays the role of a duper, and her action is both resolution and a new misdeed.

The preceding example illustrates the fact that one action can be more than one function, and likewise a character may play more than one role depending on the functions he fulfills. The most common instance of the multiple role-playing is the instance of a duper becoming a victim, or vice versa. In *Du prestre qu'on porte* (MR IV: 89), for example, the husband learns of his wife's infidelity and therefore pretends to leave on a long trip, hoping to catch the lover with his wife. She thinks she is deceiving him by acting hurt that he is leaving:

> —Sire, ore puis jou bien savoir
> Que ne m'amés ne poi ne grant,
> Quant vous m'alés si eslongant;
> Or remanrai chi toute seule."
>
> (vv. 24-27)

The husband is a victim of her infidelity, but becomes a duper when he returns and kills the lover. She then tries to deceive her husband by hiding the lover's body (who she thinks has died accidentally), but she is at the same time a victim of her husband's misdeed. Here self-deception creates a simultaneity of roles. In *De Berengier* (MR IV: 93), the change from duper to victim develops in more typical linear fashion. The wife has been taken in by her husband, who pretends to go off each morning and fight battles he always wins. She finally perceives that he is never injured in spite of the tremendous damage done to his armor, so she follows him to the forest where she discovers his mock battles. She then disguises herself and requires him to fight her or show submission in a humiliating act. In some instances an auxiliary becomes a duper also, as in *De Constant du Hamel* (MR IV: 106) when the maid carries her mistress's message to the potential lover but exacts a gratuity from him by pretending to have influenced her mistress in his favor.

Roles are not completely identified by the functions a character executes, as can be seen by referring to Figure 2. The transitional functions, F-1 and F-2, as well as the interrogation and communication, F-3 and F-4, are functions that may be executed by any character. Role differentiation is based on the other functions. Deception and misdeed, F-5 and F-6, are executed by the duper, whereas his victim must accomplish the recognition and the retaliation, F-7 and F-8. The counselor has a unique function, the resolution, F-9. The auxiliary can be seen as a *factotum* who performs any of the nine functions. He is not identified by any distinctive ones, but by his relationship to the other characters and the extent of his action. If he carries out a function for another character or is merely an accessory to the action involving a major role, then he is an auxiliary. If, however, he attempts functions such

Major Roles		Minor Roles	
Duper	Victim	Counselor	Auxiliary
F-1	F-1	F-1	F-1
F-2	F-2	F-2	F-2
F-3	F-3	F-3	F-3
F-4	F-4	F-4	F-4
F-5	F-7	F-9	F-5
F-6	F-8		F-6
			F-7
			F-8
			F-9

Fig. 2. The Roles in the Fabliau

as the deception or misdeed on his own behalf, then he has switched roles to become a duper.

Roles and relationships between characters are correlated in quite predictable ways. To return to a point made earlier, the bond of kinship seems to create the most opportunities for devious and aggressive behavior, so it is not surprising that over half (65%) of the dupers and victims are related in this way. The second most prominent relationship in the duper/victim pairs is the "negative" one, those who are not acquainted (23%). Thus in the fabliau, the polar relationships—relatives and strangers—are the dynamic ones which generate the patterns of deceit and negative social behavior, as will be seen in the discussion which follows.

The analysis by roles and functions has produced a morphology of the fabliau and a better definition of the genre. At this point then, the search for meaning must begin by taking the morphological elements and trying to understand their syntax, i.e., the text as linear narrative. What follows is not a linguistic study, however, but a critical reading of an exemplary text. It is *not* based on a self-proclaimed fabliau, because I want to demonstrate in detail the validity of the function / role model for all typical fabliaux. In choosing *Le Meunier* (MR II: 33) for this analysis, I am initiating the discussion of meaning in the fabliau by drawing on a text which represents faithfully the spirit of those texts listed as part of the 130 typical fabliaux.

* * *

Le Meunier (see Appendix D) has a tripartite macrostructure, the narrative being framed between an introduction and a conclusion. At the outset, the narrator gains his audience's attention by assuring it he will tell a good story, not one that risks any improprieties:

> Qui se melle de biax dis dire
> Ne doit commenchier à mesdire,
> Mais de biax dis dire et conter;
> Dès or vos vaurai raconter
> Une aventure ke je sai,
> Car plus celer ne le vaurai.

(vv. 1-6)

Immediately following the introduction is an initial situation (QS-2) which only presents two of the characters, Jacques the miller and Mouset the servant. We learn that Jacques lives in Palluiel but has his mill at Arleux:

> A Palluiel, le bon trespas,
> .I. Mannier i ot Jakemars;

Cointes estoit et envoisiés;
A Aleus estoit il manniers;
Le blé moloit il, et Mousès,
Qui desous lui estoit varlès.
.I. jour estoient au molin
En un demierkes au matin;
De maintes viles i ot gens
Qui au molin moloient souvent;
Il i ot molt blé et asnées.

(vv. 7-17)

Jacques must be a prosperous man because people come from many *viles* to have their wheat ground. Although the setting seems rural, four towns mentioned—Estrées, Arleux, Palluiel, and Oisi, all located between Douai and Cambrai—are referred to as *viles*. Also, in the medieval economy, Jacques is a representative of the rural elite, an enriched peasant. As Jean Gimpel points out, mills are the factories of the Middle Ages; they represent a significant investment to build and are rented to the millers for considerable sums.[5] Whether Jacques owns or rents the mill, he is clearly a "businessman" who has at least one employee, his place of business in one town, and his home in another.

The story takes place on a *mercredi matin,* an appropriate day since *mercredi* is the day named for Mercury, patron god of merchants. The object of bargaining on this day, Marie, daughter of Gerart d'Estrées, arrives (F-1a), initiating the narrative proper by trying to accomplish a task. Her request (F-3c) is simple and straightforward: she wants Jacques to grind her wheat so that she can return to prepare dinner for her father. Her sense of responsibility demonstrates that she is a serious girl who does not in any way provoke the actions which follow. With her request, the first narrative program is initiated because a contract has been offered (NP$_1$). [6]

The first part of Jacques's response to Marie might be interpreted as a truthful communication (F-4), but by the time he finishes, the reader sees that he has proposed quite a different agenda from the grinding of wheat:

Jakès li a dit maintenans:
"Ma douce amie, or vous séés;
.I. petit si vous reposés.
Il a molt blé chi devant nous
Qui doivent maure devent vous,
Mais vous morrés qant jou porrai,
Et si n'en soiés en esmai,
Car, se il puet, et vespres vient,
Je vous ostelerai molt bien
A ma maison à Paluiel.
Sachiés k'à ma feme en ert biel,
Car jou dirai k'estes ma nièche."

(vv. 28-39)

By suggesting he will take her home and tell his wife that Marie is his niece, he is making a false proposition (deception, F-5a). The implied seduction, F-6c, also constitutes a second narrative program (NP$_2$). The false nature of his story is confirmed by Mouset, the servant, who knows all their clients have been taken care of and sent home (recognition, F-7):

> Mousès voit bien et aperçoit
> Tout cho ke ses maistres pensoit:
> Andoi orent une pensée
> Por décevoir Marien d'Estrée.
> Jésir cuident entre ses bras.

(vv. 43-47)

By the forty-seventh verse, then, a classic seduction plot has been set up, and the audience smiles at thoughts of the probable outcome. The duper and victim have been identified; the auxiliary is present and his role can be anticipated. No one knows the end of the story, but the narrator does say Jacques will not be successful (vv. 48-50). His comment, however, does not spoil the fun; it adds to the pleasure because a *dupeur/dupé* plot is assured. The pleasure of the tale will also lie in the details of how the seduction will be thwarted.

Mouset's recognition of a potential misdeed could result in the victim being warned, but Mouset's role as auxiliary and his relationship to Jacques is crucial. He naturally joins in the scheme with a deceptive response of his own about the lack of water (F-5a). The victim is not a naïve girl, however, and she has a sense of impending doom. Although she says she fears being murdered, not seduced, her wariness is a recognition (F-7) of the danger Jacques and Mouset pose for her:

> La damoisièle ert plainne d'ire,
> Pleure des iex, de cuer soupire:
> "Lasse," fait ele, "que ferai?
> Or voi jou bien ke g'i morrai.
> Se je m'en vois encui par nuit,
> Jou isterai dou sens, je cuit."

(vv. 59-64)

The few details presented by the narrator depict the girl's fear, which is in comic contrast with the foolish self-assurance of her adversaries. Mouset and Jacques try to pacify her (deception, F-5a), promising that she will come to no physical harm, and Jacques promises her good food and wine (implied misdeed, F-6c). But Marie is not as naïve as Mouset must believe her to be: "Cele s'estut molt esbahie, / Qui dou mannier n'avoit talent . . ." (vv. 88-89).

In this preliminary part of *Le Meunier*, the difference between the chronological development of the action and the logical sequence of events indicated by the numerical order of functions is evident. Although F-2 (departure) logically occurs after F-1 (arrival), for example, other functions will take place between the two. In a series of actions, a function may be skipped or the sequence may move backward numerically, although the action in a fabliau never moves backward chronologically as it would if a flashback were used. If a character chooses a function of a lower number, it may in turn provoke its own logical consequences making the action more complex. It is significant that characters are not bound to only one response to a given situation.

When Marie asks a question, the duper offers a deceptive answer, F-5, rather than a straightforward communication, F-4. This deception implies a misdeed, F-6, which is recognized, F-7, first by the auxiliary. He must ask in behalf of someone else, and according to his alliances, he will either inform the victim of the misdeed or enter into league with the duper. In this case the auxiliary, Mouset, is the duper's servant, so he joins the duper and acts as his double by making a deceptive comment, F-5. It is only later that he becomes a duper in his own right. At this point, the misdeed is again implied and the girl recognizes, F-7, the threat, but she responds with a question, F-3, rather than taking clear action. Thus the numerical sequence begins to recycle again, Jacques and Mouset responding with deceptive propositions, F-5, and the veiled seduction, F-6 (misdeed). The two types of progression, chronological and logical, work independently of each other. Each time F-7 (recognition) occurs, it could lead to its consequences F-8 (retaliation) or F-9 (resolution), but the characters choose another action which delays the logical progression to the terminating functions. The repetitiveness of the action, seen in Figure 3, is not redundancy, and the skipped functions (indicated by the blanks) and implied functions (enclosed by parentheses) are not an indication of random or poorly developed action. On the contrary, they reflect reversals and delaying techniques that add complexity to the tale. Furthermore, in this particular sequence, the action is still in its preliminary stages, so there is no motivation for the entire logical sequence to be presented. The humor can also be seen to arise, at least in part, from the illogical choices so often made by the victims.

F-1, _____, F-3, _____, F-5, (F-6), F-7, _____, F-5, _____, F-7, _____, F-3,

_____, F-5, (F-6), F-7, _____, (F-2), F-1, move to Jacques's house.

Fig. 3. Sequences of Functions

With the change in scene to Jacques's house, we meet his wife, a woman who does not mince her words. In response to his query (F-3a) " 'Dame, que vous sanble? / Que mangerons-nous au souper?' " she responds, " '. . . assés. / Qui est ceste méchine ichi:' " (F-4a + F-3a, vv. 96-99). If we had any doubt that Jacques is a prosperous man, we would see by the fare they offer the girl and the costly linens on her bed that this is a very comfortable, bourgeois household:

> —Dame," fait el, "Dius bénéie."
> De mangier n'estuet tenir plait
> De chou ke promesse avoit fait;
> Pain et vin, car, tarte et poison
> Orent assés à grant fuisson.
> Quant orent mangié et béu,
> Li lis fu fais, dalès le fu,
> U la meschine dut couchier,
> Kieute mole, linches molt chier,
> Et covertoir chaut et forré.

(vv. 104-13)

These verses are typical of brief descriptive passages scattered throughout a fabliau; they strike us as significant because the action in the fabliau is sketched with such economy that any detail is outstanding. It is, in fact, these details that have led some critics to refer to the realism of the genre, but as Muscatine and Robertson have pointed out, the word *realism* can only be used in the broadest sense.[7] *Materialism* would be more appropriate because what strikes us is the attention paid to objects in a context that offers few details about characters' feelings or no more than the sketchiest details about the action. The materialism of the fabliau adds local color and a homey sense of place to these tales, but never contributes to an individualizing of the characters. They remain understandable only as people playing roles who are caught up in a rapid series of only partially motivated events.

The briefness with which actions are sketched contributes to the illusion of rapid development and change that is due in part to the numerous arrivals and departures of characters. The scene at Jacques's house has barely opened (23 verses of development) when he deceives his wife by telling her that he must return to the mill that evening (deception, F-5a, vv. 116-26). Perhaps he does need to return to the mill to finish his work; but his purpose is clearly to leave so that he can return once the women are asleep and sneak into bed with Marie. The rapidity of action here is further heightened because the function is described in less than one verse: "A tant s'en va. Cele demeure" (departure, F-2b, v. 127).

Functions are not always this succinctly presented, but neither are they elaborated upon. In fact, in a typical fabliau, a function occurs on the average of every ten verses.[8] In *Le Meunier* the total number of verses is 414, and the average number of lines per function is only seven, so this tale progresses at an even faster tempo. The rapid changes of scene and quick actions cannot be attributed to a lack of narrative technique because, as Zumthor points out, the same era that saw the rise of fabliaux also produced the elaborate prose romances and lengthy epics. The preciseness of the fabliau is related to its didacticism; it moves quickly to emphasize its final point.[9]

The tension building to that final point is increased by Jacques's hasty departure and the irony is heightened by his naïveté in thinking he has entrapped Marie. She feels so frightened and helpless that she breaks down, "Del cuer souspire et des iex pleure" (communication F-4b, v. 128), but her outburst is her salvation. The wife inquires (interrogation F-3a) why she is crying, and Marie tells her of her fears (communication F-4a + recognition F-7). The wife, apparently without a second thought, proposes a scheme that will protect the girl:

> —Or vous taisié, ma douce amie,"
> Fait la dame, ki fu senée;
> "Vous en serés bien destornée;
> Car vous girés ens en mon lit. . . ."
>
> (vv. 158-61)

Thus we have a new pair of dupers and a new intended victim within the space of two lines. As much narrative space, in fact, is given to describing the wife's preparations for bed as to proposing or thinking through the scheme to deceive her husband. Her quick-wittedness and decisiveness completely change the course of the action and create a third narrative program (NP$_3$). The succinctness of the narrative foregrounds the reversal that is about to occur and sets the pace for the other reversals awaiting all the victims.

While Jacques and Mouset are on their way back to the house, a new twist is added because Mouset offers Jacques a young pig for the opportunity of sleeping with Marie (communication F-4 + misdeed F-6). This bargain, which is referred to twice within ten verses as a "markiet," involves Mouset in the action as co-conspirator and complicates the series of exchanges that are at the heart of the plot. Jacques freely negotiates this bargain, the fourth narrative program NP$_4$, and he seems unaware of the risks involved. He enters the house without a troubled thought and performs "the game of love" five times with "Marie" before leaving. Thinking to smooth the way for Mouset, he tells her he will return (communication F-4a), and the wife, who seems to have enjoyed herself, responds, " 'Quant vous poés, si revenés . . .' " (communication F-4b, v. 235). At this point, if they had recognized each other's voices they could have uncovered the deception, but as the narrator points out, Jacques does not see she has "switched the marker" on him. "Gieut cuide avoir o la pucele: / On li a cangiet le merielle" (vv. 239-40). Jacques leaves (departure F-2a) to greet the waiting Mouset with the story of his exploits, and then he warns him to say nothing when he returns to the bed (communication F-4a + deception F-5). His advice is self-deceptive because it assures that neither Mouset nor the wife will discover each other's identity. When Mouset returns (departure F-2a) and brags in his turn about performing the game five times, the poor cuckolded husband innocently asks whether she protested! Both agree that the bargain has been concluded and that Jacques should take the pig (communication F-4c). Thus, the narrative program they initiated appears to be concluded successfully with the acquisition of their desires and a friendly exchange of goods. We might note that NP_1 and NP_2 have not been completed, and that NP_3 has had an unsuccessful conclusion for its initiator, the wife.

The truth of the situation emerges for the men when they return to the house (arrival F-1b) only to be greeted by Jacques's wife, who screams that never in fourteen years of marriage had he performed so well as he had that night, thinking it was Marie (communication F-4b). She boasts, " 'Or avés vous cangié le dé' " (v. 306); but, of course, she does not realize the degree to which the dice have also been changed on her (self-deception F-5). He recognizes the full extent of his victimization (recognition F-7); he has lost out on sleeping with a young girl, caused his wife to be angry at him, and cuckolded himself all for a pig. The narrator completely drops all mention of the wife as the pace of reversals increases. Only three verses are devoted to Jacques's recognition and reaction, which are followed immediately by Mouset's complaint that the bargain struck in NP_4 has not been fulfilled (communication F-4a + retaliation F-8). As if his cuckolding were not enough, Jacques has the tables turned on him again by Mouset's insistence that the pig was only payment for sleeping with a young, beautiful girl, not his wife. Typical of those attempted retaliations that use words rather than fists, the antagonists cannot resolve the conflict; so Mouset heads for Oisi to find someone to arbitrate between them.

Taking his case to court is an appeal for a resolution (F-9) which introduces us to the fourth role, the counselor, played by the bailiff and his magistrates. When the magistrates hear Mouset's story (communication F-4a), they agree he has kept his part of the bargain. Jacques makes a rather pitiful plea for mercy (communication F-4a), and we see the brash duper of the earlier scenes fallen to abject victim:

> Je sui vuihos et si sui cous.
> Je doi bien cuites aler par tant,
> Car sachiés il m'anuie forment
> Chou que il avint à ma feme. . . .

(vv. 350-53)

The bailiff, however, finds him highly amusing. The judgement (resolution F-9) that is rendered at first would seem to substitute a good deed for the misdeed (a trick or broken contract) because the magistrates insist that Jacques return the pig. But another reversal is effectuated as the magistrates take the pig from Mouset without asking whether he wants to sell it. They initiate their own narrative program, and it is the only one to succeed. Without bargaining, they simply confiscate the pig for a feast. They do offer Mouset thirty *sous,* which seems a handsome price. Nevertheless, neither Jacques or Mouset has obtained the goal he sought, and the narrator might well have said that the dice had been switched again. This attempted resolution, that turns out to be another reversal, is typical. The object of contention is removed and will be eliminated: "Mangiés sera à grant reviel" (v. 386). All events have been arranged to the end that dupers would be duped and victims not necessarily compensated for their losses. The resolution stops the conflict, but the laughing bailiff and the cavalier attitude of the *échevins* toward Mouset's property reveal that no serious form of justice was intended.

Le Meunier ends with the author Engerrans's conclusion that the pathetic Jacques has been appropriately punished:

> Cho fu droit que le honte en ot,
> Car raisons ensaigne et droiture
> Que nus ne puet metre sa cure
> En mal faire ni en mal dire
> Tousjors ne l'en soit siens le pire,
> Et ausi fist il le mannier,
> Qui en demoura cunquiet,
> Mais ne me chaut, chou fu raisons.

(vv. 390-97)

Surely the narrative has moved quickly toward a more important final point than that he deserved what he got. Why or how has he erred? The conclusion draws its moral not on religious values but on *raison* and *droiture.* The moral is practical; one should avoid doing or saying any evil, otherwise one risks receiving the worse end of the affair. The miller, in attempting a trick of his own, did not recognize the risks involved. He did not consider the danger of introducing a *valet* into his house and the risks inherent in making a contract with Mouset for the pig.

In the remaining verses, Engerrans tells us how the bailiff and the magistrates enjoyed their festivities. He also tells us that the story was too good to be lost, for it teaches us that anyone who tries to shame good people is not *sage.* The reiteration of terms such as *raison, droiture,* and *sage* creates an interesting contrast with the situational ethics of the narrative. In the course of the events, each character pursues his or her own self-interest and cuts deals as the opportunities present themselves. Reasoned behavior and thoughts of long-range risks or benefits are non-existent. Yet the characters do exhibit one type of intelligence—quick-wittedness in seizing opportunities and manipulating people. The narrative portrays for us a rapid series of events that do not develop characters or build toward a synthesis. On the contrary, the entire tale is about reversals and unfulfilled narrative programs. The roles the actors play are repeatedly switched, and sought-for goals turned against them. The narrative repeatedly foregrounds reversal and trickery, and the metaphors used to describe the situations are all appropriately drawn from gaming or commerce, both high risk ventures. Thus what the narrative illustrates in practical terms—cleverness and the dangers associated with clever schemes—the moral warns against in abstract terms. The wise person must use reason to avoid self-deception and its inevitable consequences.

It is fitting that the author of *Le Meunier* is a *clerc*. Who better to promote the values of *raison* and *droiture* than one who can appreciate the folly of characters who overlook the obvious, twist the truth, and purposely disregard the rights of others. We can imagine that *Le Meunier* would be especially funny to him because its victims are all would-be dupers who do show a certain amount of cleverness, but they are too clever for their own good. Although the author of *Le Meunier* is identified, we cannot make a case for all fabliaux being the works of clerics. What is apparent, however, is that this tale, in typical fabliau fashion, demonstrates love for intelligence of all types. As Alexander Murray points out in *Reason and Society in the Middle Ages*,[10] reason as a tool for gaining power was respected and cultivated as early as the twelfth century to a much greater extent than is normally recognized. He maintains that ever-increasing wealth and ambition fueled social mobility in the High Middle Ages and led to a cultivation of entirely different virtues from earlier feudal and Christian ones. Pointing to the *Coutumes de Beauvaisis* of Philippe de Beaumanoir, Murray shows that among the ten qualities needed by a *bailli*, *sapience* ranks first and loyalty last. One other quality he should have is *soutil engieng*, "a sort of business astuteness comprising an ability to do accounts and to swell the king's wealth without actually trespassing on anyone's rights."[11] Although the word *engieng* is not found in *Le Meunier*, it is commonly used to describe dupers in other fabliaux, and Jacques is described at the beginning as "cointes" (v. 9), another term meaning skillful or savvy. So the final point of this fabliau, as with so many others, is that intelligence is an absolutely crucial weapon in a battle to maintain the upper hand. The reversals and changing game plans cannot be stabilized unless a wise man steps in; but more often than not, he is filled with *soutil engieng* which allows him to manipulate the situation for his own profit.

The plot of *Le Meunier* with its typical fabliau functions and roles, its pattern of rapidly rising or falling expectations, and its use of gaming or commercial metaphors is an extremely good illustration of a very practical value system. One must use one's wits to avoid deception, for it is better to be the last duper of the series than the next victim. Furthermore, they seem to warn that no one is to be completely trusted, least of all the authorities.

This text which calls itself a *roman,* not a fabliau, conforms in almost all details to the typical fabliau patterns. It demonstrates that the structural similarities among these tales are profound even if the surface details are varied and that they do constitute a genre. Their ethic, if *Le Meunier* can be taken as typical in this respect also, is not particularly class conscious, antichurch, or antifeminist. Rather, it focuses on relationships between people and advocates a sharp wit and other pragmatic values characteristic of the great wisdom literature. The value of the intellect in these texts will be made even clearer by an examination of their forms of irony.

5

Irony as Trope and Myth in the Fabliau

Studies of humor in the fabliau are as abundant as they are diverse. Fabliau humor has been placed in traditions ranging from the Latin *comedia* to *l'esprit gaulois,*[1] and the fabliau mode has been variously identified as parody, burlesque, lowbrow *nouvelle,* or simply funny anecdote.[2] Over the years, critics have analyzed what the audience laughs at, why they laugh at certain points, and even why they do not. As the volume *The Humor of the Fabliaux* attests, these funny stories are funny to many people for many different reasons. Indeed, hardly any aspect of their humor has escaped scrutiny by critics practicing all manner of traditional, structural, and even semiotic methods.

Some of the inconsistencies among these studies may be due to the heterogeneous surface structure of the texts. It is, in fact, easy to find support for almost any theory of humor in these tales by picking and choosing one's examples. Nevertheless, the analysis presented in previous chapters confirms that structural similarities in the actions and roles of characters exist and allow us to identify tales as belonging to a well-defined genre called the fabliau. Likewise, an attempt to grasp the general nature of their humor, which is at once funny and serious, simplistic and complex, may be more fruitful than a study of how individual plots produce laughter.

The primary problems to be resolved are why these particular tales are so ambiguous, how they achieve their particular impact, and how their humor reveals an ethic different from the traditional chivalric or Christian one which informs many medieval texts. To begin, the term most descriptive of both structure and meaning in the typical fabliau is not satire, comedy, burlesque, or even *esprit gaulois.* These types of humor all exist within the tales and contribute greatly to their success, but it is *irony* which pervades their plots, their language, and the myth behind their individual faces. Pointing out those traditional ironic features that past critics have mentioned and applying to the texts various modern definitions of irony will illustrate the extent of this figure in the fabliau and how it casts a new light on the meaning of the genre.

93

Whereas most critics, Le Clerc being the most obvious nineteenth-century example, have looked for satire in the fabliau, Bédier rejected such an interpretation:

> Les portraits comiques de bourgeois, de chevaliers, de vilains y foisonnent: mais aucune idée qui domine ou relie ces caricatures; la raillerie vise tel chevalier, et non la chevalerie, tel bourgeois et non la bourgeoisie; et, le plus souvent, on peut substituer un chevalier à un bourgeois, ou un bourgeois à un chevalier . . . En ce sens nos diseurs de fabliaux ne s'élèvent point jusqu'à la satire: ils s'arrètent à mi-route, contents d'être de maitres caricaturistes. Ils jettent sur le monde *un regard ironique* [my italics]: clercs, vilains, marchands, prévots, vavasseurs, chevaliers, moines, ils esquissent d'un trait rapide la silhouette de chacun—et passent. Ils peignent une galerie de grotesques, où personne n'est épargné, où l'on n'en veut sérieusement à personne."[3]

Bédier was the first to identify their lighthearted spirit as ironic, but he did not elaborate on this notion. It is important to note his contention that individuals, not classes, are the objects of satire, because so much later criticism has failed to understand or try to substantiate his insight.

Nykrog took issue with Bédier's theory and labored to establish the texts not only as satire but very specifically as a form of burlesque that could only be understood and appreciated by the aristocracy. As has already been pointed out here and by other critics, there is no systematic satire; the diversity and contradictions central to fabliau plots disallow a narrow interpretation of their humor as antibourgeois, antifeminist, or anticlerical. For every fabliau that exemplifies such a bias, another one presents just the opposite. For example, priests may be shown to be lecherous in most fabliaux (*De celui qui bota la pierre* MR IV: 102) but are also victims of unjustifiable cruelty in others (*D'Estormi* MR I: 19). Likewise, women are not just wanton; they are also portrayed as virtuous wives (*Des .IIII. prestres* MR VI: 142) who reject unwanted advances from clergy or young *bachelers.* It is precisely the shifting focus of their humor which suggests irony, rather than satire, as a key to understanding their humor and their meaning.

Germaine Dempster, in *Dramatic Irony in Chaucer*, was the first to describe dramatic irony of the fabliau. The main purpose of her work is to point out Chaucer's accomplishments in making the irony more effective through characterization, but she does not denigrate the Old French texts. She praises their well-made plots and ironic action: "In other words, dramatic irony is the very essence and spirit of the plot as Chaucer had it from his model. . . . The irony of the French fabliaux is striking because it is excellent in itself, and because of the teller's healthy, communicative delight in a good joke."[4]

The technique of opposing reality as the audience sees it and the appearance of reality as it is understood by the victims is fundamental to the structure of almost all fabliaux. Indeed, it would be hard to identify a fabliau which does not build its plot on the type of dramatic irony that occurs when the audience has information about a situation that one or more of the characters does not have and may never acquire. In the common adultery plots, the audience is told from the outset that the woman wants to be with her lover, and the fun of watching the story unfold is to anticipate what means will be used to dupe the husband as the lovers set up or cover up their rendezvous (*Des braies le priestre* [MR VI: A-I] and *De la femme qui cunqie sen baron* [Bédier, p. 303], among others). Plots that turn on an attempted seduction are no different. For example, in *Du prestre et d'Alison* (MR II: 31), *De Constant du Hamel* (MR IV: 106), *Du segretain moine* (MR V: 136) and its variants, the audience knows of the attempted purchase of a woman's favors and the woman's subsequent plot to extort money as well as humiliate, if not kill, the seducer. The most common and least complex form of dramatic irony exists when the audience and the duper enjoy a privileged position over the victim. In a few especially clever and complicated plots, a duper befuddles first one character and then another by creating a totally false world that ensnares all victims. For example, in *Du bouchier d'Abevile* (MR III: 84) a butcher steals a priest's sheep only to later use it to pay for lodging at the priest's house. The butcher promises the pelt to a servant and the "prestresse" in return for sexual favors; he also promises it to the priest himself. All are left holding the bag—or the pelt—at the end of the story. Examples such as *Des trois avugles* (MR I: 4) and *Le Dit des perdriz* (MR I: 17) are illustrative of the same point. What is common to all of these plots is the audience's awareness of what is going on. What is left to the imagination is only what reaction the victim will have. In this sense then, dramatic irony does not create many surprise endings, unless the duper falls into a trap and becomes a victim himself.

As Norris Lacy points out in "The Fabliaux and Comic Logic,"[5] the majority of fabliaux work on this principle: the story by and large fulfills expectations because its logic mirrors a logical sense of how things will turn out. The plot creates surprise, however, when it does not follow the audience's logic but its own. In other words, a different form of dramatic irony is at work if the audience has not been given enough information to anticipate the plot. Lacy uses *De Brunain* (MR I: 10) as an example. Here the naïve *vilain* gives his cow to the priest after hearing the sermon about the cheerful giver being rewarded double-fold. The joke might stop there, but it does not because the cow comes home dragging the priest's cow with it. Naturally, the *vilain* thinks he was right. Lacy says, "no deceptions are finally practiced on the characters; the same may not be true of the audience, for we are misled by our own preconceived ideas and expectations. In this fabliau, there is a reversal of sorts, but the comic development takes place entirely within the reader or listener, and not the narrative itself."[6] I would imagine, however, that the priest in this tale is also surprised because he very obviously thought he was benefiting from the *vilain*'s naïveté. Once he realizes that he has not acquired the *vilain*'s cow and has lost his own, he will understand his own rashness and would no doubt agree begrudgingly with the moral of *De Brunain,* "Tels cuide avancier qui recule" (MR I: 10, v. 72). In other words, although the surprise ending will not be clear to the *vilain,* it would obviously be to the priest as it is to the audience. In this case, both audience and at least one character have been taken by surprise, as with Mouset's sudden grievance and the court's odd judgement in *Le Meunier.* The surprise effect is heightened by a reversal in both tales of the initial roles of duper and victim.

If dramatic irony is essential in most fabliau plots, verbal irony is a common adjunct to their effect. Although it is less obvious than in Chaucer's reworkings of similar plots, there are superb examples of ironic statements in the fabliau. From the naïve reaction of the *vilain* in *De Brunain* who says upon seeing the two cows in his pasture "Voirement est Diex bon doublère," (MR I: 10, v. 59) to the priest in *Du prestre et d'Alison* (MR II: 31) who assures Marie's mother, who is going to trick him by substituting another girl for her daughter, "Dame, ne sui pas ci por guile" (v. 266), the verbal ironies enhance already wonderful comic scenes in many fabliaux. For example, when the three blind men enter an inn and ask the host for food and lodging, promising to pay with the money they think the clerk has just given them, they say:

> "Entendez çà à nous," font-il;
> Ne nous tenez mie por vil
> Se nous somes si povrement;
> Estre volons privéement;
> Miex vous paierons que plus cointe . . .
> *(Des trois avugles* MR I: 4, vv. 81-85)

Later in the same tale when the clerk has asked the innkeeper if he would trust the local priest to repay the clerk's debts, the innkeeper says:

> "Ostes," fet-il, "vostre persone
> Du moustier dont ne connissiez?
> Ces .XV. sols bien li croiriez,
> Se por moi les vos voloit rendre?"
> —De ce ne sui mie à aprendre,
> Fet li borgois; par saint Silvestre,
> Que je croiroie nostre prestre,
> S'il voloit, plus de .XXX. livres."
> (MR I: 4, vv. 198-205)

Neither statement will be justified, of course, because the characters have no understanding of the way in which the clerk is manipulating them.

Some of the funniest ironic statements made by victims are those offered by husbands who have been totally befuddled by their wives. In *De la dame qui*

fit .III. tors entor le moustier, the husband becomes so convinced of the virtue
of his wife that he apologizes for his suspicions:

> "Dame," dist il, "je, que savoie
> Du voiage ne de la voie?
> Se je seüsse ceste chose,
> Dont je à tort vous blasme et chose,
> Je sui cil qui mot n'en deïsse
> Se je anuit de cest soir isse."
>
> (MR III: 79, vv. 161-66)

In *Des braies au cordelier,* the husband not only apologizes but also promises
a nice compensation for the pain he has caused his wife:

> . . . "Dame, ne vos desplaise,
> S'un poi vos ai faite marrie:
> Foi que ge doi sainte Marie,
> Tel amende vos en ferai
> Que jamais de vos ne serai
> En soupeçon de jalousie."
>
> (MR III: 88, vv. 342-47)

The audience always laughs at these silly statements or ridiculous circumstances created for the victims and dupers, but they may not be certain why.
Do they laugh merely at ironic reversals, at the ease with which one reality
is substituted for another, the naïveté of the victims, the bravura of the dupers,
or at the thought that they too might have been caught in similar traps? In
"De l'essence du rire," Baudelaire maintains that laughter is a symptom of
man's fallen, double nature. He is laughing at a glimpse of his other self:

> Le rire est satanique, il est donc profondément humain. Il est dans l'homme la
> conséquence de l'idée de sa propre supériorité; et, en effet, comme le rire est
> essentiellement humain, il est essentiellement contradictoire, c'est-à-dire qu'il
> est à la fois signe d'une grandeur infinie et d'une misère infinie, misère infinie
> relativement à l'Etre absolu dont il possède la conception, grandeur infinie rela-
> tivement aux animaux. C'est du choc perpétuel de ces deux infinis que se dégage
> le rire.[7]

The laugh, then, is based on the possibility of a double perspective. As
Baudelaire says, there must be two beings present; one who acts and one who
observes, for the humor is in the spectator, not the event. Spectators or readers
laugh from a sense of superiority when confronted by the weakness, stupidity,
or clumsiness of their fellow man.

Laughter of this sort, born of a sense of superiority, abounds in the fabliaux.
Consider, for example, the ugly husband in *Du vilain de Bailluel:*

> Il estoit granz et merveilleus
> Et maufez et de laide hure.
> Sa fame n'avoit de lui cure,
> Quar fols ert et de lait pelain. . . .
>
> (MR IV: 109, vv. 8-11)

Or the description of the husband in *Des trois boçus:*

> En la vile avoit .I. boçu,
> Onques ne vi si malostru;
> De teste estoit moult bien garnis
> Je cuit bien que Nature ot mis
> Grant entencion à lui fère.
> A toute riens estoit contrère;
> Trop estoit de laide faiture;
> Grant teste avoit et laide hure,
> Cort col, et les espaules lées,
> Et les avoit haut encroées.
>
> (MR I: 2, vv. 27-36)

If laughter springs from a sense of superiority over others who represent the foibles of humankind, then it is easy to understand why women are such prominent figures in these comic tales. To the medieval and perhaps even some modern minds, women represent the epitome of a doubled nature, the very incarnation of the animal and especially the devil in mankind. The women dupers are frequently compared in their capacity for deviousness to animals such as *renart:*

> Par cest flabel poez savoir
> Molt sont femes de grant savoir:
> Tex i a et de grant voisdie;
> Molt set feme de renardie. . . .
>
> (*Du prestre et de la dame* MR II: 51, vv. 169-72)

The more devastating comparison, however, is to the devil:

> Enseignier voil por ceste fable
> Que fame set plus que deiable,
> Et certeinemant lo sachiez.
> Les iauz enbedeus li sachiez
> Se n'é à esciant dit voir.
>
> (*De la sorisete des estopes* MR IV: 105, vv. 213-17)

> Trop fu ceste fame deable.
>
> (*De la dame qui se venja* MR VI: 140, vv. 270)

In *De la dame qui fit .III. tors* (MR III: 79), men are told they might as well try to trick the devil as to trick a woman. Obviously the clever woman is a reversal of hoped-for feminine traits, but her behavior is not entirely unexpected. The descriptive phrase applied to the bourgeoise in *Des braies au cordelier* (MR III: 88) will provoke a laugh and certain expectations about the plot precisely because of its familiar ring, as would a description of a lecherous priest or a dull-witted husband:

> ... une borjoise
> Qui mout estoit sage et cortoise;
> Mout savoit d'enging et d'aguet:
> A feme, qui tel mestier fait
> Et qui veut amer par amors,
> Couvient savoir guenches et tors,
> Et enging por soi garantir;
> Bien covient que saiche mentir,
> Tele eure est, por couvrir sa honte.
> La borjoise dont ge vos conte
> Fu bien de ce mestier aprise. ...
>
> (MR III: 88, vv. 7-17)

In the elaboration of this bourgeoise's powers, there is condemnation but also a hint of awe at her prowess. Her tricks and her stories are sophisticated enough to qualify as a *métier*, and one could wonder who taught her this trade. The answer does not seem to be the society, or even peers, as might be the case with a student trickster. For women, it is their nature, their base nature, as is made apparent in the analogy made between the female trickster and *renart*. The purported natural strength in manipulating people and events reminds men of their own baser nature which must be held in check.

The simple, straightforward comedy of a double perspective, what women should be—versus what they are—being but one example, Baudelaire calls *le comique significatif*. It is the essence of those particular satiric portraits we find in the fabliau and also the satire of a work such as *Aucassin et Nicolette*. There the portrait of a bumbling, wimpish Aucassin is a straightforward inversion of the courtly expectations for a knight. Humor is created in *Aucassin et Nicolette* through the reversal of sex roles, but the characters themselves remain quite consistent in the reversed roles, with the exception of Aucassin's two bursts of manly vigor when he captures Count Bougars de Valence and chastizes the King of Torelore. When an audience sees a clear and consistent inversion of the known or stereotyped behavior, the meaning is unambiguous. As Wayne Booth says in *A Rhetoric of Irony*,[8] the meaning is quite easily "reconstructed." In the case of the stereotyped lecherous priests, stupid husbands, or foxy women who populate fabliaux, the satire seems equally as unambiguous. They are inversions of the expected qualities for their role, or they illustrate laughable social behavior. If isolated from the narrative, they can easily be discussed as examples of pointed social satire. The interpretation of the whole tale is not, however, so unambiguous, and the point will be made clearer as the discussion of irony is developed. Never-theless, the contribution satiric portraits make to the humor of most fabliaux must not be overlooked.

The dramatic and verbal ironies discussed previously as well as the role reversals and awareness of man's double nature all juxtapose two realities that can provoke laughter. These ironic structures reinforce the primary message of the morals of these tales—be wary of appearances because people, events, and words are not what they seem. The fabliau may also contain the seeds of another type of comedy that Baudelaire sees as more profound and darker than the *comique significatif,* which merely makes the audience laugh and feel superior. True irony, *le comique absolu,* as Baudelaire calls it, is not just intrapersonal doubling or doubling of external realities, but a doubling of the self. For him *le comique absolu* is filled with violence and vertigenous changes from one personality to another, a doubling of the self within the work. This intrapersonal doubling is analogous to the reaction of those rare individuals, according to Baudelaire, who can perceive the humor of their own situation, those who become spectators for themselves. "Ce n'est point l'homme qui tombe qui rit de sa propre chute, à moins qu'il soit un philosophe, un homme qui ait acquis, par habitude, la force de se dédoubler rapidement et d'assister comme spectateur désintéressé aux phénomènes de son *moi.*"[9] The capacity to be a spectator for the self, or in the case of a literary character, the capacity to have a doubled consciousness, is a clear indication of our double nature; it proves, "l'existence d'une dualité permanente, la puissance d'être à la fois soi et un autre."[10]

As Paul de Man says in his discussion of Baudelaire's theory of laughter, philosophers and artists, who deal in language, would recognize that the differentiation between self and non-self necessary to irony is not only expressed in language, but is actually created by language:

> The reflective disjunction not only occurs *by means* of language as a privileged category, but it transfers the self out of the empirical world into a world consti-tuted out of, and in, language—a language that it finds in the world like one entity among others, but that remains unique in being the only entity by means of which it can differentiate itself from the world. Language thus conceived divides the subject into an empirical self, immersed in the world, and a self that becomes like a sign in its attempt at differentiation and self-definition.[11]

In other words, the only access to the double or ironic consciousness is through language, and the self that the writer or character projects in this manner overrides and denies, in many cases, the empirical self. "The ironic language splits the subject into an empirical self that exists in a state of inau-thenticity and a self that exists only in the form of a language that asserts the knowledge of this inauthenticity."[12]

Examples of the ironic consciousness in a fabliau character are not frequent

for the same reason that verbal irony is less prominent than dramatic irony—
the fabliau emphasizes the situation and plays on brief ironic descriptions
of characters and situations, rather than elaborating upon the characters'
verbalizations of their thought processes. Nevertheless, the importance of Paul
de Man's definition of irony here is his explanation of the primacy of language
in the creation of the ironfic consciousness because in the majority of the
fabliaux a doubled reality is created through language. Language is, in fact,
the primary tool of the duper. The analysis of functions in the fabliau showed
that lying in response to a question, fabricating a story, or false propositions
are the most common forms of deception, a function that is essential in all
typical fabliaux. Although some fabliau plots are based on purely physical
or material tricks, most of these are buttressed by deceptive verbiage.
Language—its use and power—is so central to the successful completion of a
misdeed that counterexamples would be difficult to find.[13]

Dupers manipulate language to make empirical reality seem a chimera (*Du
chevalier à la robe vermeille* MR III: 57 and *Des tresces* MR IV: 94) or a
fantasy seem reality (*Du vilain de Bailluel* MR IV: 109 and *Du prestre ki
abevete* MR III: 61). They create fanciful euphemisms for sexual seductions,
capitalize on the literal meanings of their language, and exploit double meanings to their fullest. What emerges in all these situations is the performatory
power of language; it makes reality rather than merely reflecting it. In *Du
clerc qui fu repus* MR IV: 91, for example, a woman entertains first one lover
then another suitor, both of whom must hide when the husband returns
unexpectedly. The wife accuses her husband of being a drunk and not provid-
ing well; he responds pointing to his jewelry and money, "ceux vont payer."
The two men think he is about to attack them, so they come out of hiding. The
plot is unveiled not because the husband was suspicious, or the wife unsuccessful at hiding the men. It is the result of a short phrase uttered in all innocence
by the husband. The number of fabliau plots dependent upon an analogous
use of language is legion.

The duper himself or herself calls attention to the power of language by the
effectiveness of its results, and the narrators warn us of this explicitly:

> Or li est bien en lieu remis
> Ses engiens, et tornez à perte,
> Dont folement estoit couverte:
> Bel s'en est ses sires vengiez,
> Qui laidement fu engingniez
> *Et par paroles et par dis;*
> Mès jamès n'en sera laidis
> Por ce qu'ele se sent meffette;
> Ses meffez a ceste pais fete;
> Bien l'en avint qu'avenir dut
> Qu'ele brassa ce qu'ele but.

(*De l'enfant qui fu remis au soleil* MR I: 14, italics mine, vv. 138-48)

As the narrator of *De la sorisete des estopes* says, men may know some tricks, but women can fool just by their language:

> Qant el viaut ome decevoir,
> Plus l'an deçoit et plus l'afole
> Tot solemant par sa parole
> Que om ne feroit par angin.
>
> (MR IV: 105, vv. 218-21)

The power of language lies in its capacity to play havoc with one's understanding of reality and oneself. For instance, one might just be beaten for saying that he is bringing "la male honte" to the king, or one might be given donkey meat instead of lamb for having mispronounced a word. But it is the ability to use language in a subversive way that the narrators underscore:

> Fame est fète por decevoir;
> Mençonge fet devenir voir,
> Et voir fet devenir mençonge.
>
> (*Le Dit des perdriz* MR I: 17, vv. 151-53)

The power of language is so great, in fact, that there seems to be no defense against it, no matter how much one might want to extricate oneself from the fabric of lies. The duper, especially if female, will maintain the upper hand.

The descriptions of some of these women express a fear of their double nature and their capacity to turn one thing to its opposite. They have, in fact, the ability to deny reality and substitute another one created through their language:

> Qui fame vorroit decevoir,
> Je li fais bien apercevoir
> Qu'avant decevroit l'Anemi,
> Le deable, à champ arrami,
> Cil qui fame viaut justisier.
> Chascun jor la puet combrisier
> Et l'endemain rest tote saine
> Por resoufrir autretel paine;
> Mès quant fame a fol debonere
> Et ele a riens de lui afere,
> Ele li dist tant de bellues
> De trufes et de fanfelues
> Qu'ele li fet à force entendre
> Que li cieus sera demain cendre:
> Ainsi gaaigne la querele.
>
> (*De la dame qui fit .III. tors* MR III: 79, vv. 1-15)

Since fabliaux include so many ironic elements, the texts foreground time and again the problem of interpretation of reality. The doubling calls into question the validity or power of its original. If, after all, the characters think or react based on a false personality or false reading of a situation, then the verbal and physical hocus-pocus they employ actually has performed as though it were real; it has created a new reality in the second instance even though there is nothing behind the new reality. This type of ironic conscious- ness has the power to make us question the validity of phenomenological reality and the relationship between reality and the language we use to repre- sent it. This does not mean that the fabliaux are fictional images of the thirteenth-century debates between the realists and the nominalists. To prove that contention one would have to demonstrate that fabliaux use language in a way unknown in folktales, jokes, and riddles of other cultures and periods. This would be difficult because some fabliaux clearly spring from folk litera- ture, tale collections from other cultures, or are in essence no more sophisticated than an expanded joke. Nevertheless, the popularity of these tales may attest to a rising interest in the thirteenth century in the power of language and the complexities of its interpretation.

A knowledge of the specific medieval context which gave rise to fabliaux is crucial to an understanding of their ethos, and that context will be discussed in the conclusion. For the present, however, it is important to see their connec- tions with a tradition that was highly valued in the Middle Ages but certainly was not created then. Beyond the pleasure principle they satisfy and beyond the resemblance they bear to humorous narratives indigenous to all cultures, the complexity of their irony and their explicit morals identify them as narra- tives belonging to the tradition of wisdom literature. They are cautionary not moral tales, not images of the ideal but reflections upon the real. As Northrop Frye points out, this type of ironic literature "takes for granted a world which is full of anomolies, injustices, follies, and crimes, and yet is permanent and undisplaceable."[14] This underlying myth of most wisdom literature advocates an awareness of the fallen nature of man: "What is recom- mended is conventional life at its best, a clairvoyant knowledge of human nature in oneself and others, an avoidance of all illusion and compulsive behavior, a reliance on observation and timing rather than on aggressive- ness."[15] Seen from this perspective, the use of language in the fabliau bears more resemblance to the Solomonic tradition than to the school of Chartres in the thirteenth century.

To maintain that the fabliaux are not so much moral as they are cautionary tales may strike some readers as troublesome because these tales so often end with a moral. As has already been pointed out in Chapter 2, these morals cannot be dismissed as afterthoughts or necessarily as satiric. They are an integral part of the didacticism of the short narrative, but that is not to say they establish moral or ethical norms. The primary reason they fail in that respect is that the narratives and the morals do not pertain to the ideal world; they are steeped in and reflect a fallen, non-heroic world that provokes laughter at the surface and disquiet at a deeper level. If the reader contemplates the implications of a non-heroic world, he must confront the chaos and lack of grounding behind the social and linguistic conventions used to maintain that social order.

Some might question the assertion that these narratives are non-heroic by pointing to the successes of the dupers. Successful schemes or outcomes are surely not the same, however, as heroic gestures. To illustrate the non-heroic nature of these tales, the reader should reflect on the configuration of characters found in the analysis of the typical fabliau. As was demonstrated, the tales revolve around victims and dupers, and the only other roles are auxiliaries or counselors. An interesting parallel can be drawn between roles and functions in the fabliau and the structure of the fairy tale as Propp analyzed it. According to him, seven functions form the preliminary part of the fairy tale: the absentation, interdiction, violation, reconnaissance, delivery, trickery, and complicity. One classic sequence described by these functions occurs when parents depart, leaving a child with specific instructions which he violates, allowing the villain to approach. In the absence of specific interdiction, the villain may seek out the victim, asking questions and receiving important information. The central action of the fairy tale begins with the next function, the villainy or a lack. Once a villainy occurs or a lack is perceived, the hero is summoned to redress the wrong. The rest of the tale relates his quest for the missing person or object, his struggle to repossess it, and his return home.

The abstract sequence of events Propp found in over one hundred Russian fairy tales may reflect archetypal myths Northrop Frye associates with the natural cycle of seasons. Indeed, the principle action of a fairy tale combines the *mythoi* of spring (comedy) and summer (romance). A new society is created through marriage when the hero redresses the villainy, and his search for the stolen object and performance of difficult tasks to achieve recognition as the true hero are the archetypal quest myth. Although it would appear that in the fairy tale the two myths are intertwined, a closer look shows a difference in the hero's two pursuit sequences. In the first, he is an outsider called in to fight the aggressor, and he wins. In the second, although the object of contention may be the same, the hero performs specific tasks and is recognized as the true hero, after which the object is restored to him. Several of the specific forms of these functions indicate that the first sequence resembles comedy, because the hero fights the aggressor and rescues the princess. He struggles against the "blocking" character, as Frye would call him, and then he creates a new society. Although the second sequence in a fairy tale may resemble the first, the two are not the same. For instance, the hero's brothers may seize his power. This implies, of course, that the hero is already an established authority figure and thus not an outsider, as in the first sequence. The nature of his struggle in the second sequence is also different because he merely performs tasks through which his legitimate status as hero/ruler is recognized. A marriage at this point, if it has not already occurred, is less important than the ascent to the throne. This second sequence of the fairy tale then is closer to the romance myth of quest and return of the true hero (*The Odyssey*) or a freeing of the kingdom from an evil power (*The Wasteland* theme) than to that of comedy.

The sequence of functions in the fabliau does not incorporate these myths; however, the myth behind the preliminary sequence of the fairy tale does bear a resemblance to the fabliau. It is important to remember that the sequences involving the hero have no parallel with the thirteenth-century French texts, but a very obvious parallel exists between the initial sequence of a fairy tale and the fabliau (see Fig. 4).

Fairy Tale: Initial Situation	*Fabliau: Major Functions*
I Absentation	F-1 Arrival
II Interdiction	F-2 Departure
III Violation	Interdiction & Violation
IV Reconnaissance	
V Delivery	F-3 Interrogation
VI Trickery	F-4 Communication
VII Complicity	F-5 Deception (implied complicity)

Main Narrative

VIII Villainy	F-6 Misdeed

Fig. 4. Fairy Tale and Fabliau Structures

The first seven functions are only preliminary ones in the fairy tale, whereas the related ones and the misdeed are the essential functions of a fabliau. If the rest of a fairy tale can be correlated to the myths that Frye calls spring/comedy and summer/romance, then it is obvious that the preliminary sequence in the fairy tale and the main sequence in the fabliau reflect the mythos of winter or irony. The fabliau, of course, goes no further than this myth because the hero never arrives and chaos is produced by the forces of disorder breaking down the status quo. Interpreting the fabliau as a fundamentally ironic genre will clarify many of the problems associated with interpreting these texts. Nevertheless, some critics may want to point out that there are functions beyond the misdeed—F-7, F-8, and F-9 (recognition, retaliation, and resolution). Are these to be interpreted as similar to the hero's victory over the aggressor in the fairy tale?

As the discussion of roles has already demonstrated, no character is identified as a hero because the only major roles played in these texts are those of victim and duper. The characters who play these roles are locked in a vicious circle of retributory justice which cannot be concluded as it would be by a heroic figure in an ideal world. As previously pointed out, the resolution in a fabliau is not a positive or happy ending. It is at best a bad fellow meeting a bad end; and, at its worst, the resolution is another trick played by the person who should have meted out justice.

Others have maintained that a *dupeur/dupé* model shows a form of rectifying an evil deed. To refute this notion, consider the numerous fabliaux (*Le Cuvier* MR I: 9, *Des trois boçus* MR I: 2, *Des trois avugles* MR I: 4, *Des braies au cordelier* MR III: 88, *Le Dit des perdriz* MR I: 17, *Du vilain de Bailluel* MR IV: 109, *De la dame qui fit .III. tors* MR III: 79, among many others) in which one character is so successfully tricked that there is no revenge taken for the misdeed, and the victim may not even be aware of what happened. There are, of course, those characters who would attempt a misdeed and who are tricked in return. Most notable are the seducers in *Du prestre et d'Alison* MR II: 31, *Du segretain moine* MR V: 136 and its analogues MR IV: 89 and MR VI: 150, *De Constant du Hamel* MR IV: 106, *Des .IIII. prestres* MR VI: 142, *Du prestre teint* MR VI: 139, and *De Connebert* MR V: 128. If the woman is virtuous, she and her husband will decide to repay the lechers by setting up a rendezvous only to take the priest's money and then punish him by setting fire to the house, by castrating him, or by murdering him. Even if the audience thinks the potential victims are justified in seeking revenge, it would be impossible to categorize them as heroes or heroines because the revenge is a comic "overkill" in the literal as well as the figurative sense.

In some tales, a victim seeks revenge by performing a trick that may not be so out of proportion. For example, in *Du bouchier d'Abevile* (MR III: 84), *Le Meunier et les .II. clers* (MR V: 119), and *Le Povre Clerc* (MR V: 132), the victims repay cheating or stinginess by sleeping with the man's wife and daughter or revealing the wife's infidelities to her husband. What the victim-turned-duper accomplishes may be no more outrageous than the initial trick, but it would be difficult to construe any of these situations as righting a wrong, such as a heroic figure might do. Thus, although the fairy tale moves from irony to comedy and romance, the fabliau remains firmly fixed in the mode of irony, for no hero ever arrives to restore the losses of the victim.

The fabliau depicts, as does all ironic literature, the eternal struggle between conflicting self-interests in fallen men and women. As an archtypal tale of trickery whether in matters of sex, money, or power, the fabliau presents characters who are all tainted by the baser characteristics of humankind. There are no pure nor redeemed types capable of heroically correcting the injustices of the corrupt world. The victimized husbands in adultery plots are not tragic figures because they are usually stupid, coarse individuals; and the intelligent wives who deceive them are not heroines because they are usually deceitful, wanton females. The two primary characters of a fabliau personify the eternal conflict between two differing self-interests which remain in an uneasy state of equilibrium until the duper, through deception and the aid of an auxiliary, swings the balance in his favor. The victim can, of course, retaliate, gaining the advantage by using similar deceptive means and an auxiliary. With very few exceptions, the characters in the fabliaux are grouped into a configuration of two against one, as the back and forth battle of wits and physical forces is waged. The majority of the tales end with one side having gained a temporary advantage, but the underlying conflict is not resolved. In those fabliaux where a counselor appears, the conflict is resolved by a simple act of neutralizing the situation—a judge may point out the basis of a verbal misunderstanding, or he may confiscate an object whose possession was in dispute. In effect, he removes an advantage held by the duper by returning the situation to a state of balance in which neither party wins. It is important to realize that he does not rectify an injustice, he merely defuses the situation. In the chaotic world of irony, a state of harmony cannot be achieved because the hero is absent.

In this non-heroic world there are, nonetheless, winners and losers in a pragmatic sense. Someone gets away with adultery, another one cheats his host out of a sheep, and another one takes the sexual favors of his host's wife and daughters. The message of the narratives and the morals, as in other wisdom literature, is that intelligence may lie in recognizing that right and wrong are not always the issue and that certainly what is right will not always triumph. Achieving success is a completely different issue, however, and the wisdom needed to attain it is not moral but practical. It is the savvy and wit so characteristic of the dupers. In fact, once the idea that the fabliau is in any important way concerned with Christian morality or the chivalric code—as image or counterimage—is put aside, the reader can focus on what is truly essential in these texts, i.e., being successful in the sense of surviving and even triumphing. An ironic vision of life is required to achieve this sort of success. A recognition that all is not what it seems to be, that reality can be manipulated to suit the moment, and that conventions will and must be broken in order for the individual to survive is crucial. So the narratives demonstrate the effectiveness of the very tools the narrators warn about in their morals. For one must be prepared, if not to use the devious means demonstrated, at least to avoid being the victim of their use. The primary means of thwarting the values of conventional society, especially for those who do not have wealth, power, or status, is cunning. From Scheherazade, who tells story after story to avoid execution, to the Aesopic tradition of weak but clever animals, narratives in wisdom collections demonstrate how to survive in a less than equitable society. The fabliau shows some of the same love of language become power, wit brokered into success, and common sense triumphing over obtuseness.

If, then, the fabliau is identified as an ironic tale of trickery which is based on an ethos of personal success and material gain, there remain a few questions, such as why it flourished particularly in Picardy and Flanders during the thirteenth century and whose values it represents.

6

A Tale of the People: Conclusions on the Fabliau Ethos

As an ironic didactic narrative about deception and the merits of practical wisdom, fabliaux present a world view that is not so much bound to a particular social class as it is common to those individuals for whom class structure is an obstacle to be overcome. All of the dictates of social standing and professionally or sexually defined roles are violated with glee in fabliaux, and much of their humor springs from their iconoclastic view of social conventions. In fact, they are not so much a literature of a class trying to define itself—as courtly literature was—as they are stories about individuals who use their wits to beat the system.

When Bédier asserted that fabliaux are bourgeois literature, he was undoubtedly influenced by nineteenth-century views on realism typified in the writings of Taine. The realism of fabliaux is, of course, quite relative, and the term is conceivable only if one is comparing these texts to epics or romances. They seem more realistic, and their humor is unrefined, so Bédier naturally attributed them to a "lower" social class than the only other class that presumably had a literature of its own at this time. They were bourgeois by default; but he also admitted that they were appreciated by a mixture of audiences. Regardless of their origins, he equated their spirit with the spirit of the emerging middle class, and the question of social origins of the genre is still debated because many contemporary critics have been influenced by Nykrog's rebuttal of Bédier.

As Charles Muscatine points out in his fine article "The Social Background of the Old French Fabliaux,"[1] Nykrog's argument that these are burlesques of courtly literature falters because his external evidence about audiences is slim, and his theory is exaggerated in order to discredit Bédier. "The main weakness of his [Nykrog's] work is the single-mindedness with which it pursues Bédier, perpetuating Bédier's presumed preoccupation with the class origins of the fabliau at the expense of serious attention to the social implications of the fabliau attitudes themselves. By presenting the fabliau as 'a courtly burlesque,' as simply an appanage of courtly literature, Nykrog diverts attention from what Faral and Olschki rightly perceived, that fabliau attitudes belong to the whole culture."[2]

Muscatine rightly argues that if one had to choose, the label "bourgeois" might be nearer the truth than "burlesque of courtly literature"; nevertheless, for him, the issue is not whether one specific class might have written and appreciated fabliaux but what particular social climate gave rise to them. "[T]he flourishing of the fabliaux, the rise of the cities, and the emergence of an urban middle class are equally visible symptoms of the same social and spiritual climate. Some phases of fabliau mentality seem more characteristic of rural society than of urban; but it is a rural society that is being transformed by essentially the same forces that are creating a bourgeoisie."[3] Nevertheless, as Muscatine points out, city environments are not the exclusive setting of fabliaux and statistics on the social origins of the characters bear this out (see p. 71 above).

As he demonstrates with numerous examples from the fabliau corpus and good historical sources, the language of the fabliaux and their social situations depict members of several social classes and reflect the movement between those classes which was characteristic of the thirteenth century. If references to artisans and agricultural metaphors are more common than typically urban expressions and occupations, Muscatine says this does not mean they are rural literature either. It means that the country life permeated the new towns and cities because their populations were drawn from the country. The opposite was also true, as Muscatine notes, because the urban mentality permeated the countryside. "The 'commercial revolution' of the thirteenth century touches the country—seigneur and peasant alike—as much as it does the city. In the rural areas of the region that concern us, the century can be generally described as a period of economic expansion and of social change."[4]

Thus there was social mobility in all directions. The upper bourgeois might move back to the country to play the role of aristocrats as their wealth increased; and, in a reverse migration, impoverished aristocrats moved to cities to take up ministerial roles. His careful presentation of historical sources fully supports his assertion that "we cannot speak of simple, homogeneous social classes, nor of simple social attitudes, in discussing fabliau origins or audiences."[5] Yet he also maintains that the tales are not preoccupied by social change; "it is not their primary subject."[6] He never tells us, however, what the primary subject of the tales is, and the final part of his article veers off into a condemnation of the ethos that he has so accurately identified. "The fabliaux, to put it crudely, seem 'lower class,' no matter whose literature they are. No matter what social biases they variously exhibit they celebrate uniformly one set of values: the ethic of cleverness, of profit, and of elementary pleasure."[7] His primary point is that fabliaux belong to the entire culture; they just seem to belong to the lower classes. Hence, the term *bourgeois* is appropriate, if we are using it as a pejorative label rather than an accurate social description.

Muscatine's corrective to Bédier and Nykrog appropriately broadens our perspective on the question of social origins; they may not be from or for a particular social class, but they reflect those bourgeois values that infected everyone in the thirteenth century. Nevertheless, we might wonder whether he marshalls all the right evidence and draws the wrong conclusion because he moves from social history to a personal condemnation of the values he uncovers. He seems offended by what he sees as their unabashed hedonism and materialism, values which he thinks only the contemporary world has made respectable. He does not consider that the fabliau ethic is a natural, healthy, even admirable one. He has overlooked the emphasis these texts place on intelligence and their implied values of spontaneity, naturalness, and even a belief in individual freedom. He is quick to dismiss the evidence he presents about their rural characters and expressions merely as evidence that the city still owed much to the rural heritage of its inhabitants. He does not consider the country as a primary source of the fabliau ethos, perhaps because he is unaware that in the northern regions of France the peasantry was a more complex social group than is generally recognized. It is my opinion, however, that members of this group, located in the new towns and villages, provided the values and images for much that informs these tales.

The history of Picardy, a region of primary interest to fabliau scholars,[8] reveals a different, if not unique, social class structure. As Fossier explains in *La Terre et les hommes en Picardie jusqu'à la fin du XIIIe siècle*,[9] this region never truly knew serfdom, was late in acquiring most customs associated with the feudal system, and had remarkably open and mobile social classes. Land was held primarily through inheritance and money made through ministerial appointments:

> Au debut de XIIe siècle, en Picardie, un homme paraît puissant non parce qu'il est chevalier, non parce qu'il est vassal ou seigneur féodal, mais parce que sa naissance, ses appuis lignagers, ses charges du cour, sa fortune lui ont procuré le droit de commander aux hommes, ou lui laissent espérer qu'il le pourra un jour; dans de telles conditions, il n'y a aucune fermeture du groupe: la richesse, fondement indispensable du succès, peut être acquise et permettre d'accéder par un heureux mariage, ou par la simple complaisance publique, au niveau des maîtres.[10]

Part of the openness of the class structure was due to the particular geographic and demographic condition of the region. By the end of the thirteenth century, the land had been largely conquered by man, and the region's well-developed agriculture provided a crucial base for the economic expansion of the area.

The history of Picardy thus is the history of rural communities, and the evolution of the peasantry does not follow the same lines as do other social groups in medieval France. "[H]istoire rurale n'a que faire des 'périodes' historiques traditionelles, celles qu'ont fixées les clercs et les gens de villes, catégorie de grand mérite, mais quantativement négligeable dans un monde médiéval où la terre est tout pour neuf hommes sur dix."[11] Fossier forces us to reconsider our preoccupation with cities as the major manifestation of the economic revival when he points out that the economic, technological, and social ascent of the peasantry was by far a more significant development:

> A y regarder de plus près, la variété et la spontanéité de l'émancipation paysanne semblent beaucoup plus révélatrice des progrès économiques et sociaux du XIIIe siècle que celle des "bourgeois," ne serait-ce qu'en raison du poids démographique de la campagne; la communauté paysanne, le groupe des villageois: voilà les fondements de la société et du droit médiévaux; la ville et le marchand ne sont que des exceptions. . . .[12]

As agrarian technology improved and money began circulating in greater quantities throughout the twelfth century, the villages' expansion, economic health, and emerging political power are signaled by documents that record the granting of *echivinages, lois,* or other legal rights. The number of villages that acquired such status was small in comparison to the total number of communes, but it is a certain indication of the growing power of the peasantry. "On voit que plus de 200 groupements villageois ont accédé certainement, avant 1300, à une situation d'autonomie. . . . Nous trouvons . . . . ce chiffre considérable; il témoigne avec éclat de la victoire arrachée par la paysannerie."[13]

What was evident in Picardy, if not so much elsewhere, was the circulation of money among the peasants who rendered various services to the landholders or merchants. With their improved iron tools, fortunate members of the peasantry pursued trades or worked clearing forest land or as *hotes,* those thirteenth-century pioneers who moved to new villages and worked vineyards and fields, earning not just subsistence in food but pay in money as well.[14] Just as one can imagine the bustling economy of towns and cities in the Ile de France where cathedrals, city walls, and other major construction projects were undertaken, so one must imagine the new village and town life in regions such as Picardy and Flanders, full of men working at various jobs for money, signing legal contracts as individuals, and associating with others who had money, regardless of their class.

A crucial point in Fossier's argument is that the increasing wealth of the peasantry created a distinction in their ranks that was perhaps as sharp as the division between burghers and aristocrats. The part a peasant played in the economic expansion was based on a simple factor—whether the man had tools, as the artisan, craftsman, or some agricultural workers had, or whether he could offer only his physical strength: "on trouve, au-dessus de la masse principale des rustiques, les hommes d'un art, le fèvre et le meunier,

bien sûr, dont l'ascension a commencé depuis longtemps, mais aussi les artisans du bois, du cuir, les maîtres du ravitaillement, brasseurs, boulangers et
bouchers."[15] These are the elite of the rural world and their presence in the
new villages not only creates a fragmentation within the peasantry but also
points to new social groupings that transcend traditional class lines. As Fossier
demonstrates, we can tell how significant newly enriched peasants are if we
look at documents that list "important inhabitants" of the villages. From these
lists we learn that approximately thirteen percent of the privileged in these
villages are peasants. It is even more interesting to note that prominent people
of these villages represent a social mixture reminiscent of the cast of characters we find in so many fabliaux:

> En 1259, à Auberchicourt, sur 67 habitants, on trouve le sire, son chapelain, le
> curé, un sergent, deux fèvres, un charpentier, un maçon, un charron, soit neuf
> privilégiés à des titres divers . . . . à Viry, sur 236 noms, deux chevaliers, trois
> officiers domaniaux, le curé, un chapelain, un mire, trois fèvres, trois charpentiers,
> trois meuniers et treize autres artisans savetiers, selliers, boulangers, bouchers,
> etc. toujours 13%. . . . Or dans les terriers du Cambrésis . . . la part du sol que
> tiennent les rustres enrichis se tient partout entre 15 et 25% du total; c'est le fait,
> à coup sur de ces "coqs": fèvre, bouchers, "franc homme," ou paysan aisé, qui ont
> pris la tête de la communauté et l'on [sic] menée jusqu'à la charte communale.[16]

The history of this region, as Fossier sketches it, is central to a reassessment
of the social background of the fabliau. The argument has previously been
couched in terms of choosing a social class these tales represent or of accepting,
as Muscatine would have us do, the whole thirteenth-century culture as a
backdrop. With Fossier's picture of the successful elite peasants and the bur-
geoning economy of the countryside in mind, the social background of fabliau
characters must be reconsidered. The most probable hypothesis concerning
their social origin places it somewhere between the narrow idea of one class
and the broad notion of the entire culture.

The statistics relating to class origins of characters in fabliaux that were
cited in Chapter 4 seem to reveal a relatively even distribution of clergy,
aristocrats, bourgeois, and a large percentage of peasants. The large group of
peasants is partially accounted for by the presence of household servants
who act as auxiliaries, but one cannot overlook the very large number of
vilains who would be examples of the elite Fossier describes. For example,
the cast of fabliau characters includes the prestigious professions: millers
(*Le Meunier d'Arleux* MR II: 33 and *Le Meunier et les .II. clers* MR V: 119)
and blacksmiths (*De Connebert* MR V: 128, *Dù fevre de Creeil* MR I: 21,
and *Le Vilain de Farbu* MR IV: 95). Other professions that may well have
been practiced by the group of enriched peasants would include butchers
(*Du bouchier d'Abevile* MR III: 84 and *Des braies le priestre* VI: A-I), healers

(*Do maignien* MR V: 130, *La Saineresse* MR I: 25, and *Du vilain mire* MR III: 74), artists (*Du prestre crucefié* MR I: 18 and *Du prestre teint* MR VI: 139), fishermen (*Du pescheor de pont seur Saine* MR III: 63 and *Du preudome qui rescolt son compere* MR I: 27), bakers (*Le Dit dou soucretain* MR VI: 150), and even *rafetiers* (*De Sire Hain et de Dame Anieuse* MR I: 6).

Although this list of specific professions and the number of examples may not be lengthy, many other tales reveal the presence of the enriched peasant who may be working the land or working at an unidentified occupation. He is, in any event, not a serf in the textbook sense.

De Constant du Hamel (MR IV: 106) is a good illustration of the presence of such peasants. The location of this tale is referred to as a *vile,* and the story has a cast representative of the medieval urban environment. A priest, a provost, and a forester in charge of the lord's woods all conspire to seduce Ysabel, the beautiful wife of the *vilain,* Constant. They mock his ugliness, lack of refinement, and manners; but Ysabel is a faithful and clever wife. Constant is repeatedly referred to as a *vilain* and *paisant,* and the reader knows that these are not mere epithets, because at several points the narrator says he is working the land with a plow. Yet, he is also not just a pathetic have-not. When the priest falsely denounces the couple to get revenge for Ysabel's rejection of his amorous advances, Constant is quick to buy him off. Later, he worries with his wife about where he will find the money he so rashly promised the priest. Ysabel responds:

> —Or ne vous chaut," fet ele, "frere.
> Toz près les ai, ses paierai;
> Ja mar en serez en esmai,
> Ne plus que por .I. oef de quaille.
> Plus avons nous deniers que paille;
> S'en donrons .X. livres ou .XX."
>
> (vv. 254-59)

It is clear that they are well-off village residents and that the three seducers want to break Constant financially. Although the couple could pay off the men, Ysabel prefers to take control of the situation by setting up a plot to punish them as well as keep their proferred gifts to her. The importance of money in this text is underscored because extortion is part of each exchange between the major characters. Even the maidservant demands money for her role as a go-between. The conclusion, not surprisingly, mentions that the priest, the provost, and the forester were punished not only for their sin but also for their envy. As the fabliau ends, two important themes are brought together—money and intelligence. The narrator merrily condones the acquisition of money through the use of intelligence:

Et la dame [Ysabel] est en sa meson,
Qui deniers a à grant plenté;
Por ce qu'a sagement ouvré,
Les deniers ot et les joiaus;
Et si furent quites de ciaus
Que dans Constans avoit promis.

(vv. 948-53)

In this case, the peasant not only escapes a potential debt, but enriches himself even further.

Even an extremely simple tale such as *Le Vilain de Farbu* (MR IV: 95) gives us a glimpse of the two levels within the peasantry, although status and wealth are not a central concern of the text. A father and son, presumably members of the large mass of ignorant peasants, make a trip to the market. The narrative turns on the stupidity of the father, who witnesses his son spit on the blacksmith's forge to prove it is hot. After returning home, the father spits in his soup. The blacksmith and the market village or town belong to the more advanced rural society which enjoys technology (and thus knowledge) which only the son is intelligent enough to understand. The father is the butt of the joke because he remains the ignorant, unliberated peasant.

Many of the occupations that figure prominently in these tales may be more common in larger towns, but they might be part of a village economy as well. There are: innkeepers (*Des trois avugles* MR I: 4, *La Plantez* MR III: 75, *Des .III. dames de Paris* MR III: 73, *D'Estormi* MR I: 19, and *Del fol vilain* G 2); money changers (*Du segretain moine* MR V: 136 and *Des .II. changéors* MR I: 23); usurers (*De la dame qui fist batre son mari* MR IV: 100); go-betweens (*D'Auberée* MR V: 110 and *Du prestre teint* MR VI: 139); jongleurs (*De jouglet* MR IV: 98 and *De Saint Piere et du jougleur* MR V: 117); con artists (*Du prestre et des .II. ribaus* MR III: 62); manure haulers (*Du vilain asnier* MR V: 114); robbers (*De Brifaut* MR IV: 103, *Le Dit dou soucretain* MR VI: 150 and its analogues, and *De Barat et de Haimet* MR IV: 97); prostitutes (*Du prestre et d'Alison* MR II: 31, *De Boivin de Provins* MR V: 116, *De la viellete* MR V: 129, and *Des .III. meschines* MR III: 64); and even a gigolo (*Du fotéor* MR I: 28). Add to these the fact that references to specific trades are less common than the ubiquitous formula *un vilain riche, une borgeoise,* or *un prestre* and we are confronted with overwhelming evidence that the majority of these tales must take place in either villages or towns, both of which have their mix of enriched peasants, clergy, *commerçants,* and feudal officers. In fact, the locations are revealed even if they are not made explicit by the mixture of characters in various occupations and from various social groups who would only have been in contact with each other in an urban environment.

It is not an exaggeration to refer to the thriving villages and small towns of vital areas in Picardy and Flanders as urban, because as Robert Lopez points out, "the crossroads within the wall" is not defined so much by population density or location of particular religious or political institutions as by the pace of development and change. "Fundamentally, what matters is whether or not the crossroads within the circle produced a quickening, a creativity that did not exist outside the circle."[17] According to Lopez, there are four types of urban settlement in the Middle Ages: the stockade city, the agrarian city, the market city, and the industrial city.[18] With this definition of city in mind, it is possible to say that all fabliaux, except those very few set in a castle or the open countryside, have an urban setting. It is true that large cities, such as Amiens or Paris are mentioned only a few times, justifying Muscatine's assertion that cities are not prominent locales in spite of numerous references to bourgeois characters. What becomes obvious on further reflection, however, is that small towns are much more significant than large cities. The towns or villages are usually not named, but they are revealed through the significant numbers of enriched peasants and the heterogeneous nature of the small societies they depict.

It is not difficult to see the connection between these settings and the fabliau world view. For if the settings are urban, so too is the mentality of these tales, and the qualities they promote are based on the new values that the economy promoted. Fossier says we may debate whether the improvements in tools and agricultural methods along with the increased circulation of money among the peasantry caused a new mentality to emerge, or whether the new mentality led to a desire to acquire material wealth. The fact that a new mentality begins to appear, however, is incontestable. "Il faut donc chercher, dans l'obscurité du Xe ou du XIe siècle la reprise de cette tendance: le sens de la précision du terme et du chiffre, le sens de l'efficacité, le goût du profit."[19] The love of profit seems naturally coupled with a desire to move up socially, and in all the areas touched by the economic revival, the conventional division among classes was seriously threatened. Alexander Murray maintains in *Reason and Society in the Middle Ages* that by the end of the twelfth century, the popularity of the doctrine of the three estates indicates not a freezing of the classes, but, on the contrary, the presence of social mobility that threatened the upper classes who promulgated the doctrine. "The doctrine of the three orders was partly a reaction against, *inter alia*, a threat to the distinction between commoner and noble. The persistence and spread of the doctrine attest the persistence and spread of the threat."[20]

Both Murray and Fossier point to a new mentality based on wealth and opportunities for upward social movement which contradicts much of the common wisdom about the medieval mind. Murray's thesis rests on numerous texts showing that an abundant flow of money made avarice and ambition so commonplace as to be considered major social problems. The texts increasingly warn of robbers, simonists, Jews, and their attendant vices. "Like avarice, ambition remained at the top of the diabolic pantheon of vices, right through the middle ages."[21] That ambition had to be so frequently condemned meant that those in power were clearly threatened by a new social trend encouraging men to seek individual advantage over others, to rise beyond their appointed stations and to amass wealth rather than land or men in the traditional feudal fashion.

Rather than decrying this new mentality, Murray points out the positive consequences of a quest for wealth and advantage. The foremost quality needed by the ambitious was a practical form of wisdom, and Murray maintains that the economic situation contributed to the enshrining of reason as a major virtue by the thirteenth century. Men began to understand the relationship between intellect and power over nature and other men. As political structures evolved in the High Middle Ages, the qualities needed to wield power and the directives designed for potential leaders show an increasingly intellectual bent. Murray points to several manuals, the *Secretum Secretorum,* Philippe de Beaumanoir's *Coutumes de Beauvaisis* (1290), and Brunetto Latini's *Li Tresors* (1268), which all place intellectual values among the most important for leaders to possess. We can appreciate how much the feudal concept of power has evolved if we consider Philippe de Beaumanoir's list of qualities needed by a *bailli*:

> The first chapter of the *Coutumes* lists ten qualities needed by the *bailli.* In the list, neither loving God nor loving the king comes higher than second place. The first is held by that virtue "which is and ought to be lady and mistress of all the others, and without which the other virtues cannot be employed. This virtue is called wisdom, which is as much as to say, being wise [*sages*]. Let us then declare: the man who sets out to hold the *bailli*'s office, and to do justice, must be wise. Nor will he be able, if he is not, to do what pertains to the office."[22]

As was mentioned in Chapter 4, another quality needed by the *bailli* is *soutil engieng,* the shrewdness so characteristic of the ambitious man, and of the fabliau duper.

In a predominately Christian culture, we expect virtues to be spiritual ones. What Murray adroitly shows is that within the Christian culture of the High Middle Ages, another set of values that included an appreciation of practical intelligence was blossoming. The medievals could justify a glorification of this type of intellect by pointing to the wise biblical kings, Solomon and David. They also idealized Alexander, whose legendary intelligence and remarkable victories were supposedly explained by the fact that Aristotle had been his tutor.[23] Through Aquinas' work, of course, Moslem and classical philosophy became legitimized; intellect could be a virtue if it aided in the search for God. Nevertheless, what Murray is referring to is a secular aspect of *prudentia* which had a practical value, not just a theological one:

It was not only knowledge, like knowledge of history, that helped a man fight his battles. It was also plain wit. Some awareness of the usefulness of wit is no doubt primeval—for example, the earliest known European folk tales include themes displaying it. But in the twelfth and thirteenth centuries this awareness was enthroned in an exceptionally high place, and an unexpected one: among the cardinal virtues.[24]

Murray believes that the glorification of *prudentia* was due to the economic revival that generated an entirely new set of values and resulted in elevating a wise man to a status enjoyed previously by *bellatores* and *oratores*:

[T]he rationalistic culture was mainly borne by the upward-moving battalions on the Wheel of Fortune; by those who responded—either consciously or unconsciously, either violently or with a gentleness baffling perception—to the pulling power of social rank; by those who knew—perhaps better than King Alfred, who had said it in an earlier renaissance—that "through wisdom you may come to power, even though you do not yearn for it."[25]

Although the characters of fabliaux do not aspire to power in any broad or lasting sense, these tales are all permeated by the ethic of practicality, ambition, and celebration of quick-wittedness that Murray finds in so many other texts in the High Middle Ages. It was not just the *bailli* who had *soutil engieng*; almost every duper in the fabliaux is accused or perhaps secretly admired for having this quality. The moral in *De l'enfant qui fu remis au soleil* (MR I: 14) repeats the word *engien* twice, in this case with its fullest negative connotations, to underscore the deviousness of the wife:

> Or li est bien en lieu remis
> Ses engiens, et tornez à perte,
> Dont folement estoit couverte:
> Bel s'en est ses sires vengiez,
> Qui laidement fu engingniez
> Et par paroles et par dis.

(vv. 138-43)

Women, as was pointed out, are often accused of being like the *bourgeoise* in *Des braies au cordelier* (MR III: 88) "Qui mout estoit sage et cortoise; / Mout savoit d'enging et d'aguet" (vv. 8-9).

In *Du vilain qui conquist paradis par plait* (MR III: 81), the power of cleverness in argumentation is illustrated as the peasant puts all the apostles who want to keep him out of heaven to shame by a recital of their failings. The fear his cleverness arouses seems to be compounded by the fact that he is a mere *vilain* using his natural and powerful gift of wit:

> Li vileins dit en son proverbe
> Que mains hom a le tort requis

Qui par plaidier aura conquis:
Engiens a fauxée droiture,
Fauxers a veincue nature;
Torz vait avant et droiz aorce:
Mielz valt engiens que ne fait force.

(vv. 154-60)

The fact that tricks, deceptive acts, and manipulative language are both celebrated and condemned by the fabliau should not be surprising. An ambitious man or woman is understandably a threat to someone about to be displaced from a position of privilege, whether it is privilege over another person, such as a wife, or privilege over an object, such as a horse or a ham.

Wit is both useful and dangerous; for every duper who uses his wits deviously there is potentially someone who could outsmart him or her and gain the upper hand. Fabliaux, of course, are full of such reversals, and they also have their share of wise men who use their wits to resolve conflict. *De la male Honte* (MR IV: 90) is an obvious example. In many fabliaux, the value of intelligence is not just demonstrated; it is explicitly stated. The count in *De la dame escolliée* (MR VI: 149) who will triumph over his wife's aggressiveness (granted, in a most sadistic manner) is successful because he is smart, and his intelligence is considered more valuable than his wealth:

Joenes estoit et de grant sens,
Et si ert plains de grant savoir,
Qui mielz li valt que nul avoir.

(vv. 48-50)

All elements in these tales reflect a genuine enjoyment of cleverness and scorn for stupidity. As was pointed out in Chapter 2, the didacticism of the fabliau is quite serious although the tales are not. A lesson is to be learned by negative example and the narrators admonish the audience to learn what is smart:

Par cest flabel poez savoir
Que cil ne fait mie savoir
Qui tot son pensé dit et conte,
Quar maint domaige en vient et honte. . . .
    (*Du provoire qui menga les meures* MR IV: 92, vv. 91-94)

Par cest fablel poez savoir
Que *cil ne fet mie savoir*
Qui mieus croit sa fame que lui:
Sovent l'en vient honte et anui.
    (*Les .IIII. souhais Saint Martin* MR V: 133, vv. 186-90)

Savoir, in the sense of *savoir faire* and *savoir vivre,* is needed to acquire those elementary objectives of fabliau dupers, or it is needed to avoid being caught in the duper's trap. From whichever perspective one views the tales, the lessons are clear. Common sense and a quick wit are indispensable survival tactics.

Like the earthy Sancho Panza whose proverbs so irritated Don Quixote, the fabliau calls attention to certain values that do have their merits. Although he was just a peasant, Sancho too had his dreams. Not knowing or caring much about the chivalric ideal Don Quixote loved, Sancho followed him for the land he was promised and the wealth and power he assumed would follow. So too, the characters in fabliaux are disinterested in ideals, be they chivalric or religious. They are out for themselves and their most immediate asset is their cunning and no-nonsense approach to life. Their goals are quite basic—sex, food, entertainment, money, or lodging; and their methods are as direct and unselfconscious as Sancho's when he tries to get Don Quixote to tell him the recipe for Fierabras' balm. Sancho did not want the balm because he believed in its healing powers, but because "I am sure that it would be worth more than two reales the ounce anywhere and that is all I need for a life of ease and honor."[26] Disinterested in matters of belief, Sancho epitomizes the quest not for a golden age or courtly ideals but a golden future of wealth and ease.

From this study of fabliaux it is clear that an ethos based on wit, pragmatism, and a quest for the good life that informs Sancho's character took shape long before Cervantes wrote the *Quixote.* Fabliau characters demonstrate the same pragmatism by extricating themselves from compromising situations, the same proverbial wisdom, and the same desire for pleasure. They are rough; they eat, sleep, and make love without false modesty or much ceremony. Just as Sancho represents modern man who must break the fetters of social class structure and impractical idealism, so the fabliau represents for the High Middle Ages an ironic casting aside of the idealism and class consciousness of the official culture by large groups of newly enriched, socially mobile country dwellers.

The fabliau, a short verse narrative about deception and misdeeds which teaches the value of cunning and aggression, reflects the fusion of a peasant mentality with the ethos of the money economy. By virture of its didacticism and celebration of ingenuity, the fabliau demonstrates its kinship with typical folk literature. But its ironic vision and strain of ambitiousness and hedonism betray the influence of the vibrant economy in the new villages and towns where modern culture was being formed. As an archetypal form of typical Gallic wit, the fabliau scorns ignorance and pretention while celebrating the new intellectual and sensual values of the commercial regions of thirteenth-century France.

Appendix A

Le Dit des perdriz (MR I: 17)

Por ce que fabliaus dire sueil,	The Introduction
En lieu de fable dire vueil	
Une aventure qui est vraie,	
D'un vilain, qui delèz sa haie	The Narrative
Prist .II. pertris par aventure.	QS-2
En l'atorner mist moult sa cure,	
Sa fame les fist au feu metre;	
Ele s'en sot bien entremetre;	
Le feu a fet, la haste atorne,	
Et li vilains tantost s'en torne;	F-2a
Por le prestre s'en va corant.	
Mès au revenir tarda tant,	
Que cuites furent les pertris;	
La dame a le haste jus mis,	F-6a
S'en pinça une peléure,	
Quar moult ama la lechéure.	
Quant Diex li dona à avoir,	
Ne béoit pas à grant avoir,	
Mès à toz ses bons acomplir;	
L'une pertris cort envaïr;	
Andeus les eles en menjue;	
Puis est alée en mi la rue	F-2a
Savoir se ses sires venoit;	
Quant ele venir ne le voit,	
Tantost arrière s'en retorne	F-1b
Et le remanant tel atorne,	
Mal du morsel qui ramainsist.	
Adonc s'apenssa, et si dist	F-6a con't
Que l'autre encore mengera;	
Moult très bien set qu'ele dira	
S'on li demande que devindrent;	
Ele dira que li chat vindrent	
Quant ele les ot arrier trètes;	

121

Tost li orent des mains retrètes,
Et chascuns la seue emporta;
Ainsi, ce dist, eschapera.
Puis va en mi la rue ester,   F-2a
Por son mari abeveter;
Et, quant ele nel voit venir,   (F-1)
La langue li prist à fremir   F-6a
Sus la pertris qu'ele ot lessie.
Jà ert toute vive enragie
S'encor n'en a .I. petitet;
Le col en tret tout souavet,
Si le menja par grant douçor;
Ses dois en lèche tout entor:
"Lasse! fet-ele, que ferai?
Se tout menjue, que dirai?
Et coment le porrai lessier?
50   J'en ai moult très grant desirrier.
Or aviegne qu'avenir puet,
Quar toute mengier le m'estuet."
      Tant dura cele demorée,
Que la Dame fu saoulée.
Et li vilains ne tarda mie,
A l'ostel vint, en haut s'escrie;   F-1b
"Diva, sont cuites les pertris?"   F-3a
—Sire, dist-ele, ainçois va pis,   F-5a
Quar mengies les a li chas."
Li vilains saut isnel le pas,   self-F-5
Seure li cort comme enragiéz;
Jà li éust les iex sachiez,
Quant el crie: "C'est gas, c'est gas.   F-5a con't
Fuiez," fet-ele, "Sathanas;
Couvertes sont por tenir chaudes."
—Jà vous chantaisse putes Laudes,"
Fet-il, "foi que je doi saint Ladre.
Or çà, mon bon hanap de madre
Et ma plus bele blanche nape;
Si l'estenderai sus ma chape,
Souz cele treille en cel praiel."
—Mès, vous, prenez vostre coutel,   (F-2b)
Qui grant mestier a d'aguisier;
Si le fètes .I. pou trenchier
A cele pierre en cele cort."
Li vilains se despoille et cort,
Le coutel tout nu en sa main.
      A tant ez vos le chapelain,   F-1a
Qui léenz venoit por mengier:
A la dame vint sans targier,
Si l'acole moult doucement.
Et cele li dist simplement:
"Sire," dist-el, "fuiez, fuiez:
Jà ne serai où vous soiez

Honiz ne malmis de vo cors;
Mès sires est alez là fors
Por son grant coutel aguisier.
Et dist qu'il vous voudra trenchier
Les coilles, s'il vous puet tenir."
—De Dieu te puist-il souvenir,"   F-3a
Dist li prestres; "qu'est que tu dis?
Nous devons mengier .II. pertris
Que tes sires prist hui matin."
Cele li dist: "Par saint Martin,   F-5a
Céenz n'a pertris ne oisel;
De vo mengier me seroit bel,
Et moi peseroit de vo mal;
Mès ore esgardez là aval,
Come il aguise son coutel."
100 *—Jel voi," dist-il; "par mon chapel,*   self-F-5
Je cuit bien que tu as voir dit."
Léenz demora moult petit,   F-2a
Ainz s'en fui grant aléure,
Et cele crie à bone éure: F-5a
"Venez-vous-en, sire Gombaut."
—Qu'as-tu," dist-il, "se Diex te saut?"   F-3a
—Que j'ai? Tout à tens le saurez;   F-5a
Mès, se tost corre ne poez,
Perte i aurez, si com je croi;
Quar, par la foi que je vous doi,
Li prestre enporte voz pertris."
Li preudom fu toz aatis,   self-F-5
Le coutel en porte en sa main,
S'en cort après le chapelain;   F-2b
Quant il le vit, se li escrie: F-6h
"Ainsi nes en porterez mie."
Puis s'escrie à granz alenées;
"Bien les en portez eschaufées;
Ça les lerrez, se vous ataing;
Vous seriez mauvès compaing
Se vous les mangiez sanz moi."
Li prestre esgarde derrier soi,   self-F-5
Et voit acorre le vilain;
Quant voit le coutel en sa main,
Mors cuide estre, se il l'ataint.
De tost corre pas ne se faint;
Et le vilains penssoit de corre,
Qui les pertris cuidoit rescorre;
Mès li Prestres de grant randon
S'est enfermez en sa méson.
A l'ostel li vilains retorne,   F-1b
Et lors sa fame en aresone:
"Diva," fet-il, "et quar me dis   F-3a
Comment tu perdis les pertris."
Cele li dist: "Se Diex m'aït,   F-5a

Tantost que li prestres me vit,
Si me pria, se tant l'amaise,
Que je les pertris li monstraisse,
Quar moult volentiers les verroit;
Et je le menai là tout droit
Où je les avoie couvertes:
Il ot tantost les mains ouvertes,
Si les prist, et si s'en fui;
Mès je guères ne le sivi,
Ainz le vous fis moult tost savoir."
Cil respont: "Bien puès dire voir;   self-F-5
Or le lessons à itant estre."
Ainsi fu engingniez le prestre
Et Gombaus, qui les pertris prist.
150   *Par example cis fabliaus dist*   The Conclusion
Fame est fète por decevoir;
Mençonge fet devenir voir,
Et voir fet devenir mençonge.
Cil n'i vout mètre plus d'alonge,
Qui fist cest fablel et ces dis.
Ci faut li fabliaus des pertris.

Appendix B

Du vilain de Bailluel (MR IV: 109)

Se fabliaus puet veritez estre,	The Introduction
Dont avint il, ce dist mon mestre,	
C'uns vilains à Bailluel manoit.	The Narrative
Formenz et terres ahanoit:	
N'estoit useriers ne changiere.	
.I. jor, à eure de prangiere,	
Vint en meson mult fameilleus:	
Il estoit granz et merveilleus	
Et maufez et de laide hure.	
Sa fame n'avoit de lui cure,	
Quar fols ert et de lait pelain,	
Et cele amoit le chapelain.	
S'avoit mis jor d'ensamble à estre	F-6b
Le jor entre li et le prestre.	
Bien avoit fet son appareil.	
Ja ert li vins enz ou bareil,	
Et si avoit le chapon cuit,	
Et li gastiaus, si com je cuit,	
Estoit couvers d'une touaille.	
Ez vous le vilain qui baaille	F-1b
Et de famine et de mesaise.	
Cele li cort ouvrir la haise,	
Contre lui est corant venue:	
Mès n'eüst soing de sa venue;	
Mieus amast autrui recevoir.	
Puis li dist por lui decevoir,	F-5a
Si com cele qui sanz ressort	
L'amast mieus enfouï que mort:	
"Sire," fet ele, "Dieus me saint!	
Con vous voi or desfet et taint!	
N'avez que les os et le cuir."	
—Erme, j'ai tel fain que je muir,"	F-3a
Fet il, "sont boilli li maton?"	

125

—Morez certes, ce fetes mon;   F-5a con't
Jamès plus voir dire n'orrez:
Couchiez vous tost, quar vous morez.
Or m'est il mal, lasse chetive!
Après vous n'ai soing que je vive,
Puisque de moi vous dessamblez.
Sire, com vous estes emblez,
Vous devierez à cort terme."
—Gabez me vous," fet il, "dame Erme?   F-3a
Je oi si bien no vache muire:
Je ne cuit mie que je muire,
Ainz porroie encore bien vivre."
—Sire, la mort qui vous enyvre   F-5a con't
Vous taint si le cuer et encombre
Qu'il n'a mès en vous fort que l'ombre:
Par tens vous tornera au cuer."
50 *—Couchiez me donques, bele suer,"*   self-F-5
Fet il, "quant je sui si atains."
  Cele se haste, ne puet ains,
De lui deçoivre par sa jangle.
D'une part li fist en .I. angle
.I. lit de fuerre et de pesas
Et de linceus de chanevas;
Puis le despoille, si le couche:
Les ieus li a clos et la bouche,
Puis se lest cheoir sor le cors:
"Frere," dist ele, "tu es mors: F-5a con't
Dieus ait merci de la teue ame!
Que fera ta lasse de fame
Qui por toi s'ocirra de duel?"
Li vilains gist souz le linçuel,
Qui entresait cuide mors estre;
Et cele s'en va por le prestre   F-2b
Qui mout fu viseuse et repointe.
De son vilain tout li acointe
Et entendre fet la folie.
Cil en fu liez et cele lie
De ce qu'ainsi est avenu:
Ensamble s'en sont revenu,   F-1b
Tout conseillant de lor deduis.   F-6b
  Lues que li prestres entre en l'uis F-5a con't
Commença à lire ses saumes,
Et la dame à batre ses paumes;
Mès si se set faindre dame Erme
Qu'ainz de ses ieus ne cheï lerme;
Envis le fet et tost le lesse,
Et li prestre fist corte lesse;
N'avoit soing de commander l'ame.
Par le poing a prise la dame;   F-6b
D'une part vont en une açainte,
Desloïe l'a et desçainte:

Sor le fuerre noviau batu
Se sont andui entrabatu,
Cil adenz et cele souvine.
Li vilains vit tout le couvine,   F-7
Qui du linçuel ert acouvers,
Quar il tenoit ses ieus ouvers.
Si veoit bien l'estrain hocier,
Et vit le chapelain locier;
Bien sot ce fu li chapelains:
"Ahi! Ahi!" dist li vilains   F-4b
Au prestre: "Filz à putain ors!
Certes, se je ne fusse mors,
Mar vous i fussiez embatuz,
Ainz hom ne fu si bien batuz
Com vous seriez ja, sire prestre."
100   *—Amis," fet il, "ce puet bien estre,*   F-5a
Et sachiez se vous fussiez vis
G'i venisse mout à envis,
Tant que l'ame vous fust ou cors;
Mès de ce que vous estes mors,
Me doit il bien estre de mieus.
Gisiez vous cois, cloez vos ieus:
Nes devez mès tenir ouvers."
Dont a cil ses ieus recouvers;   self-F-5
Si se recommence à tesir,
Et li prestres fist son plesir   F-6b con't
Sanz paor et sanz resoingnier.
    Ce ne vous sai je tesmoingnier   The Conclusion
S'il l'enfouïrent au matin;
Mès li fabliaus dist en la fin
C'on doit por fol tenir celui
Qui mieus croit sa fame qui lui.

Appendix C

De la male Honte (MR IV: 90)

Seignor, oez et entendez	The Introduction
.I. flabel qu'est faiz et rimez,	
D'un roi qui Engleterre tint.	
Toz ce fu voirs et si covint	
Que en Engleterre ert .I. rois.	
En icel tens ert us et droiz	
Que, quant .I. hom moroit sanz oir,	
Li rois avoit tot son avoir.	
Ce trovon nos avant el conte	
Qu'uns preudons morust qu'ot non Honte;	The Narrative
Honte ert le preudom apelez,	QS-2
Quant vit que tant fu adolez.	
Et que il vit qu'il ne vivra,	
.I. sien compere en apela:	F-1a
"Compere," dit Honte, "prenez	F-3c
Mon avoir que vos là veez	
En cele male qui là pent;	
Por Dieu vos pri omnipotent,	
Se ge muir, portez la lou roi.	
Si dites que ge li envoi,	
Quar ce est raison et droiture."	
Et cil respont, et si li jure	F-4a
Que il la portera sanz faille,	
Por ce que du convent ne faille.	
Honte morut de cel malage:	
Si volt garder son comparage;	
Maintenant prent la male Honte,	F-4c
De la vile ist, el chemin monte.	F-2b
Tant va, tant vient et tant demande,	
Tant a erré par Inguelande,	
Qu'il a trové, desoz en l'onbre,	F-1a
Devant le pin le roi à Londre,	
O lui grant part de son barnaige:	

"Sire," fait il en son langaige,   F-4b + self-F-5 + F-6d
"La male Honte vos aport.
Ge li oi covent à sa mort
La male Honte vos dorroie:
Prenez la, qu'il la vos envoie;
Sire, prenez la male Honte."
Quant li rois l'ot, si a grant honte: self-F-5
"Vilein," dit il, "tu me mesdiz,
Mais tu aies honte toz diz!
De honte me puist Dieus defendre!
Près va que je ne te faz pendre."   F-8
Encor voloit li vilains dire,
Mais cil le prenent à grant ire,
Qui environ le roi estoient;
Tant le deboutent et desvoient
Que tart li est, ce m'est avis,
50 *Que il se soit de cort partiz;*   F-2a
Bien li avint qu'il ne l'ont mort:
"Ha! las," fait il, "or me recort
Que mes comperes me pria,
Quant il morut et defina,
Que cest avoir au roi donasse;
Volentiers encor i pallasse,
Et donroie la male Honte;
Mais cil chevalier et cil conte
M'avroient ja mort, bien le sai.
Mais or sai bien que ge ferai:
Ge gaiterai sempres le roi,
Quant au mostier ira par soi,
Et il verra devant trestoz;
Encor serai ge si estoz,
Que li donrai la male Honte."
    A ce que ainsi dit et conte,
Voit le roi au moutier aler,
Et il le recort saluer.   F-1a
Si con il entroit el mostier,
Li commence haut à huschier,
Que tuit l'oïrent prince et conte:
"Sire," fait il, "la male Honte   F-4b + self-F-5 + F-6d
Vos aport ge encor et offre:
D'esterlins i a plein .I. coffre."
Quant li rois l'ot, si a tel raige   self-F-5
Avis li est que de duel arge:
Ne set que faire ne que dire.
Du vilein a tel duel et ire
Que la male Honte li baille,
Quant il a dit: "Où sont mi baille,   F-8
Et cil qui menjuent mon pain,
Quant ne me tuent cel vilain?"
Quant cil voient irié le roi,
Sore li corent à desroi,

Ja fust li preudons malbailliz,
Mais il s'estoit entr'aus quatiz;
Si le perdent entre la gent.
 Ez vos celui forment dolent,   F-2a
Qui preudom et loiaus estoit,
Du roi qui forment s'en iroit
Quant li offroit la male Honte.
Cil dit que à lui plus ne monte,
Mais tierce foiz li offerra,
Et puis enprès si s'en ira;
S'or le devoit li rois ocirre,
Si li era il encor dire
Tierce foiée, quar c'est droiz.
Et, quant par ot mengié li rois
Que il fut auques bauz et liez,
100 *Li vileins revint toz chargiez*   F-1a
De la male Honte qu'il porte.
A grant paor o chiere morte
Li rehuche haut et reconte:
"Sire, sire, la male Honte,"   F-4b + self-F-5 + F-6d
Fait li preudons, "quar retenez,
Quar par droit avoir la devez;
La male Honte vos remaigne,
S'en donez à vostre compaigne;
La male Honte est granz et lée,
Ge la vos ai ci aportée.
.I. mien compere, ce sachiez,
Là vos envoie, si l'aiez,
Quar vos d'Angleterre estes rois;
La male Honte aiez, c'est droiz."
Quant li rois l'ot et il l'entent,   self-F-5
A poi que il d'ire ne fent:
"Seignor," fait il, "ge vos commant   F-8
Que vos cel vilain maintenant,
Qui ne me velt laissier en pais,
Que il orendroit soit deffais."
Li preudons fust ja entrepris,
Quant .I. hauz hom s'est avant mis,   F-1a
Qui saiges ert et entendanz
Et de parole molt saichanz:
"Sire," fait il, "vos avez tort   F-4b
Se le vilain aviez mort;
Mais, ençois que li façoiz honte,
Sachiez que est la male Honte."
—Volentiers," fait li roi, "Par foi,   F-3a
Vilein," fait il, "entent à moi;
Que dis tu de la male Honte?
Tu m'en as hui fait mainte honte
En ma cort et maint grant ennui,
Ne sai quantes foiées hui."
Dont li conte cil et devise   F-4a

Con la male Honte ot emprise,
Et con Honte, son bon compere,
Li pria par l'ame sa mere
Qu'après sa mort li aportast.
Li rois l'entent, sa cuise bat   F-7
De la joie qu'il ot eüe,
Quant la parole ot entendue:
"Vilain," fait il, "or t'ai plus chier   F-9
Que de noient m'as fet irier:
Mielz m'as gabé que nus lechiere.
Or te doing ge à bele chiere
La male Honte à ta partie,
Quar par droit l'as bien gaaignie."
Ainsi ot cil la male Honte.
150   *Ce dit GUILLAUMES en son conte*   The Conclusion
Que li vilains en a portée
La male Honte en sa contrée.
Si l'a as Anglois departie;
Encor en ont il grant partie;
Sanz la male ont il assez honte,
Et chascun jor lor croist et monte:
Par mauvais seignor et par lasche
Les a honte mis en s'ataiche.

Appendix D

Le Meunier d'Arleux (MR II: 33)

Qui se melle de biax dis dire	The Introduction
Ne doit commenchier à mesdire,	
Mais de biax dis dire et conter;	
Dès or vos vaurai raconter	
Une aventure ke je sai,	
Car plus celer ne le vaurai.	
A Palluiel, le bon trespas,	The Narrative
.I. Mannier i ot Jakemars;	QS-2
Cointes estoit et envoisiés;	
A Aleus estoit il manniers;	
Le blé moloit il, et Mousès,	
Qui desous lui estoit varlès.	
.I. jour estoient au molin	
En un demierkes au matin;	
De maintes viles i ot gens	
Qui au molin moloient souvent;	
Il i ot molt blé et asnées.	
Maroie, fille Gérart d'Estrées,	F-1a
Vint au molin atout son blé;	
Le mannier en a apielé;	
Ele l'apièle par son nom:	
"Hé, Jacques," fait ele, "sans son,	F-3e
Par cele foi ke moi devés,	
Molés mon blé; si me hastés	
Que je m'en puisse repairier.	
Atorner m'estuet à mangier	
Por mon père, ki est à chans."	
Jakès li a dit maintenans:	F-4a
"Ma douce amie, or vous séés;	(F-6c)
.I. petit si vous reposés.	
Il a molt blé chi devant nous	
Qui doivent maure devent vous,	
Mais vous morrés qant jou porrai,	

Et si n'en soiés en esmai,
Car, se il puet, et vespres vient,
Je vous ostelerai molt bien
A ma maison à Paluiel.
Sachiés k'à ma feme en ert biel,
Car jou dirai k'estes ma nièche."
    Mousès ot jà moulut grant pièche;   F-7
Les gens furent jà ostelé
Et à leur villes retorné.
Mousès voit bien et aperçoit
Tout cho ke ses maistres pensoit;
Andoi orent une pensée
Por décevoir Marien d'Estrée.
Jésir cuident entre ses bras;
Mais il n'en aront jà solas,
Ains en sera Jakès décheus,
50   Tristres, dolens, corchiés et mus.
    Mousès a son maistre apielé: F-5a
"Sire" dist-il, "or entendés;
Il a molt poi d'iaue el vivier;
Il vous covient euvre laissier;
Nos molins ne puet morre tor. "
—Or n'i a il nul autre tor,"
Fait li manniers; "clot le molin."
Li solaus traioit à déclin;
La damoisièle ert plainne d'ire,   F-7
Pleure des iex, de cuer soupire:
"Lasse," fait ele, "que ferai?   F-3a
Or voi jou bien ke g'i morrai.
Se je m'en vois encui par nuit,
Jou isterai dou sens, je cuit."
    Mousès l'a prise à conforter;   F-5a
"Biele," fait-il, "or m'entendés;
Vous irés avuec mon maistre;
Il vos en pora grans biens naistre. "
—*Voire," fait Jakès entressait,*   (F-5a)
"Mais meuture n'aura huimais,
Elle, ses pères, ne sa gent."
Par le main maintenant le prent:
"Levés sus, bièle; s'en alons
A Paluiel en mes maisons;
Là serés vous bien ostelée.
Vous mangerés, à la vesprée,
Pain et tarte, car et poisson,
Et buverés vin affuison;
Mais gardés ke sace ma feme
Que soiés el ke ma parente,
Car defors ma cambre girés,
Douce amie, se vous volés,
Et jou girai à ma moillier.
A Aleus m'estuet repairier

Por mon molin batre et lever;
Adont me vaurai retorner
Et choucerai lé vous, amie."
    Cele s'estut molt esbahie,   F-7
Qui dou mannier n'avoit talent,
Ens en son cuer bon consel prent;
Dist: "Se Diex plaist, n'avenra mie."
    Tout .III. en viènent à la vile   F-1b
De Paluiel chiés le mannier.
Or sont venu au herbegier;
Li manniers apiela sa fame;
Se li dist: "Dame, que vous sanble?   F-3a
Que mangerons-nous au souper?"
    —Sire," chou dist la dame, "assés.   F-4a
Qui est ceste méchine ichi?"   F-3a
100   *—Ma cousine est, sachiés de fi;*   F-5a
Faites li fieste et grant honor."
—Volentiers," la dame respont;
"Bien soiés vous venue, amie."
—Dame," fait el, "Dius bénéie."   F-4b
De mangier n'estuet tenir plait
De chou ke promesse avoit fait;
Pain et vin, car, tarte et poison
Orent assés à grant fuisson.
    Quant orent mangié et béu,
Li lis fu fais, dalès le fu,
U la meschine dut couchier,
Kieute mole, linches molt chier,
Et covertoir chaut et forré.
Li manniers en a apielé
Sa fame, k'il ot espoussée:
"Dame," fait il, "si vous agrée,   F-5a
Volentiers iroie au molin,
Il le m'estuet batre matin;
Il i a molt blé ens ès sas."
La dame dist: "Se Diex mé gart,
Il chou est molt très bon à faire."
A tant li manniers se repaire,
Mais ainchois ot dit à sa feme
Qu'ele pense de sa parente:
"Alés à Diu," chou dist la dame;
"Pis n'aura conme se fust m'ame."
    A tant s'en va. Cele demeure;   F-2b
Del cuer souspire et des iex pleure,   F-4b
Et dist la dame: "K'avés vous?   F-3a
Dites le moi tout par amors;
Nous avons or esté si aisse
Et or nous metés en malaisse.
Qui vous a riens meffait ne dit?"
—Dame," fait el, "se Diex m'aït,   F-4a+F-7
Je me loc molt de vostre ostel,

Mais mes cuers est molt destorbés.
Se je l'osoie descovrir
J'en sui forment en grant desir. "
—Oïl," fait la Dame erramment,
"Dites le moi hardiement.
Jà ne sera si grans anuis
Ne vous en oste, se je puis. "
Dist la pucèle: "Grant merchi;
Jel'vous dirai sans contredit.
Huiman vinc por maure à Aleus,
Et vo barons si me dist leus
Que ne porroie maure à pieche.
Iluec me détria grant pieche;
L'autre gent molut erramment;
150   Le molin clot delivrement,
Car Mousès li ot ensaigniet
Qu'il ot molt poi d'iaue el vivier.
Tant iluec séoir m'i fissent
Que nuis me prist et viespres vinrent;
Chi m'amena por herbegier,
Car vaura dalès moi chouchier,
Se Jhésus et vos ne m'aïe. "
—*Or vous taisié, ma douce amie,*"   self-F-5 + F-8
Fair la dame, ki fu senée;
"Vous en serés bien destornée;
Car vous girés ens en mon lit
En ma cambre tout en serit,
Et jou girai chi en cestui.
Se mes maris i vient encui
Qu'il veulle gesir aveuc vous
Trover m'i porra à estrous
Et soufferai chou k'i vaura. "
La demoisele s'escria:
"Dame," fait ele, "grant merchi;
Bien avés dit, se Diex m'aït,
Il ert mérit, se Dius plaist bien. "
Dist la dame: "Chou croi jou bien;
C'est bien et autre tout ensanble. "
      Atant s'en entrent en la cambre   F-2a
U la pucele se coucha,
Et la dame se retorna.   self-F-5 + F-8
A l'uis s'en vint, si l'entr'ovri,
Puis est venue droit au lit,
Qui fais estoit lès le fouier,
U la pucele dut chouchier.
Ele s'i chouce, plus n'arieste;
Saingna son cors, saigna sa tieste;
A Diu se rent et au Saint pière
Qu'il li doinst bone nuit entière.
      Si fara il, mien ensient,
Se l'aventure ne nous ment,

Car ses maris, manniers qui ert,
Il et Mousès sont repairiet;   F-1b
Par mi la rue vont tout droit;
Del molin viennent ambedoit.
Por jesir avuec la meschine
Revint Jakès, ki le desire;
Mousès l'en a mis à raison:
"Sire," dist il, "par saint Simon,   F-3b + F-6c
Car faites .I. markiet à mi;
Certes j'ai un porchiel nouri,
Il a passé .V. mois entiers;
Celui aurés molt volentiers,
Foi ke doi Diu, sai ite Marie,
200 Se jésir puis o le meschine."
     —Oïl," fait Jakès entresait;   F-4b
"Se guerpir volés, sans nul plait,
Le porcelet ke nouri as,
Gesir te ferai en ses bras."
—Oïl" fait il, "par tel marchiés
Le vous guerpisse volentiers."
—Or m'atent dont à cest perron;
Je m'en irai à no maison.
Se choucerai o la pucele,
Qui tant est gentiex et biele."
Chou dist Mousès: "A Diu alés;
Quant vous poés, si revenés."
     Et Jakès li manniers s'en torne;   F-1b
Dusc'à la maison ne destorne.
Il a trové l'uis entr'overt;
Tout souef l'a arière ouvert;
Ens est entrés, puis le referme;
Mais molt se doute de sa feme,   self-F-5
Qu'il cuide k'en sa chambre gisse,
Mais je cuic la mescine i gisse.
     Au lit en vint, lès le fouier   F-6c
Dalès sa femme tost choucier.   self-F-5
Il cuide che soit la meschine;
Si l'a acolée et baisie;
.V. fois li fist li giu d'amours,
Ains ne se mut nient plus c'uns hors.
Il iert jà près de mie nuit;
Li manniers crient Mouset n'anuit,
Qui l'atent séant à la pière;
Ses demoures forment li griève.
A la dame dist: "Je m'en vois,   self-F-5c
Mais ke n'en aïés irois,
Car il est plus de mie nuit;
Je revenrai encore anuit."   F-4a
—Quant vous poés si revenés,"   F-4b
Et dist la dame, "à Diu alés."
Jakès en est dou lit partis,   F-2a

Si s'est rechauciés et viestis;
Gieut cuide avoir o la pucele;
On li a cangiet le merielle.

   A Mousèt en est retornés,   F-1b
Qui dehors l'uis est akeutés:
"Vien chà, amis, errant jesir;
Je vuel le porcel deservir.
.V. fois ai fait; bien vous hastés;
Or il para quel le ferés."
Che dist Mousès: "Que dirai jou,   F-3a
Quant je venrai en la maison?"
   Et cil a dit: "Au lit alés;   F-4a + self-F-5
250 Se vous chouciés dalé son lés;
Ne dites mot, mais taisiés vous;
Jà nel'saura par nul de nous,
Faites de li vos volentés."

   A tant en est Mousès tornés,   F-2b
Et vint au lit; si se despoulle;   F-1a
Maintenant o la dame chouce.   self-F-5 + F-6b
.V. fois li fist en molt poi d'eure.
A tant Mousès plus n'i demeure;   F-2a
Congiet a pris, si se viesti;
La dame croit, saciés de fi,
Que ce ne soit fors ses barons.
Et cil revint à Jakemon;   F-1b
Se li a dit: "J'ai fait .V. fois."
—Dont a ele éu despois?"
Chou a dit Jakès, li vuihos;
"Li porchiax esciet en mon los."   F-3c
—*Voire," fait Mousès, "en non Dé;*   F-4c
Or venés; prenc, qant vous volés,
Le porcelet, ki estoit mien;
Vous l'enmenrés par le loien."
A tant s'en sont d'illuec parti.   F-2a

     Qant li jours fu bien esclarchi,
La damoisele s'est levée;
Si s'est viestue et atornée.
A la dame congiet a demandet
Et li merchie de son hostel.
Ele li dist: "Ma douce amie,   F-4b
Perdue avés bonne nuitie,
Car mes maris .X. fois ennuit
M'en a donné par grant déduit.
Por vous l'a fait; ne l'en sai gré;
Ou lit vous cuide avoir trové."
—Gret m'en sachiés," fait la mescine.
A tant plus n'arieste ne fine;
A Hestrées tout droit s'en va.   F-2a
Et li manniers tost repaira;   F-1b
Si ammaine le porchelet;
Par dalés lui s'en vint Mousès,

Qui le porciel li ot vendu;
Bien le cuidoit avoir perdu.
   Qant la dame perçut les a,   F-4b+F-5
Sachiés ke pas n'es bienvina,
Le sien marit trestout avant;
Tost li a dit: "Ribaut puant,
.XIIII. ans ai o vous estet;
Ains ne vous poc mais tel mener,
Ne tant acoler, ne basier,
Servir à gré, ne solacier,
300   Que ja iffuse envaïe
.II. fois en une nuit entiere.
Pour la mescine euc, voir, ennuit
.X. fois, u plus, par grant déduit.
Cele m'a fait ceste bontét,
Cui vous cuidastes recovrer.
En mon lit cocha, en non Dé.
Or avés vous cangié le dé."
   Quant Jakemars l'ot, et entent   F-7
Qu'il est vuihos certainnement,
Saciés ke point ne l'abielist,
Et Mousès tout errant li dist: F-7+F-8
"Sire, mon porciel me rendés,
Car à tort et pechiet l'avés."
—Qu'esse, diable?" dit Jakemars.   F-3a
"Tu as ennuit entre les bras
Jut de ma fame et fait ton bel,
Et tu viex r'avoir ton porchiel;
Saces ke tu n'en r'auras mie."
—Si arai," fait Mousès, "biax sire,   F-4a+F-8
Car je duc gire o la pucele,
Qui estoit grasse, tenre et biele,
Ke miex vauroit ele sentir
Que de vo feme nul delit.
Sachiés je m'en irai clamer;
Tost à Oisi vaurai aler."
   Mousès en va droit à Oisi.   F-2c
Si en est clamé au Bailli,   F-9
Et li Baillius les ajorna;   F-2a
A tant Mousès s'en retorna.
   Quant li termes et li jors vint   F-1a
Que li Baillius les siens plais tint,
Li manniers i vint et Mousès
Por conquerre le porchelet.
Mousès a sa raison contèe;   F-4a
Li Eskievin l'ont escoutèe.
Que vous feroie jou lonc conte?
Toute sa raison leur raconte,
Ensi com Jakemès, li cous,
Li ot fali de tout en tout:
"O la pucele deuc jesir;

O sa feme m'a fait jesir,"
Qu'il ne prent mie en paiement,
Ains veut que Jakès li ament,
Car deut jesir o la pucele
Qui tant est avenans et biele.
Se li Esquievin li otrient;
Communaument ensanble dient
Que il li tiegne ses markiés.
 Li manniers est levés en piés: F-4a
"Signor," fait-il, "entendés nous.
350 Je sui vuihos et si sui cous.
Je doi bien cuites aler par tant,
Car sachiés il m'anuie forment
Chou que il avint à ma feme,
Car ses porchiaus ne m'atalente."
Li Baillius a grant ris éut,
Puis si lor a ramentéut:
"Volés de chou oïr le droit?"   F-9
—Oïl," dit Mousès, "par ma foit."
—Et vous, manniers?" fait li Baliu.
"Voire bien, de par Dame-Diu,
Que il me doinst cuites aler."
Li Baillius prist à conjurer
Les Eskievins por dire voir:
"Si ferons nous à no pooir,
Sire," font il, "molt volentiers."
A tant se prendent à consillier;
A ce consel en sont alé;
Plus tost qu'il peurent sont torné:
"Sire," font il, "entendé nous.   F-5d
Par jugement nous disons vous
Ke vous Mousèt faites r'avoir
Son porchelet, car chou est drois,
Et commandés à Jakemon
Qu'il li renge tout, sans tenchon,
U la meschine li r'amaint
Por faire son bon et son plain."
 Li Baillius li a commandé,
Et Jakès li a delivré
Le porchelet tout erramment,
Et li Baillius maintenant prent   F-6f
Par le loien le porchelet,
Et puis si a dit à Mouset:
"Amis, or ne vous en courchiés;
Je vous renderai en deniers
.XXX. sols por le porchelet.
Mangiés sera à grant reviel
Des bons compaingnons del païs."
Jakès s'en part tous esbahis,
Qui demeure chous et vuihos.

Cho fu droit que le honte en ot,   The Conclusion
Car raisons ensaigne et droiture
Que nus ne puet metre sa cure
En mal faire ni en mal dire
Tousjors ne l'en soit siens le pire,
Et ausi fist il le mannier,
Qui en demoura cunquiet,
Mais ne me chaut, chou fu raisons.
Et li Baillius a tout semons
Les escuiers et les puceles,
400   Les chevaliers, les dames bieles;
Si a fait mangier le porciel
A grant joie et à reviel.
        ENGERRANS, li clers, ki d'Oisi
A esté et nés et nori,
Ne vaut pas ke tele aventure
Fust ne périe ne perdue;
Si le nous a mis en escrit
Et vous anonce bien et dist
C'onques ne vous prenge talens
De faire honte à bones gens.
Qui s'en garde, il fait que sages,
Et Dius le nous meche en courage
De faire bien, le mal laissier.
Chi faut li Ronmans del Mannier.

Notes

Introduction

[1] *Recueil général et complet des fabliaux des XIIIe et XIVe siècles,* ed. Anatole de Montaiglon and Gaston Raynaud, 6 vols. (Paris: Librairie des Bibliophiles, 1872-90).

[2] Joseph Bédier, *Les Fabliaux,* 6th ed. (1893; Paris: Champion, 1969), p. 30.

[3] Per Nykrog, *Les Fabliaux* (Copenhagen: Munksgaard, 1957).

[4] Vladimir Propp, *Morphology of the Folktale,* trans. Laurence Scott, 2nd ed. (1958; rpt. Austin: Univ. of Texas Press, 1968).

Chapter 1: The Genre and Its History

[1] Bédier states, "Le plus ancien fabliau qui nous soit parvenu est celui de Richeut; il est daté de 1159. Les plus récents sont de Jean de Condé qui mourut vers 1340" (p. 40). Nykrog, who rejects *Richeut* as a fabliau, states that *Plantez,* the earliest fabliau, was composed around 1200 (p. 4). According to Charles Foulon, Jean Bodel's fabliaux were written in the 1190s (*L'Œuvre de Jean Bodel,* Paris: Presses Universitaires de France, 1958).

[2] The abbreviation MR refers to the *Recueil général et complet des fabliaux des XIIIe et XIVe siècles,* ed. Anatole de Montaiglon and Gaston Raynaud. The Roman numerals refer to the volume numbers. The Arabic numerals refer to the tales and replace Montaiglon's Roman ones. The titles are as they appear in this edition; they appear at times with the definite article, but more often preceded by *de.* Fabliaux taken from Charles H. Livingston's collection of Gautier le Leu's work will be referred to by the letter G, and other fabliaux edited after Montaiglon's collection will be fully identified as to source (*Le Jougleur Gautier le Leu,* Cambridge: Harvard Univ. Press, 1951).

[3] See the Prologue to the *Lais,* "Yonec," and "Bisclavaret."

[4] Jean Rychner, *Contribution à l'étude des fabliaux,* 2 vols. (Genève: Droz, 1960), I, 8.

[5] Of the 141 tales in MR which are considered to be fabliaux by Bédier, only eight have neither an introduction nor a conclusion.

[6] Bédier, p. 25.

[7] Nykrog, p. 3. He insists that in *fabellus* or *fabella* the intervocalic *b* would reduce to *v*: *favelle*. Tobler Lommatzch in *Altfranzösiches Wörterbuch* gives both *fable* and *fablel* as derived from *fabula*, citing the *REW*, the *FEW*, Bédier, and Robert Guiette, "Divertissement sur le mot fabliau," in *Miscellanea J. Gessler* as sources.

[8] Claude Fauchet, *Recueil de l'origine de la langue et poésie françoise, ryme et romans*, in *Les Œuvres du feu M. Claude Fauchet premier président en la cour des monnoyes*, ed. David Le Clerc (Paris: J. de Heuqueville, 1610), p. 558.

[9] Cf. *De Jouglet* (MR IV: 98) by Colin Malet. Fauchet mistook the title for the author, an excusable mistake because the main character, Jouglet, is a *jongleur*, and also because only the version in the manuscript, BM 10289, which Fauchet did not know, is signed.

[10] Fauchet, p. 578.

[11] Anne-Claude-Philippe, le conte de Caylus, "Mémoire sur les fabliaux," in *Mémoires de littérature tirés des registres de l'Académie Royale des Inscriptions et Belles-Lettres* 20 (1744-46) (Amsterdam: François Changuin, [1746?]), pp. 352-76.

[12] Caylus, p. 357.

[13] Caylus, p. 359.

[14] Caylus, p. 358.

[15] Bernard Noël, *Souvenirs de Madame de Caylus* (Paris: Mercure de France, 1965), p. 16.

[16] Anne-Claude-Philippe, le conte de Caylus, *Œuvres badines et galantes du conte de Caylus*, ed. Radeville et Deschamps (Paris: Bibliothèque des Curieux, 1921) and *Ma vie de garçon ou les faits et gestes du vicomte de Nantel* (Paris: Tchou, 1967).

[17] Lionel Gossman, *Medievalism and the Ideologies of the Enlightenment: The World and Work of La Curne de Sainte-Palaye* (Baltimore: Johns Hopkins Univ. Press, 1968), p. 136.

[18] Nykrog, p. xii. Titled *Fabliaux et contes des poètes françois des XII, XIII, XIV, et XVe siècles*, the Barbazan volumes were published as follows: Vol. I (Paris: Vincent, 1756) and Vols. II-III (Amsterdam: Arkstée et Merkus, 1756).

[19] Barbazan, I, xx.

[20] Pierre-Jean-Baptiste, Le Grand d'Aussy, *Fabliaux ou contes du XIIe et du XIIIe siècle traduits ou extraits d'après divers manuscrits du temps*, 4 vols. (Paris: E. Onfroy, 1779).

[21] Nykrog, p. xix.

[22] Victor Le Clerc, "Fabliaux," *Histoire Littéraire de la France,* 23 (1856), p. 90.

[23] Le Clerc, p. 69.

[24] *Nouveau recueil complet des fabliaux,* ed. Willem Noomen and Nico van den Boogaard (Assen: Van Gorcum, 1983-84).

[25] MR I, p. vii-viii.

[26] MR I, p. viii.

[27] MR I, p. ix.

[28] Charles Formentin, *Essai sur les fabliaux français du XIIe et du XIIIe siècle* (St. Etienne: F. Forestier, 1877); Charles Langlois, "La Société du moyen âge d'après les fableaux," *Revue Bleue,* 48 (1891), 227-36, 289-97; Gaston Paris, *La Poésie du Moyen Age,* 2e série (Paris: Hachette, 1895).

[29] Ferdinand Brunetière, "Les Fabliaux du moyen âge et l'origine des contes," *Revue des Deux Mondes,* 119 (1893), 189-213.

[30] Bédier, p. 3.

[31] Bédier, p. 340.

[32] Bédier, p. 30.

[33] Edmond Faral, "Le Fabliau latin au moyen âge," *Romania,* 50 (1924), 321-85.

[34] Faral, p. 384.

[35] Gustave Cohen, *La Comédie latine en France au XIIe siècle,* 2 vols. (Paris: Société d'Edition "Les Belles Lettres," 1931).

[36] Jürgen Beyer, "The Morality of the Amoral," in *The Humor of the Fabliaux* (Columbia: Univ. of Missouri Press, 1974), pp. 24-25. Hereafter referred to as *HF.*

[37] Charles Muscatine, *Chaucer and the French Tradition* (Berkeley: Univ. of California Press, 1957).

[38] Muscatine, *Chaucer,* p. 59.

[39] Muscatine, *Chaucer,* pp. 64-65.

[40] Muscatine, *Chaucer,* p. 66.

[41] Nykrog, p. lv. Nykrog also gives the impression that Bédier was the first to consider the fabliau as a bourgeois genre. It was characterized as such by Montaiglon (MR I, p. viii).

[42] Bédier, p. 382.

[43] Nykrog, p. 69.

[44] Nykrog, p. 104.

[45] Jean Rychner, "Les Fabliaux by Per Nykrog," *RPh*, 12 (1959), p. 338.

[46] Omer Jodogne, "Le Fabliau," in *Typologie des sources du moyen âge occidental*, ed. L. Génicot (Turnhout, Belg.: Brepols, 1975), p. 12.

[47] Omer Jodogne, "Considérations sur le fabliau," in *Mélanges offertes à René Crozet*, ed. Pierre Gallais and Yves-Jean Riou (Poitiers: Société d'Etudes Médiévales, 1966), II, 1043-55; Knud Togeby, "The Nature of the Fabliaux," in *HF*, pp. 7-13; Richard Spencer, "Generic Characteristics of the Fabliaux: A Critique of Nykrog," in *Proceedings: International Beast Epic Colloquium*, Univ. of Glasgow, Sept. 1975, mimeographed sheets, pp. 81-91; Jean Subrenat, "Notes sur la tonalité des fabliaux," *Marche Romane*, 25 (1975), 83-94; Marie-Luce Chênerie, " 'Ces curieux chevaliers tournoyeurs . . .' des fabliaux aux romans," *Romania*, 97 (1976), 327-68.

[48] Per Nykrog, "Courtliness and the Townspeople: The Fabliaux as a Courtly Burlesque," in *HF*, pp. 59-73.

[49] Rychner, *Contribution à l'étude des fabliaux*.

[50] Nico van den Boogaard, "Amplification et abréviation: Les Contes de Haiseau," in *Mélanges de linguistique et de littérature offerts à L. Geschière* (Amsterdam: Rodopi, 1975), pp. 55-69.

[51] Rychner, *Contribution*, I, 146.

[52] Rychner, *Contribution*, I, 32.

[53] Jean Rychner, "Les Fabliaux: Genre, styles, publics," in *La Littérature narrative d'imagination*, Colloque de Strasbourg, 1959 (Paris: Presses Universitaires de France, 1961), pp. 41-54.

[54] Jean Rychner, "Les Fabliaux," in *Le Moyen Age*, Vol. I of *Dictionnaire des lettres françaises* (Paris: Fayard, 1964), p. 271.

[55] Togeby, "The Nature of the Fabliaux," p. 8.

[56] Jodogne, "Le Fabliau," p. 23.

[57] The contents include: Knud Togeby, "The Nature of the Fabliaux"; Jürgen Beyer, "The Morality of the Amoral"; Stephen Wailes, "*Vagantes* and the Fabliaux"; Per Nykrog, "Courtliness and the Townspeople: The Fabliaux as a Courtly Burlesque"; Benjamin Honeycutt, "The Knight and His World as Instruments of Humor in the Fabliaux"; Howard Helsinger, "Pearls in the Swill: Comic Allegory in the French Fabliaux"; Norris Lacy, "Types of Esthetic Distance in the Fabliaux"; Paul Theiner, "Fabliau

Settings"; Thomas Cooke, "Pornography, the Comic Spirit, and the Fabliaux"; and Roy Pearcy, "Modes of Signification and the Humor of Obscene Diction in the Fabliaux."

[58] Charles Muscatine, "The Social Background of the Old French Fabliau," *Genre,* 9 (1976), 1-19.

[59] Thomas D. Cooke, *The Old French and Chaucerian Fabliaux* (Columbia: Univ. of Missouri Press, 1978).

[60] Marie-Thérèse Lorcin, *Façons de sentir et de penser* (Paris: Champion, 1979).

[61] Philippe Ménard, *Les Fabliaux: Contes à rire du moyen âge* (Paris: Presses Universitaires de France, 1983).

[62] Roy Pearcy, "Investigations into the Principles of Fabliau Structure," in *Versions of Medieval Comedy,* ed. Paul Ruggiers (Norman: Univ. of Oklahoma Press, 1977), pp. 67-100.

[63] Pearcy, "Modes of Signification," in *HF,* p. 166.

[64] Pearcy, "Investigations," p. 97.

[65] Willem Noomen, "Structures narratives et force comique: Les Fabliaux," *Neophilologus,* 62 (1978), 361-73.

[66] Nora Scott, *Contes pour rire: Fabliaux des XIIIe et XIVe siècles,* Collection 10/18 (Paris: Union Générale d'Editions, 1977).

[67] Paul Zumthor, in his *Essai de Poétique médiévale* (Paris: Editions du Seuil, 1972). See discussion in Chapter 2 below.

[68] Scott, p. 24.

Chapter 2: The Didacticism of the Fabliau

[1] MR I: 2, 4, 6, 7, 9, 10, 13, 15, 17, 19, 20, 22, 23, 28, MR II: 31, 35, 44, 46, 51, MR III: 57, 58, 61, 65, 67, 76, 79, 80, 86, 87, 88, MR IV: 89, 90, 92, 93, 94, 97, 99, 101, 104, 106, 109, MR V: 110, 111, 112, 116, 118, 121, 122, 123, 125, 126, 129, 131, 132, 133, 135, MR VI: 140, 147, 147 bis in appendix, 148, 149, 150, 151, *Trubert, Del fol vilain* (G 2), *De deux vilains* (G 3), *Disciplina Clericalis* 1, 2, and 3.

[2] Bédier, p. 34. Many of the early critics—Fauchet, Caylus, Le Clerc, and Jeanroy, among others—mentioned their didactic qualities. Most since Bédier see them as primarily comic; nevertheless, theories of their antifeminism (Charles Langlois) or antibourgeois sentiments (Nykrog and his followers) imply a serious purpose. Jodogne refers to them as "exemplaires." Zumthor, Scott, and I see their didacticism partially as a question of

form. I go further to make the case here that their didacticism is pragmatic, not moral in the usual sense.

[3] There are only nineteen introductions which have clear statements about the amusement or moral value of the tales. But of these nineteen, twelve refer to their didactic qualities: MR I: 6, 13, 20, MR III: 79, 80, 87, MR V: 135, MR VI: 140, 149, and *Disciplina Clericalis* 1, 2, and 3.

[4] Zumthor, pp. 339-404.

[5] Zumthor, p. 400.

[6] Zumthor, pp. 400-01.

[7] Beyer, p. 39.

[8] Zumthor, p. 401. See also Nora Scott's discussion in *Contes pour rire*, pp. 27-30.

[9] Zumthor, p. 395.

[10] J.-Th. Welter, *L'Exemplum dans la littérature religieuse et didactique du moyen âge*, (Paris: E. H. Guitard, 1927), p. 79.

[11] Joseph Mosher, *The Exemplum in Early Religious and Didactic Literature of England* (1911; rpt. New York: AMS Press, 1966), p. 6.

[12] Mosher, p. 6.

[13] Welter, p. 80.

[14] Marie-Magdeleine Davy, *Les Sermons universitaires parisiens de 1230-1231,* Etudes de Philosophie Médiévale, 15 (Paris: Librairie Philosophique J. Vrin, 1931), p. 34.

[15] Th.-M. Charland, *Artes Praedicandi: Contribution à l'histoire de la rhétorique au moyen âge,* Publications de l'Institut d'Etudes Médiévales, 7 (Ottawa: Institut d'Etudes Médiévales, 1936), pp. 217-18.

[16] Charland, pp. 217-18.

[17] Davy, p. 32.

[18] Davy, p. 35.

[19] Davy, p. 35.

[20] Welter, p. 102-03.

[21] Welter, p. 103.

[22] Mary Jane Stearns Schenck, "Narrative Structure in the Exemplum, Fabliau, and the Nouvelle," *RR,* 72 (1981), 367-82.

[23] For a lengthier discussion of analogues see the preceding article.

[24] The fabliau *De Guillaume au faucon* (MR II: 35) concludes by advocating perseverance in love. It is one of the fabliaux with a seemingly courtly subject and tone. The wife resists a young boy's declarations of eternal love until the husband proves himself too dense to protect her from the boy's amorous advances. It ends with a fabliau-like pun and then the moral. It may be a mixed genre, a combination of *lai* or *conte sentimentale* and fabliau. The other exception, *Des putains et des lecheors* (MR III: 76), concludes with the implication that clerics are blessed because God gave them the prostitutes when He created the world. The atypical moral goes with an atypical narrative that includes no conflict, an essential characteristic of the genre, as will be demonstrated in Chapter 3.

[25] Petrus Alfonsi, *Die Disciplina Clericalis,* ed. Alfons Hilka and Werner Soderhjelm (Heidelberg: Carl Winter's Universitätsbuchhandlung, 1911), p. 2. The italics in the quotes that follow are mine.

[26] Alfonsi, p. 14.

[27] Petrus Alfonsi, *Disciplina Clericalis: III französische Versbearbeitungen,* ed. Alfons Hilka and Werner Soderjhelm, *Acta. Soc. Scient. Fennicae* [Helsingfor, Finland], 49, No. 4 (1922), 97, vv. 1069-72.

[28] Petrus Alfonsi, *Disciplina Clericalis,* ed. William Henry Hulme, *Western Reserve University Bulletin,* 22, No. 3 (1919), p. 27. Special issue.

[29] Alfonsi (Helsingfor, 1922), see the Introduction.

[30] Alfonsi (Helsingfor, 1922), p. 22, vv. 1141-48.

[31] Alfonsi (Helsingfor, 1922), p. 4, vv. 71-74.

[32] Alfonsi (Helsingfor, 1922), p. 23, vv. 1243-48.

[33] Alfonsi (Helsingfor, 1922), p. 25, vv. 1333-34.

[34] Alfonsi (Helsingfor, 1922), p. 26, vv. 1441-49.

Chapter 3: Deception and Misdeed: The Morphology of the Fabliau

[1] Bédier, p. 187.

[2] Vladimir Propp, *Morphology of the Folktale,* trans. Laurence Scott, 2nd ed. (1958; rpt. Austin: Univ. of Texas Press, 1968). *Morphologie du conte* (Paris: Editions du Seuil, 1970).

[3] Propp, *Morphology of the Folktale,* p. 21.

[4] Propp, *Morphology of the Folktale,* p. 21.

[5] Claude Bremond, "Le Message narratif," *Communications,* 4 (1964), 4-32; "La Logique des possibles narratifs," *Communications,* 8 (1966), 60-76; "Morphology of the French Folktale," *Semiotica,* 2 (1970), 247-76. A.-J. Greimas, *Sémantique structurale* (Paris: Larousse, 1966). Claude Lévi-Strauss, "L'Analyse morphologique des contes russes," *IJSLP,* 3 (1960), 122-49.

[6] Ferdinand de Saussure, *Cours de linguistique générale,* ed. Charles Bally, Albert Sechehaye, and Albert Riedlinger (Lausanne: Payot, 1916).

[7] Bremond, "La Logique des possibles narratifs."

[8] Michel Olsen, *Les Transformations du triangle érotique* (Copenhagen: Akademisk Forlag, 1976).

[9] M. J. S. Schenck, "A Structural Definition of the Old French Fabliau," Diss. Pennsylvania State Univ. 1973; "Morphology of the Fabliau," *Fabula,* 17 (1976), 26-39; "Functions and Roles in the Fabliau," *CL,* 30 (1978), 22-34.

[10] Larry Crist and James A. Lee, "L'Analyse fonctionnelle des fabliaux," in *Etudes de philologie romane et d'histoire littéraire offertes à Jules Horrent* (Liège: Comité d'Hommage à Jules Horrent, 1980), 85-104. Crist and Lee pointed out some lack of parallelism in the labeling for subgroups which I have corrected. I have also modified some of the subgroups themselves. Crist and Lee also showed that a function I had previously identified as complicity is nothing more than a successful deception. I have therefore eliminated that function, but I do not agree with their contention that resolution is not a function. They confused resolution with the author's conclusion.

[11] Propp, *Morphology of the Folktale,* p. 67.

[12] *Du prestre qui dist la passion* MR V: 118, *De Sire Hain et de Dame Anieuse* MR I: 6, *Des putains et des lecheors* MR III: 76, *Du provoire qui menga les meures* MR IV: 92, *Do pré tondu* MR IV: 104, *De la viellete* MR V: 129, and *Del couvoiteus et de l'envieus* MR V: 135.

[13] Pearcy in "Investigations" uses examples of this common comic device to illustrate his theory that fabliaux reflect issues of medieval epistemology.

[14] Bédier, p. 31.

Chapter 4: Victims and Dupers: The Fabliau Dynamic

[1] In the first part of this chapter, the group of typical fabliaux (sixty of the sixty-six self-proclaimed fabliaux) will be the basis for my statistics. The exact figures on the social position of the characters are as follows: aristocracy 45, bourgeoisie 31, clergy 44, *vilain* or lower class 92, and those of indeterminate social standing 46.

[2] Propp, *Morphology of the Folktale,* pp. 79 ff.

[3] There are eleven tales where there is no auxiliary; this phenomenon is usually associated with a doubling or tripling of the duper and victim roles. There are two dupers in *De Gombert* MR I: 22, *Du segretain* MR V: 123, *Du prestre qui ot mere* MR V: 125, and *Le Dit dou soucretain* MR VI: 150. There are two or more victims in *Le Dit des perdriz* MR I: 17, *De deux angloys* MR II: 46, *Des .III. dames* MR IV: 99 and V: 112, and *Del couvoiteus et de l'envieus* MR V: 135. *De la viellete* MR V: 129 has duper, victim, and counselor, and *Do pré tondu* MR IV: 104 has only duper and victim.

[4] Propp, *Morphology of the Folktale,* pp. 39 ff.

[5] Jean Gimpel, *La Revolution industrielle du Moyen Age* (Paris: Editions du Seuil, 1975), p. 17.

[6] The term is used herein as Greimas would use it to designate the actions of characters who establish contracts to perform a service or obtain an object. A.-J. Greimas, *Sémantique structurale* (Paris: Larousse, 1966) and *Du sens* (Paris: Editions du Seuil, 1970).

[7] See discussion of Muscatine's work in Chapter 1. D. W. Robertson, Jr., *A Preface to Chaucer* (Princeton: Princeton Univ. Press, 1962), p. 206.

[8] In dividing a text into functions as has been done for the fabliaux reproduced in the appendices, the first verse of a function is italicized. All of the verses between functions are not necessarily part of the preceding function because they may be only descriptive. Yet, it is correct to say that a function occurs on the average of every ten verses, or that a function is described in approximately ten verses.

[9] Zumthor, pp. 399-400.

[10] Alexander Murray, *Reason and Society in the Middle Ages* (Oxford: Clarendon Press, 1978).

[11] Murray, p. 123.

Chapter 5: Irony as Trope and Myth in the Fabliau

[1] Cf. Faral, "Le Fabliau latin au moyen âge," and Bédier.

[2] Cf. Nykrog, *Les Fabliaux*; Togeby, "Les Fabliaux," *Orbis Litterarum,* 12 (1957), 85-98; and Bédier.

[3] Bédier, p. 333.

[4] Germaine Dempster, *Dramatic Irony in Chaucer,* Language and Literature Series, Vol. 4, No. 3 (Stanford: Stanford Univ. Press, 1932), pp. 28-35.

[5] Norris J. Lacy, "The Fabliaux and Comic Logic," *L'Esprit Créateur,* 16 (1976), pp. 39-45.

[6] Lacy, pp. 41-42.

[7] Charles Baudelaire, "De l'essence du rire," in *Critique d'art,* ed. Claude Pichois (Paris: Armand Colin, 1965), I, 219.

[8] Wayne Booth, *A Rhetoric of Irony* (Chicago: Univ. of Chicago Press, 1974).

[9] Baudelaire, I, 219.

[10] Baudelaire, I, 232.

[11] Paul de Man, "The Rhetoric of Temporality: Allegory and Symbol," in *Interpretation: Theory and Practice,* ed. by C. S. Singleton (Baltimore: Johns Hopkins Univ. Press, 1969), p. 196.

[12] Paul de Man, p. 197.

[13] During the final stages of preparing this ms, I read Howard Bloch's article "Le Mantel mautaillié des fabliaux," *Poétique,* 54 (1983), 181-98. It is an interesting Derridean speculation on the fabliaux which goes much further than my own ideas on their language, although my analysis of ironic doubling is similar to his final comments on their comic nature. His ideas are fascinating, but I find his examples poorly chosen for making comments about the fabliau as a genre, i.e., he uses *Le Roi d'Angleterre et le jongleur d'Ely* and *Des deux bordéors ribauz* to make a legitimate point about the role of language, but one can hardly draw conclusions about the fabliau from these two nonnarrative texts. His Freudian interpretation is credible only if one accepts traditional Freudian theories.

[14] Northrop Frye, "Archetypal Criticism: Theory of Myths," in *Anatomy of Criticism* (New York: Atheneum, 1969), p. 226.

[15] Frye, p. 226.

Chapter 6: A Tale of the People: Conclusions on the Fabliau Ethos

[1] Muscatine, "The Social Background," pp. 1-19.

[2] Muscatine, "The Social Background," p. 5.

[3] Muscatine, "The Social Background," p. 5.

[4] Muscatine, "The Social Background," p. 10.

[5] Muscatine, "The Social Background," p. 18.

[6] Muscatine, "The Social Background," p. 11.

[7] Muscatine, "The Social Background," p. 18.

[8] The predominant regions identified through either place names or authors are Picardy and Flanders. Cf. Bédier, pp. 42-43.

[9] Robert Fossier, *La Terre et les hommes en Picardie jusqu'à la fin du XIIIe siècle* (Paris: Béatrice–Nauwelaerts, 1968).

[10] Fossier, pp. 551-52.

[11] Fossier, p. 731.

[12] Fossier, p. 720.

[13] Fossier, p. 723.

[14] Fossier, p. 554.

[15] Fossier, p. 726.

[16] Fossier, pp. 726-27.

[17] Robert Lopez, "The Crossroads Within the Wall," in *The Historian and the City,* ed. Oscar Handlin and John Burchard (Cambridge, Mass.: M.I.T. Press, 1963), p. 31.

[18] Lopez, p. 32.

[19] Fossier, p. 257.

[20] Murray, p. 98.

[21] Murray, p. 104.

[22] Murray, pp. 122-23.

[23] Murray, p. 119.

[24] Murray, p. 132.

[25] Murray, p. 137.

[26] Miguel de Cervantes, *Don Quixote,* trans. Samuel Putnam (New York: Viking Press, 1949), p. 130.

Bibliography

Editions, Translations, Facsimiles

Barbazan, Etienne. *Fabliaux et contes des poètes françois des XII, XIII, XIV, et XVe siècles, tirés des meilleurs auteurs.* 3 vols. Vol. I. Paris: Vincent; Vol. II and III. Amsterdam: Arkstée et Merkus, 1756.

Dinaux, Arthur Martin. *Trouvères, jongleurs et ménestrels du nord de la France et du Midi de la Belgique.* 3 vols. Paris: J. A. Mercklein, 1836-43.

Douin de Lavesne. *Trubert: Fabliau de 13e siècle.* Ed. Guy Raynaud de Lage. Geneva: Droz, 1974.

DuVal, Jean, and Raymond Eichmann. *Cuckolds, Clerics and Countrymen: Medieval French Fabliaux.* Fayetteville: Univ. of Arkansas Press, 1982.

Eichmann, Raymond, and Jean DuVal. *The French Fabliau: The Ms. B. N. 837.* Vol. I. New York: Garland Publishing Inc., 1983. Vol. II forthcoming.

Faral, Edmond. *Le Manuscrit 19152 du fonds français de la Bibliothèque Nationale.* Paris: Droz, 1934.

Flutre, L. F. "Un manuscrit inconnu de la Bibliothèque de Lyon." *Romania,* 62 (1936), 1-16.

Foerster, W. *"Du vallet qui d'aise à malaise se met."* *Jahrbuch für romanische und englische Sprache und Literatur,* NS 1 (1874), 281-304.

Gillequin, J. *Recueil des fabliaux.* Paris: Rennaissance du Livre, n.d.

Guerrand, R. H. *Fabliaux, contes et miracles du moyen âge.* Paris: Le Livre Club du Librairie, 1963.

Guggenheim, Georges. *Trois aveugles de Compiègne.* Paris: Champion, 1932.

Guiette, Robert. *Fabliaux et contes.* Paris: Le Club du Meilleur Livre, 1960.

Harrison, Robert. *Gallic Salt.* Berkeley: Univ. of California Press, 1974.

155

Hellman, Robert, and Richard O'Gorman. *Fabliaux: Ribald Tales from the Old French.* New York: Corwell, 1965.

Johnston, Ronald C., and D. D. R. Owen. *Fabliaux.* Oxford: Blackwell, 1957.

Jubinal, Achille. *Nouveau recueil de contes, dits, fabliaux et autres poésies inédits des XIIIᵉ et XVᵉ siècles.* 2 vols. Paris: E. Pannier, 1839-42.

Lacy, Norris Joiner. *"La Femme au tombeau*: An Anonymous Fabliau of the 13th Century." Diss. Indiana Univ. 1967.

Långfors, Arthur. *"Le Dit de la Dame Jouenne."* Romania, 45 (1918-19), 99-109.

————. "Le Fabliau du *Moine."* Romania, 44 (1915-17), 559-63.

————. *Huon le roi, "Le Vair Palefroi" avec deux versions de "La male Honte."* Paris: Champion, 1912.

Lecompte, I. C. *"Richeut*: Old French Poem of the Twelfth Century." *RR*, 4 (1913), 261-305.

Le Grand d'Aussy, Pierre-Jean-Baptiste. *Fabliaux et contes du XIIᵉ et du XIIIᵉ siècle traduits ou extraits d'après divers manuscrits du temps.* 4 vols. Paris: E. Onfroy, 1779.

Livingston, Charles H. "The Fabliau *Des deux anglois et de l'anel."* PMLA, 40 (1925), 217-24.

Ménard, Philippe, ed. *Fabliaux français du Moyen Age.* Vol. I. Geneva: Droz, 1979.

Méon, M. *Fabliaux et contes des poètes françois des XI, XII, XIII, XIV, et XVᵉ siècles, tirés des meilleurs auteurs; publiés par Barbazan.* Paris: B. Warée oncle, 1808.

————. *Nouveau recueil de fabliaux et contes inédits des poètes français des XIIᵉ, XIIIᵉ, XIVᵉ, et XVᵉ siècles.* 2 vols. Paris: Chasseriau, 1823.

Meyer, Paul. *"La Housse partie."* Romania, 37 (1908), 215-17.

Michel, Francisque. *Romans, lais, fabliaux, contes, moralités et miracles inédits des XIIᵉ et XIIIᵉ siècles.* Vol. I. Paris: Silvestre, 1833.

Montaiglon, Anatole de, and Gaston Raynaud, eds. *Recueil général et complet des fabliaux des XIIIᵉ et XIVᵉ siècles.* 6 vols. Paris: Librairie des Bibliophiles, 1872-90.

Morawski, J. *"Le Prêtre pelé."* Romania, 55 (1929), 542-48.

Nardin, Pierre. *Les Fabliaux de Jean Bodel.* 2nd ed. Paris: Nizet, 1965.

Noomen, Willem, and Nico van den Boogaard. *Nouveau recueil complet des fabliaux.* 2 vols. Assen: Van Gorcum, 1983-84.

O'Gorman, Richard. *"Les Braies au cordelier": Anonymous Fabliau of the Thirteenth Century.* Birmingham, Ala.: Summa Publications, 1983.

Omont, Henri. *Fabliaux, dits et contes en vers français du XIIIe siècle.* Paris: Fondation Delrousse, Institut de France, 1932.

Raynaud, Gaston. "Une Nouvelle Version du fabliau de *La Nonette.*" *Romania,* 34 (1905), 279-83.

Reid, T. B. W. *Twelve Fabliaux from the Manuscript Fr. 19152 of the Bibliothèque Nationale.* Manchester, Eng.: Manchester Univ. Press, 1958.

Robert, A. C. M. *Fabliaux inédits tirés du MS de la Bibliothèque du Roi n° 1830 et 1239.* Paris: E. Cabin, 1834.

Scheler, A. *Trouvères belges du XIIe au XIVe siècles: Chansons d'amour, jeux parties, pastourelles, dits et fabliaux par Quenes de Bethune, Henri III duc du Brabant.* Brussels: M. Clossen et Cie, 1876.

Wright, Thomas. *Anecdota Literaria: A Collection of Short Poems in English, Latin and French.* London: J. R. Smith, 1844.

Critical Studies on the Fabliau

Bédier, Joseph. *Les Fabliaux.* 6th ed. 1893; Paris: Champion, 1969.

Bergerfurth, Wolfgang. "'Des fables fait on les fabliaus': Zum Verhältnis von Fabel und Fablel." In *Festschrift für Rupprecht Rohr zum 60 Geburtstag.* Ed. Bergerfurth, Diekmann, and Winkelman. Heidelberg, Gross: 1979.

Beyer, Jürgen. "The Morality of the Amoral." In *The Humor of the Fabliaux.* Ed. Thomas D. Cooke and Benjamin Honeycutt. Columbia: Univ. of Missouri Press, 1974, pp. 15-42. (This volume subsequently referred to as *HF.*)

————. *Schwank und Moral.* Heidelberg: C. Winter, 1969.

Bloch, R. Howard. "Le Mantel mautaillié des fabliaux." *Poétique,* 54 (1983), 181-98.

Boogaard, Nico van den. "Amplification et abréviation: Les Contes de Haiseau." In *Mélanges de linguistique et de littérature offerts à L. Geschière.* Amsterdam: Rodopi, 1975, pp. 55-69.

————. *"Le Nouveau Recueil complet des fabliaux."* *Neophilologus,* 61 (1977), 333-46.

Brewer, D. S. "The Fabliaux." In *Companion to Chaucer Studies.* Ed. Beryl Rowland. New York: Oxford Univ. Press, 1979.

Brunetière, Ferdinand. "Les Fabliaux du moyen âge et l'origine des contes." *Revue des Deux Mondes,* 119 (1893), 189-213.

Burbridge, Roger T. "Chaucer's Reeve's Tale and the Fabliau 'Le Meunier et les II clers.' " *AnM,* 12 (1971), 30-36.

Caylus, Anne-Claude-Philippe, le conte de. "Mémoire sur les fabliaux." *Mémoires de littérature tirés des registres de l'Académie Royale des Inscriptions et Belles-Lettres,* 20 (1744-46). Amsterdam: François Changuin, [1746?], pp. 352-76.

Chênerie, Marie-Luce. " 'Ces curieux chevaliers tournoyeurs . . .' des fabliaux aux romans." *Romania,* 97 (1976), 327-68.

Clouston, W. A. "The Lady and Her Suitors." In *Popular Tales and Fictions.* Edinburgh: Blackwood, 1887.

Cluzel, Irénée. "Le Fabliau dans la littérature provençale du Moyen Age." *Annales du Midi,* 66 (1954), 317-26.

Cohen, Gustave. *La Comédie latine en France au XIIᵉ siècle.* 2 vols. Paris: Société d'Edition "Les Belles Lettres," 1931.

Cooke, Thomas D. "Formulaic Diction and the Artistry of 'Le Chevalier qui recovra l'amor de sa dame.' " *Romania,* 94 (1973), 232-40.

———. *The Old French and Chaucerian Fabliaux: A Study of Their Comic Climax.* Columbia: Univ. of Missouri Press, 1978.

———. "Pornography, the Comic Spirit, and the Fabliaux." In *HF,* pp. 137-62.

———, and Benjamin Honeycutt. *The Humor of the Fabliaux.* Columbia: Univ. of Missouri Press, 1974.

Cosquin, Emmanuel. "Le Conte de l'honnête femme et les galants." In *Etudes folkloriques.* Paris: Champion, 1922, pp. 457-73.

Crist, Larry, and James A. Lee. "L'Analyse fonctionnelle des fabliaux." In *Etudes de philologie romane et d'histoire littéraire offertes à Jules Horrent.* Liège: Comité d'hommage à Jules Horrent, 1980, pp. 85-104.

Delbouille, Maurice. "En relisant Rutebeuf." *Marche Romane,* 10 (1960), 147-58.

———. "Les Romans et les contes courtois" and "Les Fabliaux et *Le Roman de Renart.*" In *Histoire illustrée des lettres françaises de Belgique.* 2 vols. Bruxelles: Rennaissance du Livre, 1958.

Dempster, Germaine. *Dramatic Irony in Chaucer.* Language and Literature Series, Vol. 4, No. 3. Stanford: Stanford Univ. Press, 1932.

———, and William Frank Bryan. *Sources and Analogues of Chaucer's Canterbury Tales.* New York: Humanities Press, 1958.

Bibliography 159

Dronke, Peter. "The Rise of the Medieval Fabliau: Latin and Vernacular Evidence." *RF,* 85 (1973), 275-97.

DuVal, Jean. "Medieval French Fabliaux." *Lazarus,* 1 (1980), 8-49.

———. *"Les Tresces*: Semi-Tragical Fabliau, Critique and Translation." *Publications of the Missouri Philological Association,* 3 (1979), 7-16.

———. "The Wright's Chaste Wife: A Satiric Fabliau." *Publications of the Missouri Philological Association,* 2 (1977), 8-14.

Eichmann, Raymond. "The Anti-Feminism of the Fabliaux." *French Literature Series,* 6 (1979), 26-34.

———. "The Artistry of Economy in the *Fabliaux." SSF,* 17 (1980), 67-73.

———. "The Question of Variants and the Fabliaux." *Fabula,* 17 (1976), 40-44.

———. "The Search for Originals in the Fabliau and the Validity of Textual Descendency." *RomN,* 19 (1978), 90-97.

Faral, Edmond. "Le Fabliau latin au moyen âge." *Romania,* 50 (1924), 321-85.

Flutre, L. F. "Le Fabliau, genre courtois." *Frankfurter Universithätsreden,* 22 (1960), 70-84.

Follain, J. "Les Fabliaux." *Tableau de la littérature française.* Paris: Gallimard, 1962, pp. 84-88.

Formentin, Charles. *Essai sur les fabliaux français du XIIᵉ et du XIIIᵉ siècle.* St. Etienne: F. Forestier, 1877.

Foulet, Lucien. "Le Poém de *Richeut* et *Le Roman de Renard." Romania,* 42 (1913), 321-30.

Foulon, Charles. *L'Œuvre de Jehan Bodel.* Travaux de la Faculté de Lettres et Sciences Humaines de l'Université de Rennes, Ser. 1, Vol. 2. Paris: Presses Universitaires de France, 1958.

Gabriel, Astrik L. "The Source of the Anecdote of the Inconstant Scholar." *Classica et Mediaevalia,* 19 (1958), 152-76.

Goodahl, Peter. " 'The Reeve's Tale,' 'Le Meunier et les II clercs,' and 'The Miller's Tale.' " *Parergon,* 27 (1980), 13-16.

Guerlin de Guer, Charles. "Le Comique et l'humour à travers les âges: Les Fabliaux." *Revue des Cours et Conférences,* 28 (1926), 325-50.

Guiette, Robert. "Divertissement sur le mot fabliau." *Miscellanea J. Gessler.* Vol. I. Ed. K. C. Peeters. Deurne: C. Govaerts, 1948, pp. 566-69.

Guiette, Robert. "Note sur le fabliau du Mari Confesseur." *Revue Belge de Philologie et d'histoire*, 20 (1941), 117-26.

Hart, Walter Morris. "The Fabliau and Popular Literature." *PMLA*, 23 (1908), 329-74.

————. "The Narrative Art of the Old French Fabliau." *Kitteredge Anniversary Papers*. Boston: Ginn, 1913, pp. 209-16.

————."The Reeve's Tale: A Comparative Study of Chaucer's Narrative Art." *PMLA*, 23 (1908), 1-44.

Henry, Charles. "The Grip of Winter in 'Des trois boçus' an Old French Fabliau." *CLS*, 17 (1980), 260-67.

Herrmann, Léon. "La Matrone d'Ephèse dans Pétrone et dans Phèdre." *Bulletin de l'Association G. Budé*, 14 (1927), 20-57.

Holbrook, Richard. "The Printed Text of Four Fabliaux in the *Recueil général et complet des fabliaux*." *MLN*, 20 (1905), 193-97.

Holmes, Urban T. "Notes on the French Fabliau." *Middle Ages, Reformation: Volkskiende, Festschrift for John G. Kunstmann*. Chapel Hill: Univ. of North Carolina Press, 1959.

Honeycutt, Benjamin L. "An Example of Comic Cliché in the Old French Fabliau." *Romania*, 96 (1975), 245-55.

————. "The Knight and His World." In *HF*, pp. 75-92.

Jeanroy, A. "Fabliaux." *Histoire de la nation française*. Vol. 12. Ed. Hanotaux. Paris: Plon–Nourrit, 1921, pp. 318-22.

Jodogne, Omer. "Considérations sur le fabliau." In *Mélanges offerts à René Crozet*. Ed. Pierre Gallais and Yves-Jean Riou. Poitiers: Société d'Etudes Médiévales, 1966, II, 1043-55.

————. "Le Fabliau." In *Typologie des sources du moyen âge occidental*. Ed. L. Génicot. Turnhout, Belg.: Brepols, 1975, p. 7.

Kasprzyk, Krystyna. "Pour la sociologie du fabliau: Convention, tactique, et engagement." *Kwartalnik Neofilologiczy*, 23 (1976), 153-61.

Kieson, Reinhard. *Die Fabliaux*. Rheinfelden: Schäuble, 1976.

Koenig, V. F. "Further Notes on Gautier de Coinsi." *MP*, 35 (1937-38), 353-58.

Lacy, Gregg. "Augustinian Imagery and Fabliau 'Obscenity.'" In *Studies on the Seven Sages*. Honolulu: ERA, 1978, pp. 219-30.

————. "Fabliau Stylistic Humor." *KRQ*, 26 (1979), 349-57.

Lacy, Norris J. "The Fabliaux and Comic Logic." *L'Esprit Créateur*, 16 (1976), 39-45.

————. "Types of Esthetic Distance in the Fabliaux." In *HF*, pp. 107-17.

Ladd, Anne. "Classification of the Fabliaux by Plot Structure." In *Proceedings: Interntional Beast Epic Colloquium*. Univ. of Glasgow. Sept. 1975. Mimeographed sheet pp. 92-107.

Långfors, A. "Le Fabliau découvert à Lyon et le MS 345 de Berne." *Romania*, 62 (1936 392-95; and *Romania*, 64 (1938), 252-55.

Langlois, Charles. "La Société du moyen âge d'après les fableaux." *Revue Bleue*, 4 (1891), 227-36 and 289-97.

Langlois, Ernest. "Fabliaux." *Jahresbericht für romanische philologie*, 5 (1897-98), 102-0!

Le Clerc, Victor. "Fabliaux." *HLF*, 23 (1856), 69-215.

Lecoy, Felix. "Analyse thématique et critique littéraire: Le Cas du 'fabliau.'" *Actes d 5ème congrès des romanistes scandinaves*. Turku, Finland: Univ. of Turku, 197: pp. 17-31.

————. "Note sur le fabliau du *Prêtre au lardier*." *Romania*, 82 (1961), 524-35.

————. "A propos du fabliau du *Prêtre au lardier*." *Romania*, 83 (1962), 407-08.

Legry-Rosier, J. "Mss de contes et de fabliaux." *Bulletin de l'Information de l'Institu de Recherche et d'Histoire des Textes*, 4 (1955), 37-47.

Lejeune, Rita. "Hagiographie et grivoiserie: A propos d'un dit de Gautier le Leu." *RPh*, 1 (1958-59), 355-65.

————. "La Patrie de Gautier le Leu." *Le Moyen Age*, 47 (1937), 1-21.

Lesouds, L. *L'Esprit gaulois au moyen âge: Les Fabliaux*. Paris: P. Sevin fils et L. Sarra 1908.

Leupin, Alexandre. "Le Sexe dans la langue: La Dévoration: Sur *Du C.*, fabliau du XIII siècle de Gautier le Leu." *Poétique*, 12 (1981), 91-110.

Lindgren, Lauri. "Courtebarbe auteur de 'Trois aveugles de Compiègne' est-il aussi l'auteu du fabliau du 'Chevalier à la robe vermeille'?" *Mélanges de philologie et de linguistique offerts à Tauno Nurmela*. Annales Universitatis Turkuensis. Ser. B. T. 103. Turkt Finland: Univ. of Turku, 1967.

Livingston, Charles. "Explication d'une allusion littéraire." *RR*, 31 (1940), 112-13.

————. "The Fabliau 'Des deux anglois et de l'anel.'" *PMLA*, 40 (1925), 217-24.

————. "The Jongleur Gautier le Leu." *RR*, 15 (1924), 1-67.

Livingston, Charles. *Le Jongleur Gautier le Leu.* Cambridge: Harvard Univ. Press, 1951.

Lorcin, Marie-Thérèse. *Façons de sentir et de penser: Les Fabliaux français.* (Essais 6) Paris: Champion, 1979.

———. "La Prostituée des fabliaux: Est-elle intégrée ou exclue?" *Sénéfiance,* 5 (1978), 107-18.

———. "Quand les princes n'épousaient pas les bergères ou mesalliance et classes d'âge dans les fabliaux." *Medioevo Romanzo,* 3 (1976), 195-228.

———. "Les Voyages ne forment que la jeunesse; ou le voyageur et l'étranger dans les fabliaux." *Sénéfiance,* 2 (1976), 453-70.

McClintock, Michael W. "Games and the Players of Games: Old French Fabliaux and the Shipman's Tale." *Chaucer Review,* 5 (1970), 112-36.

Ménard, Philippe. *Les Fabliaux: Contes à rire du moyen âge.* Paris: Presses Universitaires de France, 1983.

Micha, A. "A propos d'un fabliau." *Le Moyen Age,* 55 (1949), 17-20.

Muscatine, Charles. *Chaucer and the French Tradition.* Berkeley: Univ. of California Press, 1957.

———. "The Social Background of the Old French Fabliau." *Genre,* 9 (1976), 1-19.

Nardin, Pierre. *Lexique comparé des fabliaux de Jean Bodel.* Paris: Droz, 1942.

Noomen, Willem. "Qu'est-ce qu'un fabliau?" In *XIV Congresso Internazionale di linguistica e filologia romanza.* Ed. Alberto Várvaro. Naples: Macchiaroli, 1981, pp. 421-32.

———. "Structures narratives et force comique: Les Fabliaux." *Neophilologus,* 62 (1978), 361-73.

Nykrog, Per. "Courtliness and the Townspeople: The Fabliaux as a Courtly Burlesque." In *HF,* pp. 59-73.

———. *Les Fabliaux: Etude d'histoire littéraire et de stylistique médiévale.* Copenhagen: Munksgaard, 1957.

Olsen, Michel. "Structure de la nouvelle des fabliaux à la renaissance: Essai d'une typologie." *Actes du 5ème congrès des romanistes scandinaves.* Turku, Finland: Univ. of Turku, 1972, pp. 137-47.

———. *Les Transformations du triangle érotique.* Copenhagen: Akademisk Forlag, 1976.

Olson, Glending. "The Medieval Theory of Literature for Refreshment and Its Use in the Fabliau Tradition." *RPh,* 71 (1974), 241-313.

Olson, Glending. " 'The Reeve's Tale' and 'Gombert.' " *MLR*, 64 (1969), 721-25.

———. " 'The Reeve's Tale' as a Fabliau." *MLQ*, 35 (1974), 219-30.

Paris, Gaston. "Les Contes orientaux dans la littérature française du moyen âge." *La Poésie du Moyen Age.* 2e série. Paris: Hachette, 1895, pp. 75-108.

Patzer, Otto. "The Wealth of the Clergy in the Fabliaux." *MLN*, 19 (1904), 195-96.

Payen, Jean-Charles. " 'Trubert' ou le triomphe de la marginalité." *Sénéfiance*, 5 (1978), 121-32.

Pearcy, Roy. "Chansons de Geste and Fabliaux: 'La Gageure' and 'Berenger au long cul.' " *NM*, 79 (1978), 76-83.

———. "A Classical Analogue to 'Le Preudome qui rescolt son compere de noier.' " *RomN*, 12 (1971), 1-6.

———. "An Instance of Heroic Parody in the Fabliaux." *Romania*, 98 (1977), 105-07.

———. "Investigations into the Principles of Fabliau Structure." In *Versions of Medieval Comedy.* Ed. Paul Ruggiers. Norman: Univ. of Oklahoma Press, 1977, pp. 67-100.

———. "Modes of Signification and the Humor of Obscene Diction in the Fabliaux." In *HF*, pp. 163-96.

———. " 'Le Prestre qui menga les meures' and Ovid's 'Fasti,' III 745-760." *RomN*, 15 (1974), 1-5.

———. "Realism and Religious Parody in the Fabliaux: Watriquet de Couvin's 'Les Trois Dames de Paris.' " *Revue Belge de Philologie et d'Histoire*, 50 (1972), 744-54.

———. "Relations between the D and A Versions of 'Bérenger au long cul.' " *RomN*, 14 (1972), 1-6.

———. "Structural Models for the Fabliaux and the Summoner's Tale Analogues." *Fabula*, 15 (1974), 103-13.

Pillet, Alfred. "Ueber den gegenwärtigen stand des Fableaux-Forschung." *Neuphilologisches Zentralblatt*, 17 (1903), 98-104.

Pitcher, Edward. "A Note on the Source of 'The Child of Snow' and 'The Son of Snow.' " *Early American Literature*, 13 (1978), 215-16.

Rohnström, Otto. *Etude sur Jehan Bodel.* Upsala: Almqvist et Wiksell, 1900.

Rowland, Beryl. "What Chaucer did to the Fabliau." *SN*, 51 (1979), 205-13.

Rychner, Jean. *Contribution à l'étude des fabliaux: Variantes, remaniements, dégradations.* 2 vols. Genève: Droz, 1960.

Rychner, Jean. "Les Fabliaux." In *Le Moyen Age*. Vol. I of *Dictionnaire des lettres françaises*. Paris: Fayard, 1964.

———. "*Les Fabliaux* by Per Nykrog." *RPh*, 12 (1959), 336-39.

———. "Les Fabliaux: Genre, styles, publics." In *La Littérature narrative d'imagination*. Colloque de Strasbourg, 1959. Paris: Presses Universitaires de France, 1961, pp. 41-54.

Schenck, Mary Jane Stearns. "Functions and Roles in the Fabliau." *CL*, 30 (1978), 22-34.

———. "Morphology of the Fabliau." *Fabula*, 17 (1976), 26-39.

———. "Narrative Structure in the Exemplum, Fabliau, and the Nouvelle." *RR*, 72 (1981), 367-82.

———. "A Structural Definition of the Old French Fabliau." Diss. Pennsylvania State Univ. 1973.

Schofield, W. H. "The Source and History of the Seventh Novel of the Seventh Day of *The Decameron*." *Harvard Studies and Notes in Philology and Literature*, 2 (1893), 185-212.

Scott, Nora. *Contes pour rire: Fabliaux des XIIIe et XIVe siècles*. Collection 10/18. Paris: Union Générale d'Editions, 1977.

Spencer, Richard. "The Courtois-Vilain Nexus in *La male Honte*." *Medium Ævum*, 37 (1968), 272-92.

———. "Generic Characteristics of the Fabliaux: A Critique of Nykrog." In *Proceedings: International Beast Epic Colloquium*. Univ. of Glasgow. Sept. 1975. Mimeographed sheets, pp. 81-91.

Subrenat, Jean. "Notes sur la tonalité des fabliaux." *Marche Romane*, 25 (1975), 83-94.

Suchier, W. "Fabelstudien." *ZRP*, 42 (1922), 561-605.

Taylor, James. "Animal Tales as Fabliaux." In *Reading Medieval Studies*. Ed. John Norton Smith and Peter Nobel. Oxford: Oxford Univ. Press, 1977.

Theiner, Paul. "Fabliau Settings." In *HF*, pp. 119-36.

Tiemann, Hermann. "Bemerkungen sur Entstehungsgeschichte der Fabliaux." *RF*, 72 (1960), 406-22.

Togeby, Knud. "Les Fabliaux." *Orbis Litterarum*, 12 (1957), 85-98.

———. "The Nature of the Fabliaux." In *HF*, pp. 7-13.

Wailes, Stephen L. "The Unity of the Fabliau: Un Chivalier et sa dame et un clerk." *RomN*, 3 (1973), 593-96.

Wailes, Stephen L. "*Vagantes* and the Fabliaux." In *HF*, pp. 43-58.

Walkley, M. J. "The Fabliaux as a Guide to 'Lifemanship' in Medieval France." *Parergon*, 25 (1979), 33-38.

Warren, Glenda L. "Maris et femmes dans les fabliaux." *Chimères*, 13 (1980), 29-42.

White, Sarah Melhado. "Sexual Language and Human Conflict in Old French Fabliaux." *Comparative Studies in Society and History*, 24 (1982), 185-210.

Williams, Harry F. "French Fabliau Scholarship." *SAMLA Bulletin*, 46 (1981), 76-82.

General Works Including Other Works Cited

Alfonsi, Petrus. *Die Disciplina Clericalis*. Ed. Alfons Hilka and Werner Soderhjelm. Heidelberg: Carl Winter's Universitätsbuchhandlung, 1911.

————. *Disciplina Clericalis*. Ed. William Henry Hulme. *Western Reserve University Bulletin*, 22, No. 3 (1919). Special issue.

————. *Disciplina Clericalis: III französische Versbearbeitungen*. Ed. Alfons Hilka and Werner Soderhjelm. *Acta. Soc. Scient. Fennicae* [Helsingfor, Finland], 49, No. 4 (1922). Special issue.

Alter, Jean V. *Les Origines de la satire anti-bourgeoise en France au moyen-âge*. Geneva: Droz, 1966.

Barbazan, Etienne, ed. *Le Castoiement, ou instruction du père à son fils: Ouvrage moral en vers composé dans le treizième siècle*. Lausanne-Paris: Vincent, 1760.

Bremond, Claude. "La Logique des possibles narratifs." *Communications*, 8 (1966), 60-76.

————. "Le Message narratif." *Communications*, 4 (1964), 4-32.

————. "Morphology of the French Folktale." *Semiotica*, 2 (1970), 247-76.

Caylus, Anne-Claude-Philippe, le conte de. *Ma vie de garçon ou les faits et gestes du vicomte de Nantel*. Paris: Tchou, 1967.

————. *Œuvres badines et galantes du conte de Caylus*. Ed. Radeville et Deschamps. Paris: Bibliothèque des Curieux, 1921.

Charland, Th.M. *Artes Praedicandi: Contribution à l'histoire de la rhétorique au moyen âge*. Publications de l'Institut d'Etudes Médiévales, 7. Ottawa: Institut d'Etudes Médiévales, 1936.

Cohen, Gustav. "La Comédie latine en France au XIIᵉ siècle." *Mélanges de linguistique et de littérature offerts à M. Alfred Jeanroy.* Paris: Droz, 1928, pp. 255-63.

———. *La Comédie latine en France au XIIᵉ siècle.* 2 vols. Paris: Société d'Edition "Les Belles Lettres," 1931.

Crane, Thomas F. "Mediaeval Sermon-Books and Stories." *Proceedings of the American Philosophical Society,* 21 (1883-84), 49-78; 56 (1917), 369-402.

Davy, Marie-Magdeleine. *Les Sermons universitaires parisiens de 1230-1231.* Etudes de Philosophie Médiévale, 15. Paris: Librairie Philosophique J. Vrin, 1931.

Delbouille, Maurice. "En relisant Rutebeuf." Rev. of Rutebeuf. *Œuvres complètes.* Ed. Edmond Faral. *Marche Romane,* 10 (1960), 147-58.

Dubuis, Roger. *"Les Cent Nouvelles Nouvelles" et la tradition de la nouvelle en France au moyen âge.* Grenoble: Presses Universitaires de France, 1973.

———. "La Genèse de la nouvelle en France au moyen âge." *Cahiers de l'Association International des Etudes Françaises,* 18 (1966), 9-20.

Espiner-Scott, Janet G. *Claude Fauchet, sa vie, son œuvre.* 2 vols. Paris: Droz, 1938.

Faral, Edmond. *Les Arts poétiques du XIIᵉ et du XIIIᵉ siècle: Recherches et documents sur la technique littéraire du moyen âge.* Paris: Champion, 1924.

Fauchet, Claude. *Recueil de l'origine de la langue et poésie françoise ryme et romans.* In *Les Œuvres du feu M. Claude Fauchet premier président en la cour des monnoyes.* Ed. David Le Clerc. Paris: J. de Heuqueville, 1610.

Fossier, Robert. *La Terre et les hommes en Picardie jusqu'à la fin du XIIIᵉ siècle.* Paris: Béatrice–Nauwelaerts, 1968.

Frappier, Jean. "Remarques sur la structure du lai, essai de définition et de classement." In *La Littérature narrative d'imagination.* Paris: Presses Universitaires de France, 1961.

Frye, Northrop. *Anatomy of Criticism: Four Essays.* New York: Atheneum Press, 1969.

Gimpel, Jean. *La Revolution industrielle du Moyen Age.* Paris: Editions du Seuil, 1975.

Gossman, Lionel. *Medievalism and the Ideologies of the Enlightenment: The World and Work of La Curne de Sainte-Palaye.* Baltimore: Johns Hopkins Univ. Press, 1968.

Greimas, A.-J. *Du sens.* Paris: Editions du Seuil, 1970.

———. *Sémantique structurale.* Paris: Larousse, 1966.

Krappe, Alexander H. *The Science of Folklore.* London: Methuen and Co., 1930.

Langlois, Ernest. "Littérature goliardique." *Revue Bleue,* 50 (1892), 807.

Langlois, Ernest. *Recueil d'arts de seconde rhétorique.* Paris: Imprimerie Nationale, 1902.

Lecoy, Félix. "Sur un passage difficile de Rutebeuf." *Romania,* 85 (1964), 368-72.

Lecoy de la Marche, Albert. *Anecdotes historiques, légendes et apologues tirés du recueil inédit d'Etienne du Bourbon.* Paris: Société de l'Histoire de France, 1877.

Lenient, Charles Felix. *La Satire en France du moyen âge.* 3rd ed. Paris: L. Hachette et Cie, 1883.

Lévi-Strauss, Claude. "L'Analyse morphologique des contes russes." *IJSLP,* 3 (1960), 122-49.

————. *La Pensée sauvage.* Paris: Plon, 1962.

Lopez, Robert. "The Crossroads Within the Wall." In *The Historian and the City.* Ed. Oscar Handlin and John Burchard. Cambridge, Mass.: M.I.T. Press, 1963.

Mosher, Joseph. *The Exemplum in Early Religious and Didactic Literature of England.* 1911; rpt. New York: AMS Press, 1966.

Murray, Alexander. *Reason and Society in the Middle Ages.* Oxford: Clarendon Press, 1978.

Noël, Bernard. *Souvenirs de Madame de Caylus.* Paris: Mercure de France, 1965.

Paris, Gaston. "La Nouvelle française aux XVe et XVIe siècles." *Mélanges de la littérature française du moyen âge.* Paris: Champion, 1912.

Pauphilet, Albert. *Le Moyen Age: Histoire de la littérature française.* Vol. I. Ed. Strowski and Moulinier. Paris: Delalain, 1937.

Petit de Julleville, Louis. *Histoire de la langue et littérature française.* 2 vols. Paris: A. Colin, 1896-99.

Propp, Vladimir. *Morphologie du conte.* Trans. Marguerite Derrida, Tzvetan Todorov, and Claude Kahn. Paris: Editions du Seuil, 1970.

————. *Morphology of the Folktale.* Trans. Laurence Scott. Publications of the American Folklore Society. Vol. 9. 2nd ed. 1958; rpt. Austin: Univ. of Texas Press, 1968.

Robertson, D. W., Jr. *A Preface to Chaucer.* Princeton: Princeton Univ. Press, 1962.

Saussure, Ferdinand de. *Cours de linguistique générale.* Ed. Charles Bally, Albert Sechehaye, and Albert Riedlinger. Lausanne: Payot, 1916.

Smith, M. Ellwood. "The Fable and Kindred Forms." *Journal of English and German Philology,* 14 (1915), 519-29.

————. "A Classification for Fables Based on the Collection of Marie de France." *MP,* 15 (1917-18), 477-89.

The Fabliaux

Söderhjelm, Werner. *La Nouvelle française au XVe siècle*. Paris: Champion, 1910.

Swan, Charles, ed. *Gesta Romanorum*. London: G. Bell and Sons, 1882.

Thompson, Stith. *The Folktale*. New York: Dryden Press, 1946.

Vinaver, Eugene. "A la recherche d'une poétique médiévale." *Cahiers de Civilisation Médiévale*, 2 (1959), 1-16.

Welter, J.-Th. *L'Exemplum dans la littérature religieuse et didactique du moyen âge*. Paris: E. H. Guitard, 1927.

Wilson, G. A. *Medievalist in the Eighteenth Century: Le Grand d'Aussy and the Fabliaux ou contes*. The Hague: Martinus Nijhoff, 1975.

Zumthor, Paul. *Essai de poétique médiévale*. Paris: Editions du Seuil, 1972.

———. *Histoire littéraire de la France médiévale: VIe-XIVe siècles*. Paris: Presses Universitaires de France, 1954.

In the PURDUE UNIVERSITY MONOGRAPHS IN ROMANCE LANGUAGES series the following monographs have been published thus far:

1. John R. Beverley: *Aspects of Góngora's "Soledades."*
   Amsterdam, 1980. xiv, 139 pp. Bound.

2. Robert Francis Cook: *"Chanson d'Antioche," chanson de geste: Le Cycle de la Croisade est-il épique?*
   Amsterdam, 1980. viii, 107 pp. Bound.

3. Sandy Petrey: *History in the Text: "Quatrevingt-Treize" and the French Revolution.*
   Amsterdam, 1980. viii, 129 pp. Bound.

4. Walter Kasell: *Marcel Proust and the Strategy of Reading.*
   Amsterdam, 1980. x, 125 pp. Bound.

5. Inés Azar: *Discurso retórico y mundo pastoral en la "Egloga segunda" de Garcilaso.*
   Amsterdam, 1981. x, 171 pp. Bound.

6. Roy Armes: *The Films of Alain Robbe-Grillet.*
   Amsterdam, 1981. x, 216 pp. Bound.

7. *Le "Galien" de Cheltenham,* edited by David M. Dougherty and Eugene B. Barnes.
   Amsterdam, 1981. xxxvi, 203 pp. Bound.

8. Ana Hernández del Castillo: *Keats, Poe, and the Shaping of Cortázar's Mythopoesis.*
   Amsterdam, 1981. xii, 135 pp. Bound.

9. Carlos Albarracín-Sarmiento: *Estructura del "Martín Fierro."*
   Amsterdam, 1981. xx, 336 pp. Bound.

10. C. George Peale et al. (eds.): *Antigüedad y actualidad de Luis Vélez de Guevara: Estudios críticos.*
    Amsterdam, 1983. xii, 298 pp. Bound.

11. David Jonathan Hildner: *Reason and the Passions in the "Comedias" of Calderón.*
    Amsterdam, 1982. xii, 119 pp. Bound.

12. Floyd Merrell: *Pararealities: The Nature of Our Fictions and How We Know Them.*
Amsterdam, 1983. xii, 170 pp. Bound.

13. Richard E. Goodkin: *The Symbolist Home and the Tragic Home: Mallarmé and Oedipus.*
Amsterdam, 1984. xvi, 203 pp. Paperbound.

14. Philip Walker: *"Germinal" and Zola's Philosophical and Religious Thought.*
Amsterdam, 1984. xii, 157 pp. Paperbound.

15. Claire-Lise Tondeur: *Gustave Flaubert, critique: Thèmes et structures.*
Amsterdam, 1984. xiv, 119 pp. Paperbound.

16. Carlos Feal: *En nombre de don Juan (Estructura de un mito literario).*
Amsterdam, 1984. x, 175 pp. Paperbound.

17. Robert Archer: *The Pervasive Image: The Role of Analogy in the Poetry of Ausiàs March.*
Amsterdam, 1985. xii, 220 pp. Paperbound.

18. Diana Sorensen Goodrich: *The Reader and the Text: Interpretative Strategies for Latin American Literatures.*
Amsterdam, 1986. xii, 150 pp. Paperbound.

19. Lida Aronne-Amestoy: *Utopía, paraíso e historia: inscripciones del mito en García Márquez, Rulfo y Cortázar.*
Amsterdam, 1986. xii, 167 pp. Paperbound.

20. Louise Mirrer-Singer: *The Language of Evaluation: A Sociolinguistic Approach to the Story of Pedro el Cruel in Ballad and Chronicle.*
Amsterdam, 1986. xii, 128 pp. Paperbound.

21. Jo Ann Marie Recker: *"Appelle-moi 'Pierrot' "*: Wit and Irony in the *"Lettres" of Madame de Sévigné.*
Amsterdam, 1986. x, 128 pp. Paperbound.

22. J. H. Matthews: *André Breton: Sketch for an Early Portrait.*
Amsterdam, 1986. xii, 176 pp. Paperbound.

PURDUE UNIVERSITY MONOGRAPHS IN
ROMANCE LANGUAGES, an ongoing series, contains
critical studies dealing with literary or philological
topics as well as critical editions. The books average 200
pages in length, with texts in English, French, or Spanish.
Inquiries concerning the publication of manuscripts should
be sent to the General Editor, William M. Whitby, Dept. of
Foreign Languages & Literatures, Purdue University,
West Lafayette, Ind. 47907 USA.
Orders to: John Benjamins B.V.,P.O.Box 52519,
1007 HA AMSTERDAM, Netherlands.
Customers from North America please order directly from:
John Benjamins North America, Inc.,
One Buttonwood Square
PHILADELPHIA, Pa. 19130 USA